ASIAN AUNTIE-JI

ASIAN AUNTIE-JI

MIKE CURTIS

Matador
9 Priory Business Park
Kibworth Beauchamp
Leicestershire LE8 0RX, UK
Tel: (+44) 116 279 2299
Fax: (+44) 116 279 2277
Email: books@troubador.co.uk
Web: www.troubador.co.uk/matador

ISBN 978 1784620 790

British Library Cataloguing in Publication Data.
A catalogue record for this book is available from the British Library.

Typeset in Aldine401 BT Roman by Troubador Publishing Ltd
Printed and bound in the UK by TJ International, Padstow, Cornwall

Matador is an imprint of Troubador Publishing Ltd

For my family and friends who told me to get on with it.
For the 'friends of family' who challenged, celebrated and connected.
And for the restless, the scenesters and the contented who listened.

Contents

CHAPTER 1

proclamAsian

For the parents of many of my Asian friends and colleagues, their first memories of BBC radio were tied up with the come and go signals of the World Service abroad and the Sunday morning broadcasts for Asians in the UK. As for me, I remember Jack de Manio stumbling over time checks as the *Today* programme burbled out of my bedroom's old steam radio that could be tuned to more exotic names than the BBC's Home, Light or Third. Away from 'Auntie', you could rough-tune through the atmospherics to Allouis, Athlone, Moscow, Hilversum and Luxembourg.

'The Great 208', Radio Luxembourg burst out from my portable transistor with sparky jingles, adverts for Goya Aqua Manda and verbose disc jockeys introducing 'powerplay super hits' by the Rolling Stones, the Monkees, the Supremes, Marvin Gaye, the Seekers and Manfred Mann. Then there was Radio 270, the pirate station anchored off Scarborough for a year or so in the mid-1960s. All I remember of Radio 270 was that it seemed to have 'I'm Your Puppet' by James and Bobby Purify on heavy rotation. In 1967, all these offshore radio stations like Caroline and London played the single 'We love the Pirates' by the Roaring 60s. This sang the praises of all pirate radio as Harold Wilson's Labour government moved to close them down in August that year and get them replaced by the BBC.

I got my first name-check on the radio towards the end of 1967 on *Junior Choice* on the new BBC Radio 1. Among the favourite requests in those days were 'Goodness Gracious Me' by Peter Sellers

1

and Sophia Loren – Doctor Peter Sellers intoning in a mock Indian voice that from New Delhi to Darjeeling, he had done his share of healing, and he'd never been beaten or outfoxed…and so on in the lyrics of Herbert Kretzmer. Then there was 'Nellie the Elephant', 'Donald Where's Yer Troosers' and 'The Laughing Policeman'. I sent in a request for my school friends asking for 'Death of a Clown' by Dave Davies of The Kinks and it actually got played.

The radio was on around Sunday lunchtimes for *'Two Way Family Favourites'* with Cliff Michelmore and, when no one else was around, *'Round the Home'*. Years later in the mid-1970s, I battled with weak and crackly medium wave signals trying to listen in the dead of night to the Wolfman Jack shows on the American Forces Network beamed out of what was then West Germany. From AFN

*MC at his hirsute height aged 23 (see 'rejuvenAsian'),
providing the anaesthetic from the hospital radio
studio in Boston, Lincolnshire in 1977*

and the weekly *Melody Maker*, I picked up the latest music coming out of the United States and added them to my own collection and thus to the playlist for my weekly music show on hospital radio. People recovering in the Pilgrim Hospital at Boston got a Sunday evening diet of comedy clips, Steely Dan, Bob Seger, Donna Summer, Tamla Motown, Boz Scaggs, the O'Jays, the Doobie Brothers and Bob Marley and The Wailers.

I also went in to read the local news on Radio Pilgrim every Thursday evening after the paper I worked on as a reporter, the *Lincolnshire Standard*, had hit the street. After years of listening to the radio, I was now actually broadcasting, albeit on a closed circuit to an audience that was on drugs and drips, comatose, hallucinating, asleep, unable to escape or too exhausted to reach the 'off' button. The BBC beckoned in the shape of a reporter contract at BBC Radio Oxford followed by other moves around England before I ended up, somewhat surprised, at the BBC Asian Network.

This tale of the Asian Network is a story of highs and lows, of expansion and contraction, of dismay and triumph, and clarity and confusion. It follows the BBC as it grappled with the concept of properly serving a rapidly growing ethnic community in an age of increasing multiculturalism and diversity. It charts courageous decisions to expand a service and seriously invest in it, only to backtrack at signs of trouble and then dither and agonise over how to proceed. It highlights the genuine desire of the BBC to reflect the lives, culture and experiences of the UK's incredibly diverse and growing South Asian population.

It tells the story of the BBC Asian Network from its roots in local radio in the 1970s through its gradual expansion across the 1980s and 1990s. It follows the subsequent move onto a national digital platform and then, in 2006, into another major development which was given the name 'TransformAsian' – a marketing buzz-word which informs the chapter titles in this book. This expensive overhaul did not deliver the big audiences that were hoped for, precipitating three unsettled years in which the station was recommended for closure then reprieved at the cost of half the staff and half of the budget.

It is certainly not an academic analysis of 'Auntie's' history of ethnic broadcasting. I never was academic and the last qualifications I achieved were three low grade 'A' levels in English Literature, Geography and French when I fell out of school. I will leave analysis and interpretation to the media students who write their university dissertations about the BBC and its forays away from the mainstream. Elsewhere the Asian Network remains a mere footnote in more weighty works about the wider BBC and the history of broadcasting in the UK, but I felt it deserved to have its own story told as a stand-alone epic tale. I had thought initially that this book could be an 'official' history of the BBC Asian Network but my own experiences and memories across the years soon put paid to that lofty idea.

This is nevertheless the story of the BBC Asian Network but from my personal perspective and my own archives. It reflects the people who worked for the Asian Network, who cared about it and criticised it, and who followed it throughout its roller-coaster ride. It is also about the people at the top of the BBC who supported its expansion and its reason to exist, but who also succumbed to doubt, and murmurs and mutters off-stage, when falling audiences around 2009 made it look unsustainably expensive.

Underpinning it all is my affection for an organisation that I was part of for most of my working life. There was always a sense of awe walking through the main doors of (the old) Broadcasting House and indeed Pebble Mill. I remember my first visit to BH, getting into a black cab at Paddington and, in old 1950s movie style, barking to the driver 'Broadcasting House please' and then banging my head as I climbed in. Moment ruined. I would sometimes claim that working on the deck chairs on Filey beach in my teenage summers was the best job I ever had, but in fact nothing could beat being part of the BBC, both in local radio and the Asian Network.

The BBC has been known as 'Auntie' since the 1950s, when its more restrained, cosy, prudish style was contrasted with the new brash ITV. The nickname grew out of the phrase 'Auntie knows best' and she did not need to listen to criticism or advice from others. In South Asian culture, the word 'ji' is used as a respectful form of address to someone older than you, hence 'Asian Auntie-ji'.

The Asian Network, from its roots in local radio through to its reprieve from closure in 2012, became known as 'the difficult one' as well as 'the noisy neighbour'. It never fitted easily into the portfolio of either BBC English Regions or network Radio and Music. It was unique in the Corporation – an oasis of diversity in what was memorably described by one Director General as a 'hideously white' BBC. We always felt we were on our own – challenging, different and complicated. The radio station survived several reboots and rode out the threat of closure before its importance to the BBC in a growing multi-cultural UK was really recognised. It was also a lot of fun, and a privilege to be part of the Asian Network story.

CHAPTER 2

immigrAsian

Forty five years before the BBC decided it should close its national radio station for the UK's South Asian population, the Corporation's bluntly named 'Immigrant Programmes Unit' in the Gosta Green and Broad Street studios in Birmingham started a weekly nation-wide programme for the newly arrived Asian immigrants.

One of the presenters, Mahendra Kaul, said the aim of the programme was to 'demystify' British life. Tensions had been running high about the new immigrants and Kaul, along with co-presenter Saleen Shahed, said that frankly they had to get their people to adapt to the new life so that they would be accepted rather than rejected. Contributors explained how gas boilers worked, how to change a plug, the necessity for an NHS registration card, how to find a number in a phone book and why the neighbours left empty bottles on their door steps every night.

They got Prime Minister Jim Callaghan on the show but Enoch Powell, whose inflammatory and infamous speech on immigration in 1968 caused a huge political storm, declined. The emphasis at the start was to target recently arrived wives and schoolchildren who were joining their Asian husbands and fathers. David Gretten, the producer of the programme, said: 'Our task here is to answer questions and to sweeten the jaw-breaking complexities of housing or nationality with a little traditional song and dance'. Gretten also said the English lessons within the programme would help immigrants to cope with everyday situations and give them 'reassurances that these situations were not too difficult to be faced'.

The programme, which was initially broadcast at 8.10am on the Midlands opt-out of the BBC Home Service, was introduced on the orders of the then Director General Hugh Carleton Greene who was responding to calls for broadcasters to consider serving a growing immigrant population. The Postmaster General had to push through an emergency measure to allow television transmitters to operate on a Sunday morning to broadcast the 15 minute television version which went out at 9am. Maurice Foley, a junior government minister with special responsibility for immigrants, said in the introduction of the first radio programme: 'I hope you will find them entertaining and useful, so that you can settle happily amongst us. In the world of today we all need to know a great deal more about each other. This is one small contribution towards showing you something of ourselves and the society in which you live'.

Initially called *'In Logon Se Miliye'*, translated as *'Can I Help You?'*, its presenters spoke a combination of Hindi and Urdu and offered informal lessons in English. A few months after it was launched in October 1965, its name was changed to *'Apna Hi Ghar Samajhiye'*, which was *'Make Yourself at Home'* in English. Jeff Link, a long time radio training instructor at the BBC, remembers as a young studio manager playing in the Asian film music on 45 rpm discs which were made from beautiful marbleized colour vinyl.

The television show eventually threw off its educational role and became an iconic showpiece for the Asian communities. Called *'Nai Zindagi Naya Jeevan'* (*New Way, New Life*), it brought families together in front of the television every Sunday morning to watch performances by some of the legends of Asian music and entertainment. It was believed that most of the UK Asian population watched the programme every week.

This early decision by the BBC to serve the new and growing Asian communities was like the proverbial snowball rolling down the hill. It triggered a series of developments over the years which allowed the service to get bigger and better and whose momentum was hard to rein in. The ideas behind the Home Service programme in 1965 were picked up by BBC local radio, especially in Leicester where this radio service was expanded out of its once a week tokenism. Millions of pounds were thrown at what became the Asian Network as it competed with Asian commercial stations and satellite television for a slice of the audience that would make it good value for money. In the bid to offer what was expected of the BBC (such as strong news, debate, drama and new unheard music), the station eventually lost its balance with a family audience that really wanted familiar Bollywood and bhangra.

A generation earlier, Radio Ceylon became the most famous radio station in South Asia and could be heard across India where it was loved for the Hindi film music that it pumped out across the 1950s and 1960s. Major brands flocked to its marketing team to get their products advertised on its airwaves. It is said that when Edmund Hillary turned on his transistor radio after reaching the summit of Everest in 1953, the first station he heard was Radio Ceylon.

One of the station's best-loved broadcasters was Vernon Corea, the 'golden voice of Radio Ceylon', who joined the station in 1956. He championed the musical talent of Ceylon but also played western stars on his shows like Louis Armstrong, Cliff Richard and Elvis Presley. After nearly 20 years at the station and shortly after Ceylon became an independent republic called Sri Lanka, Vernon Corea and his family moved to London in the mid-1970s where he joined the BBC.

BBC Radio London was running a Hindi-Urdu show on Sunday evenings for its growing ethnic community. The programme was called *Jharokha*, a Hindi word for a stone viewing platform projecting from a building and often used for addressing the public. *Jharokha* started at 7pm and lasted 45 minutes before Radio London switched to Radio 2 for the rest of the evening and overnight. However the BBC was starting to change the way it did programmes for immigrants, acknowledging a growing awareness that the understanding of English in Asian communities was actually quite high and therefore the programmes did not need to be in Hindi-Urdu.

Consequently Radio London dropped its Hindi-Urdu programme in 1976 when Vernon Corea fronted a new programme for London's Asians called 'London Sounds Eastern' which was broadcast entirely in English. Corea got the big South Asian stars like Ravi Shankar and Usha Uthup as guests, and the programme attracted huge audiences on a Sunday evening. Vernon Corea went on to become the Asian Programmes Officer for BBC Local Radio and later the Ethnic Minorities Advisor to the BBC.

'London Sounds Eastern' ran each Sunday evening from 1976 to 1985. While believed to be the first BBC Asian show to be broadcast in English, it was overtaken in the same year by much more ambitious Asian programming in the Midlands where Radio Leicester introduced daily programmes for the city's Asian communities and where the seeds for a regional and ultimately a national service were being sown.

A combination of events after the Second World War brought Asians to Leicester. The violence and upheaval around Partition in 1947 – when India and Pakistan became independent countries – forced many to emigrate, encouraged by the British Nationality Act of 1948 which effectively gave UK citizenship to everyone in the Commonwealth. The post-war demand for workers in the UK persuaded others to start a new life in a new land, particularly in the 1960s.

But for many, there was no choice. In 1972, President Idi Amin of Uganda gave Asians 90 days to get out, accusing them of hoarding wealth and sabotaging the economy. He wanted the 'Africanisation' of Uganda. In neighbouring Kenya, the 180,000 Asians faced unrelenting pressure after Kenyan independence in 1963 and in the late 60s and early 70s, many chose to utilise their British passports and move to the UK.

Leicester City Council actually placed adverts to try and dissuade the Ugandan and Kenyan Asians from coming to Leicester. The adverts, widely criticised and later withdrawn amid grovelling apologies, only highlighted Leicester to more people and it became one of the key resettlement cities. Ultimately it became one of the most diverse cities in the UK with around half of its population from the ethnic minorities. The Asian communities were the biggest of these ethnic groups, especially those of an East African and Indian background and speaking Gujarati.

A quarter of those initially ejected from Uganda came to Leicester – around 6,000. More followed, settling mainly in the north of the city around Belgrave, Melton Road, and Rushey Mead. In the decade up to 1978, it was estimated that 20,000 Asians relocated to the city, bringing the Asian population up to nearly 60,000. The Melton Road – the 'Golden Mile' – bears testament to this influx today with its branches of the Bank of India, its restaurants and its plethora of sari and gold shops.

A mile away from this bustling road, which vibrates with colour and music during the festivals of Diwali and Vaisakhi, stands a bleak office block. Epic House is one of those architecturally dull towers that dominate so many city skylines, boasting 'luxury office space'. It was also the home of BBC Radio Leicester for some 40 years. In the gathering gloom of a Friday evening in 2001, the BBC's Director General Greg Dyke stood outside this block and turned to an in-house BBC camera crew making a video for him. He pronounced it 'the worst office in the BBC'.

Back in 1967, the BBC had opened its first local radio station in Leicester. It was the year that the pirate radio stations were closed down and Radio 1 took over the prime role of providing 'pop' music to the nation. Radio Leicester was only doing a few hours a day but it was pioneering the most successful project that the BBC had ever embarked on to take its London-centric, somewhat stuffy image out to the real people, including the immigrant population.

On the top floors of Epic House, a new team of BBC managers, presenters and producers began the task of reflecting the lives, concerns and gossip of the communities of Leicester, Leicestershire and Rutland. Early trailers for the station said it would have something for everyone, including 'something for the immigrants'.

Radio Leicester could not reflect its communities without acknowledging the fast-growing Asian population in its city. Someone came up with the idea of a weekly programme aimed specifically at Asians, and presented by Asians. Volunteers from the Asian community came in to pull this weekly programme together, lightly supervised by one of the professional producers at Radio Leicester. The programme was in Hindi Urdu and called '*Milan*', a Hindi word meaning '*a coming together*'. The early presenters were Bhupinder Attwal, Yusuf Choudhry and Kartar Singh Sandhu.

This weekly show was firmly part of the Radio Leicester schedule when Owen Bentley was appointed as the station's new manager towards the end of 1975. A year earlier, Owen had been running Radio Botswana on the border of South Africa at the height of the apartheid era. This had made him acutely aware of 'race issues' and he immediately felt that his new radio station in the East Midlands was not reflecting the ethnic mix of its local population.

'I saw a multi-racial city but heard a white radio station', he said. 'If Radio Leicester was going to be attractive to Asian listeners, then we should give them a substantial amount of programming stripped across the week, mainly in a language – English – that more than 90 per cent of them understood and used daily. It was my hope that once we had hooked the Asian audience with its own programmes, Asian listeners would gradually tune in to the rest of the station which itself would make an effort to be more welcoming and relevant to new listeners'.

Owen Bentley took the decision to upgrade this once a week programme run by volunteers and broadcast it across the week from Mondays to Fridays. Radio Leicester's education producer Paul Cobley was given the task of setting up the new programmes and the team behind them. Cobley was helped by the enthusiasm and drive of the station's junior assistant producer Greg Ainger, who later got the education producer job after Cobley moved on.

Radio Leicester advertised 'on air' across all of its output for a team of presenters and, from a strong list of applicants, appointed Mike Allbut (who was not Asian), Mira Trivedi, Don Kotak and Vijay Sharma, a Leicester social worker and race relations advisor. The programme was called '*The 6 O' Clock show*' and had a remit similar to the '*Make Yourself at Home*' show in that it featured information to help the Asian community understand life in Leicester and the UK. Always 'live', it included local news, interviews, phone-ins, Bollywood music, children's entertainment and a series aimed at increasing fluency in English. '*Milan*' remained as the Hindi programme on Tuesdays, another was in Gujarati and the other three were in English.

Five years later, Don Kotak was recruited by Leicester's first commercial radio station Centre Radio which also targeted the Asian community with hour-long programmes called Sabras ('all tastes' in Hindi). In the history of commercial radio franchises in Leicester,

Some of the team behind the first daily programme for UK Asians – the '6 O' Clock Show' on BBC Radio Leicester which actually started at 6.05 after the news bulletin. The photo is a page from a Radio Leicester magazine around 1976, preserved by the manager at the time, Owen Bentley.

the name of Sabras became a daily evening show and eventually, from 1995, a radio station in its own right with Kotak at the helm. Before Sabras, there was Sunrise East Midlands – put on air in September 1992 which provided Leicester with its first 24 hour Asian radio station. On the day it launched, BBC Radio Leicester tried a 'spoiler' by running Asian programmes all day on its medium wave frequency of 837 AM. This must have come as a shock to the mainly elderly non-Asian listeners whose radios were welded to the AM frequency and who had perhaps never heard bhangra and Bollywood, although there were remarkably few complaints.

Apart from trying to stop Radio Leicester's Asian listeners defecting to this new commercial upstart, it may have been one of the first exercises to encourage people to listen to their favourite station by other means where that option was available. Years later the radio industry spent thousands trying to encourage FM listeners to buy a digital DAB radio – and car manufacturers to install a DAB radio by default.

'*The 6 O' Clock Show*' on BBC Radio Leicester revolutionised Asian broadcasting, setting a template for the fully fledged Asian Network in later years and showing up the inadequacies of the once a week programmes elsewhere on BBC local radio. Audience research claimed that 67 per cent of the Asian communities in Leicester were tuning in each week. Six years later, Radio WM in Birmingham started daily programmes for its Asian communities and won a significant audience as well. This in turn led to the idea of a seven day Midlands-wide service and in 1988, the name 'The Asian Network' was first bandied about in BBC circles.

A year later – on 30th October 1989 – the Asian Network was born with a substantial increase in hours on both stations. From five hours a week on each, the output increased to 35 hours – a total of 70 hours across the Midlands. BBC World Service bulletins in Hindi, Urdu and Bengali were broadcast nightly, and the WM programmes were also carried at times on the newest local radio station, BBC Coventry and Warwickshire. The Managing Editor of the BBC World Service at the time, John Tusa, was invited to formally launch this expansion at the Diwali celebrations on Leicester's Melton Road.

The programmes proved popular but were interrupted every hour by a complete change of style when the Asian Network dropped back to Radios Leicester and WM for the news bulletins. Presenters had to 'opt in' to local radio news and hope that the local journalists had found some story relevant to the Asian audience. It would be nearly ten years before it got its own newsroom and regional reporters.

One of WM's Asian presenters did get a national airing once a week. Samantha Meah was described a funny, sassy Asian female who attracted a loyal audience on Radio WM and Stoke with her range of music and particularly her gossipy 'motormouth' chat. Her style was sometimes cited as an influence on Radio 1's Chris Moyles. It earned her show a once a week simulcast on the new Radio Five, launched in 1990.

As the Asian Network expanded on its medium wave frequencies across the Midlands, a new threat was emerging from the Conservative government. The 'Broadcasting in the 90s' White Paper, although largely about television, signalled the Government's desire to encourage the expansion of commercial radio. In the Commons in February 1989, Home Secretary Douglas Hurd said the independent sector was booming with profits up by 24 per cent the previous year.

The plan was for the BBC to give up its AM frequencies to the Radio Authority who would distribute them among commercial franchises. This was a real threat to the Asian Network – and indeed to many BBC local stations whose elderly listeners were wary of retuning the 'wireless' onto the new fangled FM band.

The BBC still went ahead with the expansion of the Asian Network even though it accepted it could eventually lose its AM frequencies. John Major had replaced Margaret Thatcher as Prime Minister in 1990 and seemed less aggressive towards the Corporation than his predecessor, particularly after its coverage of the 1991 Gulf War.

The key word in the AM debate was 'simulcast'. The government did not want BBC stations to hang onto AM frequencies just to broadcast exactly what they were doing on FM. In 1990. Radio Five (now Five Live) had launched on the Radio 2 AM frequencies and in 1994, Radio 1 gave up its AM transmitters to Talk Radio (now Talksport). The battle was on to enable the Asian Network and many BBC local radio stations to hang onto their medium wave lifelines.

innovAsian

The Asian Network started the 1990s in a precarious position. The argument that the BBC wanted to retain its AM frequencies to enable it to serve the Asian minorities had not been won – indeed the Home Office banned further splitting of frequencies to serve minority groups. It did not want the BBC to create a false expectation that its Asian Network could be sustained. Nevertheless in the midst of this uncertainty, Owen Bentley successfully lobbied the government in the late summer of 1990 to allow the Asian Network to extend its broadcasting to include weekends during the first Gulf War, which had UK troops fighting again in a Muslim country.

The Radio Authority was concerned that the expansion of commercial radio would be inhibited if the BBC hung onto its AM frequencies. It also felt that the commercial sector could serve the ethnic marketplace, although the BBC would wave its 'public service broadcasting' flag at any opportunity.

Meanwhile the Asian Network's pioneering work in reaching out to the Asian population in the UK was being noticed in the BBC's upper circles. One of the 15 'task forces' pulling together the BBC's Charter Review presentation was charged with examining the 'BBC and the Communities' and was recommending that an Asian Community Network should be set up.

Owen Bentley was, by 1991, the Senior Manager for Local Radio in the Midlands. He was tasked to flesh out this proposal, examine evidence of the demand for such a Network, flag up the potential pitfalls and political factors, suggest a programme schedule and have a shot at estimating what it might all cost.

In July 1991, Owen sent off an eight page report from his office on the fourth floor of Pebble Mill. It went to the chair of the Communities Task force – and Director of BBC News and Current Affairs – Tony Hall, who became Director General of the BBC more than 20 years later. It was copied to his boss in Pebble Mill, to the Controller for Regional Broadcasting and the regional heads across England in places like London and Leeds.

Owen concluded that the 1.5 million Asians in the UK at that time were not great devotees of mainstream radio with nearly half not catching any of it each week. But they did like programmes aimed at them – a trend proved by the popularity of the six hours each weekday on Radios Leicester and WM. In the 1980s, reports by the Commission for Racial Equality and the Home Office confirmed a substantial interest in ethnic radio. The demands from an Asian audience were clear. They wanted music (Bollywood film sound tracks cited by 79 per cent), relevant news and information (54 per cent) and programmes in an Asian language (58 per cent).

Based on the successful Midlands project, Owen suggested that the Asian Network could be rolled out across other AM frequencies owned by BBC local radio stations serving the most significant Asian areas – London, Manchester, Sheffield, Leeds and Lancashire. Leeds and Sheffield were already running shared Asian programmes – and Radios Manchester, Lancashire and Three Counties (Bedfordshire, Buckinghamshire and Hertfordshire) already had some Asian output.

The principle of regional franchises in significant Asian areas in England surprisingly reappeared nearly 20 years later. It was the first shot from BBC strategists and senior management as they struggled to find a replacement for an under-performing and expensive national Asian Network.

Everyone in radio knows that Breakfast is peak time listening – get your Breakfast Show right in presentation and content and the rest of the day will benefit even though the audience steadily falls away. But these Asian programmes on local radio were running in the evenings where research showed the Asian communities were more prepared to listen. For years the audience figures for the Asian Network's Drive (teatime) programme mirrored and sometime eclipsed its Breakfast show figures.

Owen's initial proposals had the Asian Network coming on air at 1pm each day, with the mornings being filled by the mainstream programmes from the area's BBC local radio station. Asian programmes would thus run from 1pm to midnight. The principle language would be English but it would broadcast programmes in the five most popular Asian languages – namely Hindi, Urdu, Punjabi, Gujarati and Bengali. The majority of the output would be generated locally rather than centrally from somewhere like Leicester. The new money required would be just over half a million pounds, including staffing, needletime (the cost of playing music), office kit, expenses and broadcast lines between the production centres.

Owen's report also highlighted arguments that followed the Asian Network down the years and were rolled out alongside every new strategy launch, closure threat and fluctuation in audience figures. Why should the BBC spend money on providing a specific service for a particular ethnic community? If the BBC is going to have output for the South Asian communities, then what does it do for its African-Caribbean, Chinese or Polish listeners? But Asians pay their TV licence fee and aren't they under-served by the BBC mainstream?

The proposal in Owen's document of July 1991 was scuppered by a significant development in the AM frequencies debate. The 1458 kilohertz frequency was held by the BBC in three cities – London, Manchester and notably Birmingham, where it was one of the Asian Network's key platforms.

The BBC agreed to give up the 1458 AM frequency in both Manchester and more significantly London – a decision which came to haunt the Asian Network over the years. It meant that the Network had no analogue platform to bring its programmes to London and the southeast, where nearly half of the UK's Asian communities were living.

Consequently someone living in Southall, Croydon or Bethnal Green would not be able to switch on a radio for the Asian Network until DAB arrived in 2002 – and by then it was too late. Asians – particularly the younger ones – never took to DAB when it launched. They could get their music – and radio – off their mobile phones and satellite television.

Meanwhile Sunrise Radio was formally launched in November 1989 and moved onto the 1458 frequency in January 1994. Based in Southall, Avtar Lit's commercial enterprise became the default radio station for the South Asian communities in London and overshadowed the efforts of the Asian Network, battling on satellite television, on-line and eventually DAB, for years. The Asian Network team felt that, when London Asians did tune into the Asian Network, many still confused it with Sunrise.

If the Asian Network had got its London AM frequency in the early 1990s, it might have captured the audience that found Sunrise. It may have at least doubled its UK audience and thus never have faced closure nearly twenty years later.

Having lost London and Manchester, Local Radio Advisory Councils on the other stations with big Asian communities started a publicity campaign to hang onto AM in the Midlands and the north. These volunteer groups made up of local figureheads and ordinary listeners did much to save many aspects of BBC local radio over the years, petitioning and nagging the upper echelons of the BBC and writing to MPs and councillors.

Every opportunity to highlight the threat to the Asian Network and its AM frequencies was seized upon. During an acceptance speech for an award at the One World Broadcasting Trust in 1992, Vijay Sharma told the audience that 'dark clouds are gathering over the horizon which could affect our ability to continue to produce such programmes'. The winning programme was a documentary called '*Uganda Revisited*' in which journalist Nand Sall examined how Asians were returning to Uganda 20 years after being expelled by Idi Amin.

Across two years of wrangling, the BBC's Director General, Michael Checkland, who had taken over in January 1987, refused to concede the Midlands AM frequencies to the Radio Authority. In 1993 it was announced that the single Leicester and two WM frequencies would be retained by the BBC, which identified other frequencies to hand over instead. (For example, the Radio 1 AM frequency that went to Talk Radio).

With its medium wave platforms in the Midlands secure, the Asian Network could now consolidate and build its reputation further both inside and outside of the BBC. Network radio bosses in London were starting to pay more attention to what this new team was doing up in Leicester. Vijay Sharma, who had been appointed as Senior Producer after an 18 month spell as Education Producer on Radio Leicester, was asked to look at all Asian broadcasting across BBC local radio including stations like Sheffield and Leeds which, like Leicester, were in the first group to be opened back in the late 1960s.

In September 1991, a recording of '*The Six O' Clock Show*' was submitted to the Radio Programme Review Board in Broadcasting House, where Controllers and senior editors from all the radio networks listened to each other's output and picked it apart. There was warm praise for what Vijay Sharma and the rest of her team were achieving. Ron Neil, then Managing Director of Regional Broadcasting, said he read the Review Board's comments with 'great delight'. In a note to Vijay, Neil said; 'They are a pretty critical lot and this level of praise reflects wonderful credit on you and the whole team. Please pass on my warmest congratulations to everyone involved for producing a product that passes radio's severest quality test with such flying colours'.

The dispute over the site of the Babri mosque in Ayodhya in Uttar Pradesh in India erupted in violence in 1992. Many Hindus believed the mosque was built on the foundations of the Ram Janmabhoomi temple – and a rally over the issue turned into a riot with an estimated 150,000 participants. The mosque was burnt down – and the story reverberated around the world. It was big story for the Asian Network, which had the delicate task of honestly reflecting all sides of this ancient dispute to its diverse audience.

The coverage won a top award in the annual Sony Radio Awards – regarded as the 'Oscars' for the UK radio industry. It got the Gold in the 'Response to a News Event' category – a tough section which attracted entries from all the major radio news outlets inside and outside the BBC. Another 'delighted' note was sent to Vijay from the top – this time from the Chairman of the Governors, Marmaduke Hussey. 'This is extremely well-deserved and a credit to both yourself and the BBC', he wrote. 'Please pass on my congratulations to everyone concerned'.

The coverage and subsequent Sony Gold also highlighted the Asian Network's link to the BBC World Service in Bush House through the magnificently named 'BAPS'. It was a rite of passage for everyone who worked on the Asian Network up until 2005, when it was shipped off to English Regions, to explain 'BAPS' to some smirking editor or producer elsewhere in the Corporation.

BAPS stood for 'Bush Asian Programmes Service' and was a unit tucked away in a corner at Radio Leicester, presided over by a seasoned producer called Hisam Mukaddam. Set up in January 1991, it gathered together all the South Asian material from the BBC

World Service in Bush House in London and despatched it round the wires each evening to 16 BBC local radio stations with Asian programmes. The written cue material for each piece of audio was sent out on the BBC's internal wire service GNS (General News Service) with Hisam routinely marking everything as 'Urgent', to the exasperation of GNS' legendary editor Dave Dunford.

This link enabled the Asian Network to enhance its coverage of the Ayodhya story. In another congratulatory note to Vijay about the award, the World Service Eastern Service boss William Crawley wrote; 'Can I say that we are also very pleased that the BAPS connection played a part in the material collated and presented in the winning output. This further strengthens a system which serves the Asian community here. There can be no better illustration of how you are serving them than to win this award in reaction to an event which would have had such a big impact on virtually all Asian homes in Leicester on that day'.

It was a hell of an achievement for a group of people who were all relatively inexperienced in dealing with big news stories and working on a part-time radio station without a dedicated news room. They were ready for the next development – becoming full time across the Midlands and led by someone with the title of Editor.

CHAPTER 4

regionalisAsian

T he Asian Network launched as a regional radio station at 9am on Monday 4th November 1996 with Sonia Deol as the first voice on-air. Her daily (weekday) programme had an immediate impact with stories and opinions from the UK Asian communities which had never been heard on-air before. Where else on the radio would you hear a young Asian woman explaining (anonymously) how she left her home for work or college each morning wearing a sober traditional outfit approved by her parents, and then change on the train or at work into the 'western clothes' which she loved? And then change back again on the journey home.

As part of the launch, the Asian Network got its first Breakfast Show – in fact it got two of them. It was now a full-time radio station in that it started broadcasting at 6am each day, with separate shows from both Leicester and Birmingham fronted by Kamlesh Purohit and Ray Khan respectively. The Drive programmes remained separate too – Rupal Rujani in the East Midlands and Nasser Hanif in the West – but the mid morning, afternoon and evening shows were shared across the Midlands, bouncing off the three AM transmitters at Freemans Common in Leicester (837), Sedgely south of Wolverhampton (828) and Langley Mill near Sutton Coldfield (1485).

At one of those BBC 'boards' (BBC slang for job interviews), Vijay Sharma faced three senior BBC managers to explain why she wanted to be the first Editor of the Asian Network. On the panel were two people who would play a significant part in the development of her corner of the BBC – Nigel Chapman and Richard Lucas. Vijay got the job – and the rest of the staff and casuals were kept on in Birmingham and Leicester to sustain this expanded operation. This split-site scenario was a challenge to manage, with Vijay spending half her life on the M69 and M6. It set a pattern for successive senior staff who at one point had a radio station based across five buildings in three cities.

On the hour each hour, the Asian Network continued to drop back to Radio Leicester or Radio WM (Birmingham) for the news bulletins – a cost effective but ultimately unsatisfactory compromise. Its own newsroom and dedicated reporters were still only a BBC 'development bid' in 1997 when the team covered the fiftieth anniversary of Partition and the establishment of India and Pakistan as independent countries, the deaths of Diana Princess of Wales and Mother Teresa of Calcutta, the General Election which brought Tony Blair to power,celebrations around the thirtieth anniversary of BBC Local Radio, and its first solo venture on the BBC's *Children in Need* night.

Across the Midlands in April, May and June 1997, research showed that 164,000 were listening each week but over the following three months it dropped to 128,000. Most of the BBC listeners were aged between 45 and 54 with an equal balance between male and female. The main competitors, apart from BBC national and local stations, were Sabras in Leicester (showing 35,000 a week across April, May and June), and the Asian commercial station in Birmingham, XL, which did not subscribe to the independent audience research and whose figures were somewhat anecdotal. The other significant competitors were the Asian satellite and cable TV services – Asian Net, Namastee, Asian TV and Zee – and a growing number of 28 day RSL (restricted service licence) stations set up to cover particular events or religious festivals.

People also listened to the Asian Network for shorter lengths of time than to the commercial stations. The average weekly listen to the Asian Network in early 1997 was under five hours – but the average for Sabras in Leicester was 12.4 hours. This underlined the fear that, by going regional across the Midlands, the Asian Network risked upsetting its Leicester listeners who were not interested in what was going on in Birmingham. Consequently the challenge was to stop the local BBC listeners defecting to the still local Sabras and thus defeating the aim of boosting the audience. That challenge was to become even greater when the Asian Network eventually went national.

The audience figures for the BBC and commercial stations were provided by RAJAR, an independent organisation owned by the BBC and the RadioCentre (on behalf of the commercial sector). It sent out diaries to targeted groups of people asking them to make a note of what they listened to, when and for how long. Four times a year, the RAJAR figures came out and caused agony and ecstasy as presenters assessed their egos and popularity, managers contemplated their careers, and strategists unpicked the details to establish trends, failures and future budgets.

If your figures were up, RAJAR was a wonderful, reliable and thoroughly respectable independent organisation. If the figures were down, RAJAR was unreliable, had sent its research diaries into the wrong places and should re-assess its criteria and methodology. Certainly when the Asian Network figures dropped, questions were asked if Asian areas were being targeted correctly by the researchers.

The Asian audience seemed to like what they were hearing, especially the up and coming Sonia Deol on the sparky phone-in. Bollywood music shows were very popular but there was a problem getting music from Lollywood – Pakistan's film industry based in

Lahore. Some of the compact discs were of dubious broadcast quality – and some of the very popular older music was only available on cassette. It took a few years to completely ban presenters playing music from cassette – its audio quality being further compromised by transmission on mono AM.

The South Asian news stories carried within the programmes were split between India (40 per cent), Pakistan (30 per cent), Bangladesh (20 per cent) and Sri Lanka (10 per cent). The music was a mix of Indian, Pakistani and Western – the audience wanted their Michael Jackson as much as Bollywood, Bhangra, Nusrat Fateh Ali Khan (who died in 1997) and Pakistan rock bands like Junoon and Vital Signs.

The Asian Network was also unique among BBC stations in carrying devotional music every day. In the early days, it was an hour between 6am and 7am, split equally into 20 minutes sections reflecting the Islamic, Hindu and Sikh religions. Zeb Qureshi, Ashwin Mahli and Ravinder Kundra were the three main presenters from the start until this 'daily dose of devotional' was axed in the radical cuts of 2012.

Vijay and two SBJs (senior broadcast journalists – one each in Leicester and Birmingham) presided over 10 staff posts, 27 freelance presenters (boosted by the need for specific presenters to front specific language shows) and six people on contract. The Performance Review for the year noted that 'great strides have been made in bringing the freelance staff under the Editorial control and supervision of the SBJs' – a comment that subtly hinted at the challenges of reining in so many part-timers who came from so many diverse backgrounds, broadcasting in different languages, and most of whom only appeared in the evenings.

The 7pm-9pm language programmes in both Leicester and Birmingham had different presenters every night to cover all the Bengali, Gujarati, Urdu, Punjabi and Hindustani languages – plus a couple of production staff for each slot. The weekday 9pm to midnight shows had four different presenters across the five nights – Amarjit Sidhu, Pam Sambhi, Tony Mandez and Danny Choranjj.

Some of the schedule was mercifully simpler. Navinder Bhogal hosted the weekday afternoon show with its news from the BBC World Service in Hindi. Mike Allbut, Rajni Sharma and her husband Sanjay, Rabia Raza, Neeta Kara, Kanwal Qazi, Gurpreet Grewal, Daljeet Neer and Najma Sayeed were among those who held court on-air over the weekends – and the World Service South Asian programmes were fed into the three AM transmitters from midnight to 6am.

To ensure accountability, the Asian Network got its own Advisory Council, drawn from outsiders across the Midlands and reflecting a mix of gender, religions, interests and ethnicity. It first met in May 1997 under Shama Sharif who chaired it until its demise in 2002. Meeting every three months, members reviewed the output, made suggestions, gave feedback from their respective communities and generally made supportive noises. Although they sometimes got side-tracked by wider BBC issues such as the controversial television programmes depicting Asian issues, the Council proved a strong ally of the radio station until it was disbanded when the Network went national.

Shama wrote to Greg Dyke soon after his appointment in 2000 to thank him for supporting the expansion of the Asian Network. She said that the members of her Advisory Council felt that 'only the BBC with its knowledge, expertise and skills is best placed to corner the market and become a leader providing national and international radio broadcasting of quality to Asian people'. A secretary in the DG's office asked Louise Hall in English Regions for some background information so that she could 'draft a reply for Greg's signature. Please can you also tell me if Shama Sharif is a man or a woman'.(the latter).

—⟶⟵—

And how much did it all cost? The total budget for 1997-98 was just under a million (£991,000) with another £87,000 for BAPS (remember them?). The Network was excused 'efficiency savings' that year as it expanded – it cost £111 per hour (£128 an hour with BAPS) which made it the best 'value for money' station in English Regions.

The forecast 'cost per listener per hour' (CPLH) was 2.46 pence compared with the English Regions average of about 3 pence. The CPLH figure nearly destroyed the Asian Network some ten years later as it shot up above other national stations as the audience fell away.

The Performance Review document summing up the financial year up to April 1998 hinted at long term dilemmas as a result of expansion and development. It stated there was 'an overwhelming need to revisit our vision and strategy'. What if the Network went 'national' (as it eventually did)? What if its programmes were broadcast on other stations (they eventually were)? When it gets its own Newsdesk, what will its news agenda be? Where should it be based? Should it still be split across two sites? Should it have its own radio car for broadcasting out and about? Should it leave the cramped 9th floor of Radio Leicester and move to the top floor of Epic House at Leicester? How will the audience respond to on-air changes?

Another line in the Performance Review read: 'Sections of (the) Muslim community have pressed for better representation in the Network staffing profile. This is going to be a subject of on-going debate and correspondence'. This note foreshadowed a long running and sensitive issue which was raised by external pressure groups and some staff over the years. It led to formal reviews on recruitment policy and whether Muslims, Sikhs and Hindus were fairly represented in a team that was broadcasting to an incredibly diverse diaspora.

So how did a white, son of a Church of England vicar, with no real experience of working with any ethnic community other than the Cornish, end up running the Asian Network news and sports operation?

CHAPTER 5

desperAsian

A few months after joining BBC Radio Oxford in March 1978, I was called out on strike with my colleagues in the National Union of Journalists. The cause was threatened cuts to local radio and I wondered if my year-long contract with the BBC, of which I was so proud, would survive. Last in, first out – the contracts would go before the staff.

Twenty years later I faced a more personal threat. Nigel Chapman, the Controller of English Regions, was implementing the latest 'efficiency savings' cascading down from the current Director General, John Birt, who had taken over in 1992. This particular round of cuts aimed to save a million pounds immediately, and eventually four million over five years, and zeroed in on various levels of management within English Regions including Assistant Editors in local radio.

I was one of this endangered species – Assistant Editor running the news at BBC Radio Lincolnshire and deputy to the station's manager. I was invited to apply for what the BBC called 'closed boards' for certain relevant jobs at my level. I went for the vacancy for the top job at BBC Radio York, which was an area I knew and loved having grown up on the Yorkshire coast. Nearly a dozen local Editor posts were ultimately vacant but gossip had most of those earmarked for someone.

On Tuesday 2nd December 1997, I sat in my car in the Pebble Mill car park feeling awful. It was about 2pm and I would be on in half an hour. I had done all my research but I knew my recall of the right information at the right time and in an articulate way would dissolve once I had sat down in the 'board'. I was sure that I was just cannon fodder and that someone was already lined up. I took a shot of bourbon from a pathetically small hip flask and headed for the gallows pole.

I had only met Nigel Chapman once, when he made a visit to Radio Lincolnshire after he took over in the Midlands. He had a perceived reputation as a disciple of John Birt and as someone whose experience of local radio was measured in weeks with a menial job at Radio Humberside at the beginning of his career. Now he was in front of me, chairing the interview panel with the head of programmes in Yorkshire Colin Philpott and the senior HR manager in English Regions, Alistair Currie, whose main interests were, I was told, beer and Scottish football. I do not remember much about my disastrous performance other than offering up the idea of Judi Dench as a new presenter on Radio York. Well, 'M' was born there...

Any solid reputation I had through work at Radio Oxford, Radio Cornwall, the Local Radio Training Unit in London and Radio Lincolnshire had not echoed down the corridors of Pebble Mill or Leeds. I was n't good at networking – certainly networking with anyone who had power and influence. My honest assessment of myself was a good and supportive deputy but not good enough or indeed driven enough to be the figurehead.

A short time later, I was with a gaggle of local radio News Editors who bumped into Mark Byford bouncing along outside Henry Wood House near Broadcasting House in London. Byford, who was then the Director of Regional Broadcasting, greeted us enthusiastically, enquiring if we were all alright and if everything was tickety-boo in local land.

'No, I'm not, Mark!' I shot back. 'You're trying to make me

redundant'. I have no idea if he remembered me particularly from his visits to Radio Lincolnshire when he was running BBC Yorkshire at Leeds. His father had been Chief Constable of Lincolnshire and had chaired the Radio Lincolnshire charity appeal for a while. He seemed slightly taken aback at this unexpected response but recovered to say: 'Don't worry, you'll be alright!'

The BBC boss in the East Midlands, then covering Nottinghamshire, Derbyshire, Leicestershire and Lincolnshire, was Richard Lucas. He had two problems in this round of Assistant Editor cuts – Mr D'Arcy and me. Mark D'Arcy was the political correspondent for the East Midlands and secured a place in the Millbank team in London covering Parliament. So that left me.

On a Friday afternoon nearly 20 years earlier, I was on shift in the Radio Oxford newsroom. Like every newsroom, we were getting reports on the teleprinter that there had been an explosion at the House of Commons. I answered the newsroom phone – it was Richard Lucas, then Chief Parliamentary Correspondent for BBC. 'This is strictly off the record for now but we think the Commons explosion involves Airey Neave'. Two days earlier on the 28th March 1979, the Conservatives under Margaret Thatcher had won a Vote of No Confidence in the Commons, defeating James Callaghan's Labour government and triggering the 1979 General Election campaign which brought Thatcher to power. Airey Neave was her Northern Ireland spokesman and, more significantly for Radio Oxford, the MP for Abingdon.

It was later confirmed that Airey Neave had indeed been the victim – blown up in his car as he drove up the ramp out of the Palace of Westminster underground car park. The Irish National Liberation Army claimed responsibility. Richard's early tip off enabled us to get a head start on a special tribute programme later that evening, fronted by Nick Utechin, who later went on to become a respected producer of Radio 4 topical programmes. The programme that evening included my telephone interview with Airey Neave, recorded immediately after the Commons vote on the Wednesday night. The two minute long exchange on a five inch reel-to-reel spool had to be retrieved from dozens of other tapes in the big recycling dustbin.

By coincidence Richard and I were both appointed to management jobs at Radio Lincolnshire within weeks of each other in 1984 – he as Programme Organiser and me as News Editor. He left a couple of years later to open and lead BBC Essex before returning to the East Midlands as HRLP – Head of Regional and Local Programmes.

Two days after my interview for the Radio York job, Richard rang me with the expected news of my failure. He suggested I go and talk to Alistair Currie in Pebble Mill about my options. After a miserable Christmas, I went to see Currie in the first week of January but he obviously regarded me as a lost cause and I was running out of BBC options. The person who did get the York job was, ironically, someone I had appointed to her first BBC job at Radio Lincolnshire. With hindsight, I know I had a lucky escape by not getting York but it did not feel like that at the time.

While I was contemplating the end of my BBC career thanks to BBC cuts, expansion plans were being considered elsewhere in English Regions. Richard Lucas had submitted a development bid for a bespoke News service for the Asian Network. Being headquartered in Leicester, it fell within his remit. The Midlands station was still taking hourly bulletins from Radio Leicester and Radio WM in Birmingham but it had extended its editorial patch (and audience research) into Nottingham and Derby without covering their news.

The idea of putting the Asian Network onto a national digital radio platform was also concentrating minds about a bespoke news service. There were other pressure points – for instance the evening programmes were woefully understaffed at a time when they were being carried in full by another station – BBC Three Counties Radio based in Luton.

Richard's submission prioritised the needs for reporters, radio cars to allow them to broadcast directly from Asian areas, closer links with the mainstream regional and local news operations, and a core-hours bulletins desk. He also said the introduction of a news operation would make the addition of a third SBJ (senior broadcast journalist) to run it as essential.

His submission, in July 1997, had two costing options. The newsdesk, a reporter in both Leicester and Birmingham, and one radio car for the Midlands would be £215,000. Two reporters at each site would bump it up to £283,000. The project got the approval – Nigel Chapman even added money for an extra half a post to give the newsdesk three fulltime Broadcast Journalists. The radio cars could wait but Richard, and Editor Vijay Sharma, could have the third SBJ to run the news operation, two reporters and three newsdesk journalists who would prepare and read the Asian Network's own bulletins.

Richard asked me to drop into his office after we had finished a regional editors' meeting in Nottingham. He needed someone with senior journalistic experience and an organised mind to spend six months setting up a news operation for the Asian Network in Leicester and wanted to sound me out about leading that project.

The suggestion took me by surprise. My first reaction was that I knew nothing about the Asian communities, did not speak the languages and that I would be out of my depth. But I had always embraced new challenges at work and I really had nowhere else to go. It was also a very exciting task and I was flattered that he felt I could sort it. Ofcourse it also neatly solved his dilemma around his last redundancy case in the East Midlands – for six months at least. I have always credited Richard with kick-starting my career again. Did he persuade Nigel Chapman that I was not the gibbering wreck that Chapman had witnessed a few weeks back? Did my exchange with Mark Byford have any impact? Had 'M' intervened?

The deal was not totally closed. Richard said I should meet my potential new boss first – Vijay Sharma. If Vijay was happy, we were 'go'.

Thus it was on Friday 13th February 1998, I went to Leicester to meet Richard and Vijay for lunch. I was not feeling that good. The night before, there was a farewell party for Sharon Peach, one of the Radio Lincolnshire reporters who was leaving for another station. It was in a Mexican restaurant in uphill Lincoln. One of the sports team thought it would be a good idea to end the evening with tequila slammers. It was not.

By the time I got to Leicester for lunch in one of Leicester's finest Asian restaurants, a curry was the last thing I wanted or needed. Confessing to not being at my sharpest due to the previous evening, we nevertheless had a positive discussion about the project. Slumped in the back of Vijay's car going back Radio Leicester, I asked them both: 'Oh, do you want me to do Sport as well?'

Vijay seemed happy to take on this stranger from Lincolnshire – after all it was only for six months. I suspect she checked me out with Dave Wilkinson, my boss at Radio Lincolnshire, to confirm that I was usually of sound mind and clear head. Dave was one of the buccaneering breed of local radio managers who was ready to bow out as the new austerity and the radical changes being introduced by John Birt kicked in. I spoke at Dave's retirement party (or 'dog hanging' as he called such events) the following year. He was an innovative and legendarily hospitable manager whose radio station was always in the vanguard of new technology, came in on budget and also delivered high audience figures.

At that time, most local radio station managers kept a 'drinks cabinet' in their office to entertain visiting BBC top brass, local dignitaries and programme guests and indeed their own staff. For years, there was folklore that each station should always have a bottle of the finest malt in the manager's office in case of a surprise visit by a Director General of the time who was of proud Scottish descent. After Nigel Chapman was appointed as Head of BBC Midlands and East, and then later Controller of English Regions, word came down that he would not welcome a large gin and tonic – or indeed a decent malt – whenever he made a state visit to one of his radio stations.

Consequently on his debut at Lincolnshire and out of respect to him, the drinks cabinet was cleared out and the contents hidden except for a forlorn, nearly empty bottle of dubious sherry and some orange juice. Shortly after Nigel Chapman left, the intercom on my desk in the newsroom upstairs burst into life. 'He's gone!'. I came down to Dave's office to find him restocking the cabinet only minutes after the Head of BBC Midlands and East had left the building. I considered aloud the scenario of Mr Chapman remembering he had forgotten to ask something and turning round and coming back in again. 'It's alright', said Dave, 'If he re-appears, I've told the receptionist to hit the fire alarm!'.

My colleagues at Lincoln gave me a fine send-off – gifts including a Nick Drake box-set, books and an Asian-themed buffet lunch for all staff on the last day. I would like to have taken the ultra-efficient newsroom secretary Su Whitaker with me to Leicester but, even if she had any remote interest in working 50 miles down the A46, there was no money for such a post in the new Asian Network newsroom. A few years later I asked the record library custodian at Lincolnshire, Linda Rust, to come and help the Asian Network unravel the new music logging technology in the Midlands. Linda had patiently indulged my passion for trawling through the reject pile of LPs and CDs by artists who would never make the local radio playlist, letting me escape with obscurities by people like Daniel Lanois, Millie Jackson, Warren Zevon and Charles Mingus. At every local radio station I worked on, I always got the 'gram librarian' and the engineers on-side as quickly as possible.

On Monday 2nd March, I started work at the BBC Asian Network, nearly 20 years to the day since I first joined the BBC. My target audience changed overnight from predominantly white over fifty to overwhelmingly Asian under forty. I was on my way to earn my Desi DNA.

CHAPTER 6

intrepidAsian

I had my first serious brushes with south Asian culture and history as a teenager in 1971. The Concert for Bangladesh, now described as the first 'Live-Aid', captured my imagination as George Harrison pulled together a stellar cast of rock musicians to raise funds for the children and refugees of that new country as it recovered from civil war and a cyclone. Ravi Shankar, who had ancestral roots in Bangladesh, brought the scale of humanitarian crisis to the attention of his Beatle friend, who in turn persuaded Bob Dylan, Eric Clapton, Ringo Starr, Leon Russell and Billy Preston to join him in two charity concerts at Madison Square Garden in New York.

I bought the subsequent box set from a second hand record shop in Sunderland. The first side of the three LPs featured Ravi Shankar (sitar), Ali Akbar Khan (sarod), Alla Rakha (tabla) and Kamala Chakravarty (tamboura) performing a 16 minute piece called Bangla Dhun. The largely young white audience wildly applauded after the tuning up, believing it to be the first part of the show. On film, it was a joyous and beguiling performance to watch as the incense smoke curled up and Shankar's fingers flew up and down the neck of the sitar. In the absence of anything else, this LP side was invariably played (on repeat) as the backdrop to any Indian takeaways brought home. As Ravi Shankar said later, the concert ensured that the name of Bangladesh was thereafter known throughout the world.

One of my friends at the time, after flirting with the hippie scene, picked up on the Indian spiritual guru Sri Chinmoy and inveigled some of us non-believers to a couple of meditation sessions. I could n't sit still long enough and slipped off to the pub, but I was intrigued that one of my favourite musicians was also a follower at the time – the Mexican-born Carlos Santana, whose band bearing his name exploded onto the scene at the 1969 Woodstock Festival (which also had Shankar on the bill). Another high profile follower was jazz guitarist John McLaughlin, who had played with Miles Davis and was now fronting his new band called the Mahavishu Orchestra.

My friend went off on a pilgrimage to one of Sri Chinmoy's meditation centres in New York. He brought me back a couple of drum sticks – one broken – which he insisted had been used by the Mahavishnu Orchestra's legendary drummer Billy Cobham. I treasured them for some years but, to my eternal shame, they eventually got used as paint stirrers and ultimately disappeared.

All of this was hardly enough to prepare me for my new role in life. I needed to listen and learn – and immerse myself in Asian culture, music and stories. The Asian Network team welcomed me warmly and several people indicated in private conversations that, actually, my complete lack of knowledge of all things Asian was a good thing. They said there were always some tensions between the different religions and cultural backgrounds of the staff, and to have someone with no such Asian 'baggage' was seen as fairer and thus made me more approachable.

Still I trod carefully. Offering a bag of smoky bacon crisps round a group of Hindu and Muslim colleagues at the BBC Club in Pebble Mill was not a smart thing to do – needless to say there were no takers. It was the last bag of smoky bacon crisps that I ever bought.

A couple of weeks after getting my bearings, Richard, Vijay and I met up in Nottingham to sort out a timeline for the project. The launch date was early June although it did slip slightly to Monday 22nd June. So we had three months to recruit five people, sort shift times for only three newsreaders across seven days a week, decide on bulletin lengths and frequency, clarify the scope for news bulletins, build a news broadcast studio from scratch and move up a floor in Epic House.

The decision was also taken to stop doing separate Breakfast and Drive shows in Leicester and Birmingham. To coincide with the newsroom launch, there would be a Breakfast show from Leicester for the whole of the Midlands, and Birmingham would originate the Drive programme. It made economic sense and freed up staff on both sites.

The adverts for the five posts were already published when I arrived. It said the expanding Asian Network was looking for five 'go-getting' broadcast journalists to cover the Midlands, UK and overseas news of relevance to an Asian audience. 'If you have a good understanding of Asian affairs and you have a feel for the kind of stories that interest an Asian audience, read on...'

I was given a list of objectives. Apart from setting up the news operation and recruiting the people to run it, I was also asked to oversee the move of the Asian Network to the 10th floor. This involved everything from getting a local house clearance character called Bunny to come and shift the rubbish to chasing up engineers to construct a News booth with all the required kit for hourly bulletins and getting it all hooked up to the transmitters so people could hear them.

With news and sport came weather and travel news – all to be negotiated. A new desktop system called ENPS for compiling and rolling out BBC News was being introduced at this time and we needed to be on board with that project. And BAPS was coming upstairs with us. I was introduced to McIndians, a fast food outlet across the road that sustained many of my new colleagues and boasted the slogan 'You've tried the cowboys, now try the Indians'.

I also had to tell other BBC people about this development. We needed good relationships with the BBC Newsgathering set-ups in Birmingham and Nottingham where the regional television programmes originated and into which the local radio stations fed their stories. There was also the Regional News Service desk in London, which pulled together the national and international news for local radio, and Bush House and its South Asian offices in places like Delhi and Islamabad.

My trump card was the offer of more stories and issues from the UK Asian communities which mainstream newsrooms did not pick up. They did not have a high number and wide range of contacts in those communities – and back in 1998 there was still a lot to learn about Asian news and culture. I was guilty of that myself. In 25 years as a journalist since leaving school, I had not been inside a mosque or a gurdwara until I joined the Asian Network.

A crucial debate in the news desk planning was the type of news that we would carry and in what format. Nearly 80 per cent of the Asians in the UK were under the age of 45 so we needed to target the younger end of the age spectrum. All the research into Asian audiences and Asian demographics in the UK told us to target the 22 to 44 year olds. In a note to Richard Lucas in late April, Owen Bentley, about to retire as Senior Manager for Network Radio in the Midlands, thought Sonia Deol's mid-morning programme was the right mix with its 'young and lively' feel, but the Breakfast shows sounded unsure of their role and 'unrooted' in the Asian community.

Even so the audience figures were on the up. The last three months of 1997 hit 181,000. After the RAJAR figures were released in February 1998, Nigel Chapman wrote to Vijay saying how pleased he was with the improvement in reach, share and hours per listener. 'As a new service, this is very encouraging. I am sure that, with the extra investment, we can go from strength to strength'.

The interviews for the new journalists were held in mid-April.

There were 42 applications for the three newsdesk journalists and 36 for the two reporters. Some people had applied for both. We drew up a shortlist of 18.

Apart from the interviews, candidates faced a written test of choosing from a list of stories and compiling a bulletin that was logical and legal. They all had a voice test, reading news and sport liberally sprinkled with names they would have to come across, sometimes without prior notice, such as the Sri Lankan cricketers Muttiah Muralitharan and Chandika Hathurusingha (the Sri Lankans were touring England later in the year).

Various project people responsible for phones, computers, furniture, transmission and ISDN lines, fire extinguishers, coat stands, First Aid boxes, mini-disc portable recorders, photocopiers and radio cars swept in and around the 10th floor at Leicester. The builders finished work in the first week of April and the new carpets were laid.

Shabina Akhtar, Vanita Patel, Rahul Tandon, Siobhann Tighe and Aasmah Mir had their group photograph taken on 8th June. These were the pioneers of the newsroom – and much was expected of them. Four of them had an Asian background.

Shabina and Aasmah became the two reporters, working the West and East Midlands respectively. Shabina could present programmes as well as report – and went onto work for BBC local radio in Birmingham and Oxford. Aasmah had a contract with commercial regional television and needed some persuading to come to radio. She gave us a good six months before bailing out, later becoming one of the main news sequence presenters on Five Live.

Some Asian journalists understandably did not like to be 'pigeonholed' into Asian radio and television services. I discovered that Asian students on broadcast journalism courses were routinely directed to us for work experience simply because we were the Asian Network. They were very welcome but I always urged them to get experience in mainstream newsrooms as well. Other Asian journalists and producers preferred the comfort zone of broadcasting to the communities they knew – which in turn underpinned the credibility of the output.

Siobhann Tighe, Vanita Patel and Rahul Tandon made up the news desk team. Siobhann later moved onto World Service and Radio 4, while Vanita remained a stalwart on the Leicester team for many years.

Rahul Tandon had to be persuaded to join for different reasons to Aasmah. He was working for Asian commercial radio in Yorkshire and living at home. His father had been very ill and Rahul was uneasy about moving south. I convinced him this was too good an opportunity to miss and that he could whizz up the M1 at any time if his father took a turn for the worse.

Brought in as a newsdesk journalist, he proved to be a good reporter, moving subsequently to Five Live and then to India where he continued to report on Indian matters for the BBC. He found his wife at the Asian Network, marrying BAPS producer Rumella Dasgupta in a lavish Hindu ceremony at Leicester racecourse. True to tradition and appropriate to the location, Rahul arrived on a horse.

I had particular sympathy with Rahul as my own father became ill at the same time – on the other side of Yorkshire in Scarborough. I went home for his birthday at the beginning of May when he was waiting for a heart bypass operation.

The five journalists that we appointed started to arrive towards the end of May. They were in for an intensive few weeks of training before the launch – both editorial and technical. I was calling in favours from or formally booking in colleagues from around the BBC to help – people like David Martin (digital editing), Sarah Fuller (legal training), Kevin Steele (mini-disc recorders), Andy Farrant (World Service sport), Nick Wilmott (voice training) and Bob Chesworth, a 'can-do' engineer made redundant mid-April at Radio Lincolnshire who found himself contracted by me almost immediately to help local engineers Malcolm Pugh and Bob Smith to build the News studio.

One week to go and there was still a lot to do. We declared the Newsroom operational six days before the launch and started sending stories around the BBC system. There was full day 'dress rehearsal' on the Thursday with everyone doing it for real – although none of it being broadcast. The on-air trailing about the news service was ramped up. The pigeonholes arrived for the daily post.

My big day was looming large – and then I missed it. In the middle of the dress rehearsal day, I got a call from home to say Dad had taken a turn for the worse. He had suffered a serious stroke after the bypass operation. I drove up to Yorkshire to be with my mother – and on the other side of the world my elder sister Alison prepared to set off from Perth as the news sounded bad. On Friday afternoon, three days before the newsroom launch, my father died in a Hull hospital. He was 73.

Instead of overseeing my project go 'live' in Leicester, I spent the morning of Monday 22nd June at the Registrar's office and the funeral directors in Scarborough. That evening I watched England lose to Rumania on television – the football World Cup was in full swing. I made a call to Vijay to see what I had missed – apart from a couple of minor technical hitches, it had all gone remarkably well and everyone was pleased.

Leaving my Mum with brother Chris and sisters Alison and Kate, I drove back to the Midlands on the Wednesday. I had a ticket for a rare double bill at the Birmingham NEC – Bob Dylan and Van Morrison. Dylan was on first. Towards the end of his set, Morrison wandered on stage to duet on one song. I later discovered it was the only time on the UK tour that they had both been on the stage together – and the song they went for was 'Knocking on Heaven's Door'. For me, between my father's death and his funeral, it was a poignant moment.

CHAPTER 7

consolidAsian

At the end of the first week of the Asian Network news
operation, Nigel Chapman hosted a reception in Leicester
for around 100 presenters, staff and management. He also
had his photograph taken with Sonia Deol, who had won the 'Top
Radio Presenter Award' at the Asian Music and TV Artists Awards.
Chapman congratulated us on the launch, the transition to 'a proper
news service' and the start of the new Breakfast and Drive shows.
He also found the reception 'very lively – it was good to see so many
happy staff'.

The audience figures were up again across April, May and June
to 188,000 a week. Another handwritten note from Nigel was
unpicked: 'Each time we're going up towards the 200,000 weekly
reach figure – you're doing *very well* for such a young station'.

The Asian Network audience was not matching the
demographic profile of the UK Asian population though. It was
heavily skewed to the older age groups and away from the younger
ones. For example, 52 per cent of our audience was under 45 – but
77 per cent of the Asian population was under 45. Only ten per cent
of the Asian population was over 55 but 37 per cent of our audience
was over 55. In London, Sunrise had a growing audience that *was*
matching the Asian demographic.

Despite efforts to reach out to all Asian groups, the Asian
Network audience still seemed biased towards those of an Indian
background. Listening in the Bangladeshi community was very low

– a community particularly underserved by the BBC and, being mainly centred in east London, out of reach of the Network's Midlands transmitters. Nevertheless audience figures and staff morale got a further boost across July, August and September when the weekly reach figure went over the 200,000 mark. However the amount of time that people were listening for was still low compared to the Leicester Asian commercial station Sabras.

The Asian Network was trying to be all things to all listeners at different times. In the autumn of 1998, the British Sikh Federation complained about the news and music on the Asian Network. It claimed most presenters only spoke in English and Hindi even if they could speak Punjabi, and it wanted them to be more welcoming to Punjabi speakers. An analytical monitoring of the main sequence programmes, establishing where presenters, guests or listeners spoke Punjabi, actually disproved the Federation's claim. Sections of the Pakistani community continued to lobby for more Pakistani music – in fact they wanted it to be 50 per cent of all the music played.

In the newsroom, we dealt with the nuclear weapons testing by both India and Pakistan – one of the many editorial tightropes that the young team had to tread. The ongoing dispute around Kashmir was another issue to be carefully reported. Most news agencies in the region would refer to parts of Kashmir as being 'occupied' by either India or Pakistan. BBC policy was to say 'administered by'. We were urged to think carefully about generalisations in the way we wrote stories and not just follow mainstream phraseology. For example, should 'Kashmiri separatists' be also called 'Muslim militants'? Was the religion of the Indian prime minister relevant to every story about him? You did not automatically add the religion to the name of European heads of state when you broadcast a story about them.

We were asked to check most of our Kashmir stories with the local expertise in the BBC offices in the sub-continent. Colleagues in Bush House briefed us on the pitfalls of reporting the region. India had a general election that year, there was a civil war raging in Sri Lanka, and Pakistan was worried about the 'cultural invasion' of satellite television.

Before I joined the Asian Network, 'Kashmir' was primarily a slow burning blues stomp by the popular musical combo Led Zeppelin rather than the beautiful piece of disputed land in the north west of the sub-continent. One morning I took a phone call about our coverage of Kashmir and the 'line of control' separating the Indian and Pakistani areas. The complainant said our reports were not balanced and he accused me of being an agent for the Pakistani government. I reflected that, only a few months earlier, I had been overseeing balance in reports about Lincolnshire County Council.

At least I understood the language of the news bulletins that I was responsible for. Elsewhere in the output, there was a lack of what they now like to call 'compliance' about what was being broadcast. In the early days of the Network, rumours abounded that the evening language shows would drop in a plug for a mate's restaurant now and then, or that a presenter would play a disc on heavy rotation as a favour for a friend who was a musician or record producer.

One afternoon shortly after I joined, Kamlesh Purohit, a senior producer at Leicester, suddenly leapt up from his seat opposite me and swore at the speaker on his desk. Somewhat alarmed, I enquired what the bloody hell was wrong. 'We're playing an advert for Tilda rice', he fumed.

I learnt that companies often sponsored soundtracks of Bollywood films, putting short adverts on the front of tracks on CDs. Presenters were supposed to check first that the track they were about to play would start on the music and not on the advert. Sometimes they forgot. As the Hindi-Urdu from the afternoon show burbled away in the background, I had absolutely no idea what was being said or sung. Many of my colleagues were multi-lingual, speaking English as their first language but also fluent in one, two or possibly more South Asian languages. The perfect manager really needed to understand all the swear words, slang and nuances of English, Punjabi, Hindi, Urdu, Bengali, Gujarati and Mirpuri.

Years later, I would be one of the senior managers at the Asian Network who was authorised to sign off the pre-recorded Devotional Sounds strands which would be broadcast for three hours early on Saturday and Sunday mornings. I was approving this for transmission even though I had no idea what the words were about in the music. All I had was the assurance from the producer who compiled the programmes that there was nothing controversial, blasphemous, slanderous or obscene.

With increased tensions in the workplace, particularly after the closure announcement in 2010, it was clear that the use of languages could occasionally be deployed by some toxic individuals to abuse a colleague. The target, who only understood English, would be blissfully unaware that a colleague had just sworn at him or her in Punjabi or another South Asian language. If the vitriol had been in English, there would have been hell to pay.

As 1998 drew to a close, my attachment to the Asian Network was extended by a further six months. I was still facing a potential redundancy but was hopeful of staying on at the Asian Network as its news editor. I was thoroughly enjoying the job and working with the people around me. I was learning so much and growing more confident about my new world.

I learnt that there was more to Bollywood films than a young couple falling in love, running round a tree, invoking parental disapproval of the liaison, and then it all ending happily ever after. I heard stories of the casual and constant racism endured by my new friends growing up in Leicester. The walk home from school could be character building.

Diwali, Vaisakhi and Ramadhan had been just words to me at the beginning of 1998. Now I understood their significance and what they meant to the people around me – work colleagues and listeners. In the office, desks groaned under the sweets and chocolates brought in for Diwali. Exotic smells of Asian cuisine drifted around the office in the evenings of Ramadhan as Muslim team-mates broke their fast, having put in a full shift with no food or water since the early hours. Famous Punjabi singers that I had never heard of were booked in to celebrate Vaisakhi.

In early November, I had my first experience of those award ceremonies that I had only seen on television. Now it was our turn to look shocked, arise from the table in the spotlight and lurch towards the stage to thank everyone that we could remember and everyone else who knew us.

We had two nominations in the British Diversity Awards. A group of us threw on our glad-rags and headed for the Lancaster Gate Hotel in London for the ceremony. Nigel Chapman offered to buy us all a drink before it started. 'I'll have a Jim Beam please!'. He looked rather blank. 'It's a bourbon, Nigel, an American bourbon'. With a large round looming, he decided to write it all down, pointing at me and saying 'Right, you're a Jim Bourbon'. He got to the bar just as they rang the bell for us all to find our tables – I never ever got a drink out of Nigel Chapman.

There was plenty to celebrate. The new Newsroom won the Gold award for Innovation, and our coverage on the national appeals for victims of the Bangladesh floods and the Gujarat cyclone got the Silver in the Social and Community Responsibility section. Vijay, Kamlesh Purohit, Perminder Khatkar and my bow-tied self had our photo taken with Ian McCartney, Minister of State at the Department of Trade and Industry, who presented the award.

There was another awards dinner at the end of November, tied in with yet another new experience for me. The Mega Mela at the NEC was a three day festival and celebration of Asian culture, fashion, cooking and music and a tremendous opportunity to push our brand at younger people. It was also like living in an Asian discotheque. Three days of pulsing Asian funk music and dhol drumming, booming out from various stages and stalls across the Halls, left me with a reeling head. However it did prepare me for subsequent Asian Network parties across the years where, to avoid exhibiting my Dad-dancing style of bhangra, I would prefer to talk but would have to spend the evening shouting above the music in the ear of someone then turning my head for him or her to shout back at me.

The Birmingham staff really got involved in the Mega Mela. As one of the senior managers, I also got willingly caught up in its organisation as an escape from news. We brought in an outside event organiser Janet Scull from Manchester to help with the meticulous planning. Engineers like Bob Chesworth and Ian Oakland were drafted in to look after the stage sound and the live radio inserts.

Asian Dub Foundation was a cool band of the time (still are) and had been booked to do a slot on our Mega Mela stage. Half way through their set, someone decided to go out for a cigarette and asked me to take over the lighting. I took to moving the sliders back and forth in rough time to the beat of the song, making the coloured lights fade up and down somewhat dramatically. It probably gave the band a headache but they smiled politely at the end. If I ever needed to boost my credibility with Asian youth, I could now fall back on the line: 'You're talking to someone who did the lighting for ADF'.

CHAPTER 8

accommodAsian

B
ack in Lincolnshire, someone whose job was to badger the BBC for fair coverage of Lincolnshire County Council (as opposed to Kashmir) was hatching a plan. Steve Jackson was a public relations manager with the council but away from work he was a musician and music fan. Steve was obsessed with the American band The Byrds. The group – once dubbed the American Beatles – had numerous incarnations but one of them included the drummer and guitarist Gene Parsons.

Through some convoluted means, Steve ended up being the promoter of a Gene Parsons concert in Nettleham village hall near Lincoln one night in 1999. I came back from Leicestershire to support his venture and enjoy an evening of fine musical entertainment. Gene and his wife actually stayed overnight with Steve and his family.

I have never forgotten Steve telling me later that he suddenly stopped himself at breakfast the following morning and thought: 'Bloody hell, I've got a Byrd in my kitchen'. The remark may have sounded like a Sid James line from any of the '*Carry On*' films but it perfectly reflected his sense of disbelief and I knew exactly what he meant. I had many moments of wonder and disbelief in 1998 and more were to follow in 1999.

For a start, I was invited out of the blue to be a judge at the Sony Radio Awards, those so-called Oscars for radio. I have no idea why but needless to say I accepted and about 50 entries – all on cassette – landed on my desk. Our panel of three was judging the Short

Form Award and gave the Gold to John Peel for features from his Saturday morning programme on BBC Radio 4, '*Home Truths*'.

I was never asked to be a judge again. Nevertheless, my name as a judge appeared in the 1999 Sony Awards programme for the awards night at the Grosvenor House Hotel in Park Lane. I wrestled with what was described as a cannon of lamb on a tapenade-flavoured chargrilled slice of courgette and mused that, for the first and only time in my life, I was on the same list as such icons of the media as Ken Bruce, Michael Buerk, Nicky Campbell, Lynsey de Paul, Germaine Greer, David Jensen, Rod Liddle, Gillian Reynolds, Brian Sewell, Feargal Sharkey, Moira Stuart, Richard Whiteley and Dale Winton.

On the night, the table plan put me next to Sebastian Coe (now Lord Coe of Twenty Twelve) who was then the Conservative MP for Falmouth. Coe and I talked Cornwall – I had been on the launch team of BBC Radio Cornwall back in 1983 – before moving onto William Hague, who was then leader of the Conservative party. Coe was Hague's Chief of Staff at the time.

In the same way that a local radio station will ask a national politician about something specific to its patch, so the Asian Network would 'Asianise' an interview. It was invariably the answer to the Asian question that was lifted out of the interview for the news bulletin. Hague had recently done an interview over the phone with us and, in response to a question about Asians in UK politics, had expressed a hope that someone from the Asian communities would indeed lead the Tory party one day. Obviously not immediately as he rather hoped to hang onto the job.

As the evening wore on, I think we agreed that Seb Coe would bring William Hague to the Midlands to meet the Asian Network team. It never happened. Two months later, it was announced that the Labour supporter Greg Dyke would be the next Director General of the BBC. Hague's reaction was to hire a firm of media specialists to monitor BBC news and current affairs very closely for political bias. I wondered if they ever got round to our Mirpuri or Punjabi bulletins.

A month after the Sonys, we were at the awards again. This time it was the Ethnic Minority Media Awards at another posh hotel in London – this time the Dorchester. The Awards gave a lifetime achievement award to Muhammad Ali who unfortunately could not actually be there but sent this message: 'As in the United States, Britain is lucky to draw from the talents of a community rich in ethnic diversity'. Comedians Richard Blackwood and Nina Wadia were among those at the Awards who had their photos taken with Asian Network 'slebs' like Vijay Sharma, Ishfaq Ahmed, Kamlesh Purohit, Mintu Rahman and me.

At the 1999 EMMAs – the Ethnic Multicultural Media Awards. From left, Kamlesh Purohit, Ishfaq Ahmed, Nina Wadia ('Goodness Gracious Me' and later 'Eastenders') and MC

Our coverage of the 1999 Cricket World Cup, which was staged in England and the Netherlands, won us a Silver award at that year's British Diversity Awards. Kamlesh Purohit and Deepak Patel endeavoured to cover as many of the matches involving the South Asian teams as possible. Australia won the Final at Lords, beating Pakistan by eight wickets. The Asian Network rightly made a big fuss of cricket, sending Kamlesh and Lee James to South Africa and South Asia in following years to provide either commentary or updates on significant matches.

My threat of redundancy finally disappeared in February with the decision to make turn my 'acting' Senior Broadcast Journalist post into a fulltime substantive role. With the newsroom launch and award behind me, I was actually the front runner this time but nevertheless took the preparation for the interview very seriously. I cunningly failed to suggest Judi Dench as the new Punjabi presenter and buried the Radio York attempt once and for all and got the job.

The problems around our Leicester building were starting to mount up. Long before Greg Dyke condemned it, staff were living with numerous issues day to day. Although the actual offices themselves were not bad and commanded a view over the Leicester skyline to the rolling hills of Charnwood, everything around it was depressing.

The lift frequently jammed, resulting in calls to the Fire Brigade to rescue some hapless hack heading for the early shift. The front door lock was filled with superglue on a couple of occasions. The BBC had no control over the floors below and Security was non-existent. There were a couple of incidents with intruders. There was a janitor in a cubby hole at the entrance but he seemed to disappear most afternoons. There was the bonus of a staff car park but it was round the corner down a dark lane and not for the faint-hearted on early and late shifts.

One morning, someone opened a window and it slipped out of its hinges and hung perilously over the bus queues ten floors below. The engineers brought gaffer tape to try and secure it until the owners got a contractor to come and sort it. I imagined a Daily Mail headline: 'Pensioner slain by BBC window'.

In 1999, Mark Thompson spent a year as Director of Nations and Regions, responsible for the BBC in Scotland, Wales, Northern Ireland and England. In June, he made a state visit to Leicester to meet the Asian Network and Radio Leicester teams. It was an awful day weather-wise and as he waited in reception for the managers to come and get him, rain was pouring in through a closed window while the Receptionist shouted for buckets.

It was a perfect illustration of the state of Epic House. The timing of the cascade was exquisite. It was as if we had one of the staff on the roof with a high pressure hose pipe. Mark Thompson actually helped mop up. He needed no further convincing that the complaints from staff about their building were genuine. However he was gone by the end of the year to another top job – but would reappear years later as Director General to play a significant part in the Asian Network story.

The building issues in Birmingham were simpler but the Asian Network team had to share an office with some of the Radio WM team. Although people generally got on, there were occasional tensions over printers, photocopiers or people eating pungent curries at their desk. WM owned the little studio used for swapping audio between Leicester and London – and they liked to lock it at 4.30pm each day. Asian Network did eventually get its own production office in Pebble Mill but plans were in hand for the BBC to leave the Mill and move into the city centre.

What really concentrated a lot of minds about Epic House in

Leicester was the looming Millennium. The BBC started to gear up for 'Y2K' (Year 2000), summoning people from all over the Corporation to dozens of meetings to discuss nightmare scenarios, civil disobedience, power failures, computer meltdown, emergency broadcasting, spare batteries, standby typewriters with spare ribbons, cans of soup, tin openers, whistles, torches, first aid kits, soap, toilet paper, water supplies and chocolate hobnobs.

The BBC was convinced that everything that it was responsible for would be fine, but companies providing us with facilities may have failures. In Leicester, BBC Property was having trouble getting assurances that Epic House was Y2K compliant with alarms and emergency lights. A full evacuation exercise was planned. If the power went off on the night, everyone would head down the ten flights of stairs and go and assemble outside a nearby fabrics shop. To add to the concerns, the ground floor of Epic House was used by a big DIY store with loads of inflammable liquids.

Across the BBC, plans were laid for managers to have cash in case ATMs failed. HR updated Next of Kin details on all staff. Hundreds of phone numbers were distributed around the system in the hope that if everything failed, the mobile network would not. 'Protected' mobile phones which should work regardless were distributed to a few senior figures. We only had one which was given to Vijay who thus would not be able to ring anyone else on her staff if the mass mobile signals were cut off. Each BBC outlet fed its details into the regional broadcasting's so-called 'Intelligence Centre'. BAPS had the right idea – it closed down for its Christmas break on 13th December and did not reopen for business again until 3rd January.

If Leicester failed – and people assured us that if anywhere was going to, it would be Epic House – a small group of Asian Network staff led by myself would drive to Pebble Mill in Birmingham (full tank? – check). If Birmingham fell over, they would come to

Leicester. Our colleagues at Radio Leicester would go to Derby to help with an East Midlands emergency programme. Someone asked what we would do if there was then a Royal death at midnight.

On the night, a small group gathered in the newsroom at the top of Epic House awaiting Armageddon. The main programme was coming from Birmingham with news and other inserts from Leicester. We had a programme team in Leicester ready to take over if Birmingham failed. Half the nation was out celebrating. Crowds lined the Thames awaiting the River of Fire and Concorde but the weather, rather than a Millennium bug, scuppered that somewhat. The minutes ticked round to midnight.

Big Ben boomed midnight out of the radio speaker. On the newsroom television, the Queen linked arms with the Blairs at the Millennium Dome. Nothing happened. The lights did not even flicker. Stone cold sober at the top of Epic House at the start of the new Millennium, I gazed miserably at Blair and Mandelson on the box and then out of the window as a handful of limp fireworks spluttered into the night sky above Leicester. We hung around until 1am and then went home. Happy bloody New Year – it's a new dawn.

CHAPTER 9

digitalisAsian

'**B**ottom line is… we do not want too many Chiefs and not enough Indians', explained a senior manager in Radio and Music. 'What about Pakistanis or Sri Lankans?', I murmured audibly. 'Oh God, sorry, I did n't mean…' exclaimed the reddening back-tracking executive.

We were at a meeting in W1A to discuss the first steps to develop a website for the Asian Network. We needed help from the national interactive team and this senior figure was earnestly outlining his thoughts on whom we could refer up to and how all this would fit in with the current Radio and Music staffing organogram. Clichés were being scattered like confetti, he was flying by the seat of his pants, had got off on the wrong foot and probably would have continued until the (sacred) cows came home. So that's all good then.

The Asian Network contingent consisted of Vijay and me along with Mintu Rahman, who was a programme broadcast assistant in Leicester. Full of energy and enthusiasm, he was desperately keen to be involved in the website and we knew he was the man for the job. Working with Mintu, I was reminded of the British Leyland Unipart advertising slogan when I was working at Radio Oxford – 'The answer is Yes, what's the question?'

Mintu – or Minty or Minto as he occasionally got called at those London meetings – was in on the website from the start. In the very early days, I wrote the content and he did the rest, designing the pages and putting them on-line. After all the preparatory work and the necessary training, the website was launched in March 2000. Apart from the web pages, it also streamed the 'live' Asian Network radio programmes.

The number of weekly hits was around 7,400 initially. Once we got Mintu working on it fulltime and were able to update it daily, the hits soared to nearly 16,000 hits a week by the end of the year. It peaked at 35,000 at the end of Ramadhan, helped by some unexpectedly welcome cross-trailing from Radio 1. The Messageboards added extra input to the programmes, especially Sonia's phone-in. There were the fasting times for Ramadhan, a link to a web-cam in a north London registrar's office where many Asian couples married, and the opportunity to listen again to big interviews with Bollywood stars.

Along with the website, another significant development was quietly kicked off – the aspiration to go national. Both projects would accelerate over the years and give the Asian Network a global platform, with the website meaning it could be heard in the South Asian diasporas across the world including countries such Canada, Kenya and Fiji as well as the sub-continent. Its publicity leaflet at the time – an A4 sheet folded into three – featured the outline of the sub-continent on the front. Unfortunately it was totally dominated by India with very little of Pakistan and Bangladesh on either side. Consequently it did not represent the aim of broadcasting to everyone from the South Asian diaspora nor the main target audience – UK Asians – and it was quickly dropped.

On a weekend in November 1999 that coincided with our second Mega Mela at the NEC and that year's British Diversity Awards, the Asian Network was switched on to digital satellite. This meant that it was not restricted to AM transmitters in the Midlands and could be listened to through the televisions of people who had cable or satellite dishes. It would another two years before the Network made it to DAB digital radio but it was a significant step forward.

In one of those 'water cooler' conversations about broadcasting on digital satellite, one of the part-time presenters asked 'How would we get up there?'. We assumed this was side-splitting jocularity but it soon became clear it was a serious question. He was quickly assured that each week he would get a plane ticket to the Kennedy Space Centre in Florida 24 hours before his programme was due to start. Everything became clearer after that. Thankfully he did n't ask us how the output got up there to be bounced back to the dishes – that *would* have shown how little we knew.

In addition to the digital development, the Asian Network was evaluating its expansion onto AM frequencies outside the Midlands. London remained a priority – but the BBC had already given up the 1458 frequency in the capital. Suggestions around medium wave transmitters used by Radio 4 in Chelsea, BBC Essex at Chelmsford, and BBC Radio Thames Valley (as a joint Oxford and Berkshire station was briefly called) at Slough were floated but came to nothing.

Instead the BBC concentrated on expanding into the north and east. Five public meetings were set up in the targeted areas and off we went to meet the locals in Bradford, Sheffield and Blackburn in the north, and Peterborough and Derby on our doorstep in the Midlands. The Blackburn meeting was held at Rover's Ewood Park, overlooking the pitch. The other meetings were in town halls and civic centres. Between 70 and 90 people were invited to each meeting although attendance ranged between 15 and 38.

There had been a plan late in 1998 for BBC Radio Lancashire to link up with the Asian Network for a high profile programme once a week. It was kicked around in a meeting with Steve Taylor, the Editor at Lancashire, Richard Lucas and Martin Brooks, who was running regional television and radio in the north west. The station, which was already doing an average of 10 hours a week for the Asian communities, was keen to have a Lancashire-originated programme on the Asian Network without diminishing its current hours. The idea never got off the ground but it did take the Asian Network's evening programmes for a while, even though they were on the AM frequency whose reception after dark was notoriously patchy.

The overall response to the expansion plans was very welcoming, although many expressed a desire to retain their local Asian programmes as well as calling for a greater integration of Asian issues into the mainstream BBC output. There were calls – heard repeatedly down the years – for the output to be on FM and preferably available across the UK.

Some feared that Asian-only programmes would ' ghettoise' Asian issues, meaning they would not be heard elsewhere. They wanted programmes that related to younger people, that reflected music and religion and news from the sub-continent, more sport, and coverage direct from the heart of communities. The BBC nationally was accused of still treating Asians as immigrants after 40 years. There were conflicting opinions on the BBC television comedy *'Goodness Gracious Me'* which had successfully transferred from Radio 4 the year before.

In November 2000, the Asian Network appeared on the AM transmitters in Lancashire, Leeds, Sheffield, Derby and Peterborough. Only Peterborough (the Gunthorpe transmitter) was 24 hours – the others appeared around teatime and went through until midnight. Three Counties Radio in Luton also took the evening programmes, and for a while so did Radio Manchester (GMR). Some evenings, the Asian Network listeners in Leeds and

Sheffield would still lose their AM service to a football commentary from the lower divisions, bhangra giving way to the exploits of the likes of Huddersfield Town.

—⟋⟋⟍—

Greg Dyke had became the BBC's thirteenth Director- General on 29th January 2000, taking over from John Birt who had held the post for eight years. According to his book '*Inside Story*', he was deeply depressed by the end of the first week by discovering that the main activity at the executive level of the BBC seemed to be writing and reading documents, reports and policy papers. He also felt it was 'risk averse' whereas his approach to organisations, business and life was to 'try things'.

So it was that, in one of his executive meetings getting to grips with the monolithic BBC organisation, Greg had Jenny Abramsky, Director of Radio and Music, and Andy Griffee, the new Controller of English Regions, in the same room. The Asian Network was now on digital satellite and on more AM transmitters – and it was now being talked of as part of the BBC's new digital radio portfolio.

'If the Asian Network is going to be heard across the UK, it should be part of network radio, should n't it?'. If the DG thinks it's a good idea, it is – and Andy conceded his regional station, complete with its significant contribution to the ethnic make-up of English Regions, to Jenny Abramsky.

The first I got to know about this decision was after a regional meeting in Nottingham. As the local radio editors dispersed to their outposts across the East Midlands, Vijay said she would give me a lift as she had something to tell me. As we drove past Trent Bridge cricket ground, she uttered these seven words: 'Greg thinks we should be under Jenny'. There was little detail but clearly a new and major upheaval was looming for our young, small team which had only graduated to a Midlands regional station four years earlier and which had only got its own newsroom and journalists two years ago.

By the end of 2000, Jenny Abramsky had announced that five more BBC radio services would be available through digital audio broadcasting (DAB). Joining the existing networks, there would be three new ones – Radio 1Xtra, 6Music and Radio 7 (later rebranded as 4Extra). In addition, Five Live would get an extra platform to enhance its sports coverage and the Asian Network would go national.

Jenny Abramsky came to talk to the Asian Network staff and explain the plan for the next couple of years. The target date for the transfer to Radio and Music was April 1st 2001. In the meantime, the expansion would continue with extra reporters to support the Network's increased presence in the north, a first Management Assistant for the station based in Leicester, and all Personnel functions to be handled by the English Regions HR team in Nottingham. The long awaited radio car for the Midlands was due – and we were starting to flirt with satellite phones that would enable us to broadcast from anywhere in the world, despite costing about £8,000 each with calls at £5 a minute.

The move to R&M was going to be underpinned by investment of 1.5 million pounds. This included a plan to establish a sports unit of three people, enhance weekend news coverage and bring in a 'Trailblazer' for the three months (this person would ramp up the on-air station identity). We also asked for another journalist on the newsdesk as the East Midlands reporter based in Leicester was repeatedly drawn into the news bulletin rota to cover holidays and sickness. We desperately needed our own engineer in the Midlands. In London, the Network had reporters Poonam Taneja and Tanjua Solanki, who had come from the capital-based units that served local radio. They often worked out of a small Asian Network studio on the seventh floor of Bush House, next to the World Service's Bengali unit, if they could reminder how to find it.

Sixteen people applied to be the Asian Network reporter in Manchester, covering the north-west. There were twelve applicants for the Leeds/Bradford post. Rahila Bano and Sanjiv Buttoo got the jobs – both of them were already working in the areas and had good contacts and a solid understanding of the Asian communities there. A handful of the strongest unsuccessful candidates would later join the Network as it expanded – Inderpreet Sahota, Ranjit Chohan and Rabiya Parekh.

During 2000, Sonia Deol left for other broadcast work in the UK (she'd be back), with Shabina Akhtar or Osma Malik taking over the phone-in. Sameena Ali Khan hosted the Drive programme, with Gagan Grewal and Ray Khan opening and closing the Network each weekday. At weekends, programme presenters included Kanwal Qazi as the breakfast host, Mike Allbut, Rabia Raza, Najma Sayeed, Amarjit Sidhu, Daljit Neer and Rajni Sharma, who fronted the Bollywood show '*Filmi Duniya*' .

BBC English Regions, which still included the Asian Network, won the Diversity Champion 2000 award at the British Diversity Awards. It recognised the work done across English Regions to further the awareness of disability, equality and racial and cultural awareness. Controller Andy Griffee, receiving the award at the Park Lane Hotel in London, said: 'This is a fantastic achievement for everyone in BBC English Regions. Diversity is one of the five main planks of our strategy in Connecting England. It is vital for all of us, as the front door of the BBC in so many communities, to properly reflect the diverse audience we serve, both in our programming and our workforce.'

Asian Network got nominated (but did not win) in the category for Enhancing Race Equality Practice. This was for our news coverage of the Runnymede Trust report on '*The Future of Multi-Ethnic Britain*', for which we *did* win at the Campaign for Racial Equality's 'Race in the Media' Awards. The year also saw us covering the military coup in Pakistan which brought General Musharraf to power and the 300th anniversary of the creation of the Sikh Khalsa.

It was also finally announced that the BBC would be getting out of Epic House in Leicester. Staff at the Asian Network and Radio Leicester were given the choice of decamping to some industrial estate on the edge of the city or waiting a bit longer for brand new, specially built premises in the city centre. The wait for this new landmark building would only be six to eight months longer than the cheaper, out of town option so it was no surprise that everyone voted for St Nicholas Place in the city centre near the Cathedral.

Jenny Abramsky and other senior managers decided to give staff the choice because, they said, they were acutely aware of the unacceptable conditions at Epic House. In the meantime, they were planning to recruit a full-time property manager to be based in Epic House for at least six months to monitor the cleaning and security contracts, and to act as the BBC's property champion. In addition, work started to refurbish the toilets and lifts.

The Head of Regional and Local Programmes for the BBC in the East Midlands, Craig Henderson, could barely contain himself in a news release: "Our new building will be fresh, and rise up as the modern face of the BBC in Leicester. It will be much more than just a home for our broadcasting activities. We plan to encourage local people to come in and see how the BBC operates. The details are still being finalised, but we envisage an internet café providing people with an opportunity to broaden their education."

Greg Dyke, welcoming the purchase, said: 'I'm delighted the deal has gone through. St Nicholas Place will provide an excellent base in Leicester for a forward-looking BBC. I hope to be invited to open the building!'

diversificAsian

There were those who thought I had a passing physical resemblance to Greg Dyke. I conceded a bit on the height and hair view, adding that both of us also started our working lives in local newspapers. A few colleagues remarked on more than one occasion that I could probably get away with walking around Television Centre and Broadcasting House, ordering more funding for local radio and telling everyone to 'cut the crap' – his widely publicised comment about making life and programmes in the BBC much simpler.

Greg Dyke appeared at the Asian Network in Leicester a couple of times. His first visit coincided with the interviews for the two Assistant Editor jobs which Jenny had approved to strengthen the management structure of her new radio station. A couple of us got 'done' in the morning but the afternoon interviews were shuffled around as we awaited the arrival of the new DG. He turned up on his own, without the entourage that always seemed to surround his predecessor.

Apart from 'cut the crap', another notorious phrase from Greg Dyke was that the BBC was 'hideously white'. Quoted out of an interview with BBC Radio Scotland in January 2001, it resonated with my colleagues at the Asian Network. Dyke said he looked around at a Christmas party he had hosted a couple of weeks earlier and saw only one person who was not white. He claimed 98 per cent of BBC management was white.

The BBC was not racist, he said, but it was failing to represent the diversity of the population that it served. He set a target for 2003 to ensure that 10 per cent of the BBC's UK workforce and 4 per cent of its management were from the ethnic minorities. He said many ethnic staff seemed to leave before having the opportunity to rise through the ranks, and he wondered if they just did not feel welcome in the Corporation. Eleven years later, Neila Butt, one of the longest serving and most senior Asian editors at the Asian Network, remarked on her still being the only 'brown' face at a big meeting of senior management people from all the BBC radio networks.

Greg Dyke's second visit to Leicester was when he condemned Epic House as the worst offices in the BBC. 'As I said when I spoke to staff on day one, people are entitled to decent accommodation to work in' said Dyke. 'A lot of our accommodation right across the BBC simply is n't good enough. The aim is to improve our properties at no additional cost to the BBC'. The new Leicester building, superbly designed by architect Colin Bass, cost about four million pounds. The plan was to gut the building and start again, incorporating an 'inviting' public access space where people could see into Radio Leicester's studios, use a learning centre, loiter in a café and browse in a BBC shop. An 11th century Norman stone undercroft was buried under the site and would have to be preserved.

On Sunday 28th October 2001 at about 4.30pm, a significant earth tremor rumbled across the East Midlands. It was felt across Nottinghamshire, Leicestershire, Lincolnshire and Derbyshire. A child was reportedly thrown out of bed but there were no reports of serious injuries or damage. The British Geological Survey said it registered 3.8 on the Richter scale and that the epicentre was in the Leicester area. Asian Network staff working in Epic House certainly felt they were at the 'epic-centre'.

There were nine Asian Network people working on a Diwali special programme on the tenth floor of Epic House. Some Radio Leicester staff were on the floor below. Mintu Rahman rang me at home to say the whole building shook twice and they were all very concerned. The building was apparently designed to have some 'give' in it but this was of little consolation to people in it at the time. We decided that, if it happened again, they should put on the 'emergency tape' until someone in Birmingham could take over output and then get out.

Numerous BBC offices and email accounts could now boast an impressive collection of notes about Epic House in Leicester and the trials and tribulations of working there – but an earthquake was a new avenue to explore. Attaching the news bulletin from Radio Leicester, I sent an email to the 'Senior Facilities Manager, Regional Premises, English Regions'. 'We have various contingencies for Epic House scenarios – but earth tremors is a new one. Is it BBC practice to request a structural survey of any of its premises after such an occurrence (not least in the view of the Epic House history)?'

One of the people that I copied into the note was Caroline Elliot, a senior Radio 4 producer who was now responsible for all kinds of projects and strategies at Radio and Music headquarters. Initially Claire Paul was the link between the Asian Network and Jenny Abramsky but over the years, it was Caroline who got the calls and emails about the latest drama unfolding in the Midlands or convoluted explanations as to why the Asian Network could not operate in the same way as Radio 3. She was relentlessly gracious and patient.

Many new people were now beating a path to our door before and after we formally joined Radio and Music on 1st April 2001. We did not sever our ties with English Regions and Vijay was still reporting to Andy Griffee, the Controller of English Regions, as well as Jenny Abramsky. Owen Bentley, who had retired as senior manager for network radio in the Midlands, was persuaded to come out of retirement to help us prepare for the DAB roll-out. His part-time consultancy role proved invaluable and he stayed on-call for us for another five years. Sangeeta Kotak, the long serving finance assistant who worked for me in my Network Manager years, got her foot in the BBC door with a job on Leicester reception.

Three years after the newsroom was established, we started to get visitors from the top of BBC News. Steve Mitchell, then Head of BBC Radio News, and Bill Rogers, Managing Editor of the same parish, came to visit, bearing gifts of better co-operation and support from the centre and a 'rolling attachment' of an experienced Five Live journalist to sit across our news bulletins. Bill was named as our point of contact and would organise the attachments and also arrange for our journalists to spend time in the London newsroom. Ceri Thomas, then the Five Live Breakfast Editor and later Editor of the Today programme, was another visitor.

The terrible earthquake in Gujarat in January 2001 was the sort of story where we really needed help. It killed 20,000 and injured nearly 170,000. Many of the Asian Network's listeners had strong connections with this region, and those people – as was the case in other major tragedies over the years in Pakistan, Bangladesh and Sri Lanka – expected the BBC to give them fast and accurate information.

We pushed for better links with BBC correspondents such as Owen Bennett-Jones in Pakistan. Bennett-Jones was familiar with some aspects of the Asian Network as he regularly got emails which should have been sent to Owen Bentley.

So it was that people like Dafydd Rees and later Stephanie Hyner, both senior broadcast journalists from Five Live, came to Leicester to lend their experience and get a crash course in all things Asian. Like me before them, there were pitfalls to be avoided that could show up your lack of knowledge about your new constituency.

The name Piara Khabra may initially appear to be a female first name to a non-Asian but ofcourse it was not – Piara was a man and, at the time, the longest serving Asian MP in the House of Commons. And how many famous Imran Khans were there? The Pakistani international cricketer turned politician certainly, but there was also an actor (a nephew of established Bollywood star Aamir Khan) and the increasingly high profile London solicitor who represented the parents of the murdered black teenager Stephen Lawrence.

'Asian Life' website was run by the Asian Programmes Unit in Birmingham which produced the 'Network East' television shows that were tucked away late night on BBC2. The website was launched in 1998 and was more of a magazine and lifestyle format than the Asian Network one, which primarily supported the on-air offering. Both were getting around 25,000-30,000 hits a week – Asian Life users being older and more representative of the whole UK Asian population than the Asian Network's which was more Midlands-orientated.

Both web-teams viewed each other suspiciously and believed each was taking users from the other. But both suffered from a lack of funding and resources, an ineffective management structure and no long term strategy. The sites were also starting to duplicate ideas and material, especially in the news, sport, music, faith and film areas, so London sent someone called Rhiannon Lewis to unpick the mess. The idea of having only one entry portal for all the BBC's Asian presence on-line was agreed but ultimately 'Asian Life' disappeared anyway, along with the Asian Programmes Unit.

Over the years, I had got used to public speaking. In Lincolnshire and Cornwall, I was often invited to speak about the BBC to the emergency services, councillors, magistrates, business groups,

Women's Institutes and the like. It usually involved an overall plug for the BBC, a plea to listen to the local radio station, an explanation of how we got our news and it ended with me playing a tape of some radio 'bloopers' (on-air cock-ups) to leave them smiling before the warm white wine and the rubber chicken.

However it was still a surprise and somewhat unnerving to be asked to talk on 'Communication in a Multi-Cultural Society'. The invitation came from the Celebrating Diversity Working Group of Accrington Church and Great Harwood Partnership in Lancashire. It was a sobering reminder of the responsibilities that came with being the news editor for the BBC Asian Network. I was now talking with some authority about a world that I had only known for three years.

Mind you, I could also get away with talking with no authority whatsoever. As the band Joi played at the 1999 Mega Mela awards dinner, English Regions' Controller Andy Griffee leaned over and shouted; 'They're good, are n't they? Are they on your playlist?'. I had no idea. 'Absolutely, oh yes!'

It was now clear that the Asian Network was going national on DAB with a target date of May 2002. Staffing levels were being increased in preparation, with two Assistant Editors reporting to Vijay. I was appointed as the News one based in Leicester and Ishfaq Ahmed, already an SBJ on the network and who had worked at Five Live, got the Programmes remit. In turn we became responsible for more broadcast journalists and assistants rolling out at some 60 full time posts, prompting concerns that there might not be enough room for everyone in the new accommodation planned in both Leicester and Birmingham. The ten desks initially allocated for the Asian Network in the new Birmingham Mailbox building were flagged as totally inadequate.

Some of the external applicants who did not get a job nevertheless got a second chance. Described as 'full of potential but not immediately appointable', they were invited to an assessment day and the top five embarked on a specially devised four week training course in Leicester. Organised by the ubiquitous Mr Bentley, the course covered all the practical journalism and production skills and offered a four week placement off the end of it. Funding was provided by the BBC's Diversity Centre and the course won a nomination for innovation at the British Diversity Awards.

All five got jobs with the BBC, with three of them joining the Asian Network in the following months. Devan Maistry, who had worked as a journalist in South Africa, joined the language programmes while Anubha Chaturvedi and Rozina Iqbal both joined the newsteam. Anubha later went on to work for the main BBC newsroom in London and rose to became assistant editor at Radio 1's *Newsbeat*, while Rozina became the main news presenter for the Asian Network. They came on board to help in a busy year which included two of the biggest stories the network ever covered – the riots in the north and the 9/11 terror attacks.

CHAPTER 11

confrontAsian

A new system for playing out news bulletins and programmes was being rolled out across BBC English Regions. It was imaginatively called 'Radioman' and would change the way in which everyone worked. Although we were now part of network radio which used a system called Dira VCS, it was decided that, out in the provinces, it made sense for the Asian Network to go with the system that everyone around it was using.

At 2pm on Tuesday 11th September, a Radioman training session was set up for about 15 staff in the top floor conference room of Epic House in Leicester. As I went off to the session, the newsroom television was showing a pall of smoke coming off the side of one of the Twin Towers in New York amid reports that a light aircraft had hit it. I asked the newsreader to let me know if anything significant developed.

A short time later, one of the Broadcast Assistants, Panna Mawji, put her head round the door of the conference room and beckoned to me. I arrived back at my desk to see a replay of an aircraft hitting the tower – it clearly was not a 'light' aircraft. The scale of what was happening was beginning to unfold and it was obvious that this was now a huge story for every news organisation across the globe. I returned to the conference room and pulled all the journalists out of the Radioman session.

Navinder Bhogal was on-air hosting her gentle programme of music, competitions and features in Hindustani. It was being broadcast from the Leicester studio on the floor below the newsroom. I went down with a news flash, explained what was happening and asked her to introduce me as soon as possible. Understanding only the words 'Mike Curtis' from Navinder, I read out in English what we knew so far and said I would be back with more details. I duly returned 15 minutes later with another update.

There were not many of us in Leicester. Kamlesh and Deepak were on a sports course in Bristol. Another of our senior team, Perminder Khatkar, was on a Social Action course in London. Navinder's programme was due to run on until 4pm when our Drive programme picked up from Birmingham. The Drive team, with presenter Sameena Ali Khan, was already on the case, lining up interviewees and plucking out audio from the GNS circuits, Five Live and the BBC TV news channel.

There was more than an hour to go before Drive would start in Birmingham and they were not ready to go early. It would be unfair to expect Navinder to suddenly anchor a rolling news programme in English – and we did not have the resources in Leicester to stretch beyond a longer bulletin on the hour and news flashes. There was only one thing for it. I gave Navinder a note for her to translate for her listeners. It read that, after the 3pm bulletin, 'in view of the events unfolding in the United States, we would be joining our colleagues at BBC Radio Five Live for an hour'.

Although we carried World Service South Asian programmes and later Five Live as our overnight sustaining service between 1am and 6am, the only time it was likely that you would go to another radio station in your core hours would be in the event of a Royal death. But as Five Live expertly channelled the devastating breaking news out of our Asian Network speakers, I was convinced I had taken the right decision. That hour gave our small and relatively inexperienced team a breathing space to deliver some superb output for the rest of the day and the following morning.

The terror attacks in the United States had huge implications for our audience. There was a rise in Islamaphobia, and Sikhs were abused in the street simply because they wore a turban. The news team and importantly our morning phone-in charted the developments and our reporters went deep into the Asian communities.

The coverage was shortlisted in the Radio News category in the 2002 'Race in the Media Awards' run by the Commission for Racial Equality. The judges said: 'The tragedy of September 11 posed unique reporting issues for BBC Asian Network as it became apparent their audience, especially Muslim and Sikh, were directly affected by reprisals. Media coverage could have aggravated various factions or produced rising anger and panic. Staff briefings and input from community advisors ensured sensitivity in all reporting and analyses'.

The BBC conducted a survey among British Muslims a month or so after 9/11. More than 80 percent said there was no justification for the Twin Towers attacks – and a similar percentage said the resulting war in Afghanistan was unjustified. More than 90 per cent said the USA and its allies should have pursued the individuals suspected of being behind the attacks through diplomatic efforts alone. A quarter of those Muslims questioned said they or a member of their family had faced hostility or abuse from non-Muslims as a result of 9/11.

A year later, we sent a small team to the United States to talk to Asians living in New York and compare their experiences in the aftermath of 9/11 with those of Asians in the UK. Their broadcasts from the USA on and around the first anniversary of 9/11, along with our reflective reporting in the UK, were later reviewed by the Radio and Music Programme Review Board.

'We heard things that we have never heard before' was typical of the comments. Senior managers and producers from all the other networks were generally effusive – the Asian Network's coverage of

9/11 one year on and the subsequent impact on UK Asians was 'refreshing', 'remarkable' and used radio in a 'fantastic' way. The emotional impact was remarkable and the interviews were intelligent and gave the listener the ability to stand back and reflect. The Asian Network reporters had also been to the Regent's Park mosque in London to talk to Muslims about how they were now perceived – and they interviewed Sikhs who had been targeted for abuse simply because they were 'Asian'. Jenny Abramsky, chairing the meeting, described the output as 'terrific' and said it was a real example of knowing your audience. 'We really need to hear Asian voices on other networks', she added.

The BBC is often accused of making too much of stories from the USA compared to similar tragedies or incidents elsewhere in the world. There was no question that the 9/11 attacks deserved the huge coverage but it was interesting to see how lesser American stories could dominate BBC bulletins. In 1999, the BBC television bulletins made much of preparations along the East coast of the USA for a violent hurricane. On the Asian Network, we were leading with a cyclone that had already hit the east coast of India. Ten thousand had died in Orissa already but it took some time for the mainstream BBC news to catch up with the scale of that tragedy.

On 21ˢᵗ September 2005, I sent a gentle reminder to the Asian Network news team: 'Please keep across the storms in the Bay of Bengal. Other BBC outlets are paying more attention to Hurricane Rita and its potential impact on the southern US states – the storms hitting India and Bangladesh have already caused death and chaos (hundreds missing, 30,000 evacuated)'.

—∽∽—

In the months before 9/11, there were riots in Burnley, Oldham and Bradford. News stories told of 'Asian' youths rioting but it was a lazy description. The youths were predominantly of a Pakistani background – a point that Indian listeners made repeatedly to the BBC. At the time Bradford had 68,000 Pakistanis, around twelve and a half thousand Indians and five thousand Bangladeshis. The same argument has been raised repeatedly over the years. In 2012 British Sikhs and Hindus criticised the BBC and the media for the use of the term 'Asian' in connection with child sex grooming by gangs of men who were mainly of Pakistani Muslim background.

Frustration at lack of opportunities and anger over right wing anti-immigrant demonstrations were blamed for the youths taking to the streets. Police faced around a thousand rioters across three nights in Bradford. It was a dangerous story to cover. Our Bradford reporter Sanjiv Buttoo was forced to run for safety with other BBC colleagues as the rioters breached the police barricades and petrol bombs rained down. A BBC cameraman was slightly injured. Events in Bradford dominated the Asian Network news agenda for days and the number of calls to the phone-in doubled.

Sanjiv's local knowledge meant he was in demand across many BBC outlets over the weekend. He told the BBC's in-house staff newspaper Ariel: 'We were surprised by the severity of the violence but behind the mindless thuggery, there were stories of real cross-community support – local people going out of their way to keep each other safe'.

On the other side of the Pennines, our Manchester reporter Rahila Bano fired off a very long email to Steve Mitchell, Head of Radio News. She was angry about the relationship between the Asian Network and the rest of BBC News, saying it consistently failed to tackle Asian stories in the north west. She cited the examples of police in Oldham leading football supporters through an Asian area which led to violence, and also comments made by a senior police commander about the number of racist attacks on white people by Asians.

After the riots in Oldham, Rahila said many Asians were telling her that the BBC had 'watered down' its coverage as it did not want to upset the police and the authorities. They said the media generally did not report racial attacks on Asians and, when it did try to reflect the Asian communities, it usually went to the self-appointed 'community leaders' who were not representative. She also felt her expertise was overlooked, despite having passed on her best contacts to the national and regional correspondents.

Rahila had made her point to the top of BBC News, albeit in a long-winded way. It was a familiar cry – BBC local radio stations had long complained that national news outlets only wanted contact names and numbers from them. They did not trust the local journalists to cover the story properly. I had sympathy with Rahila but Vijay told her that she was seriously worried when reporters, who should be out and about gathering news and digging out original stories, felt compelled to spend their time writing very long notes of this nature!

There was criticism of the wider BBC's coverage of the riots in the north west – and the BBC's Manchester boss Martin Brooks said feelings were running high in his patch. Steve Mitchell suggested taking some of his network editors up north to brief them on what to do differently if riots broke out again. The Asian Network would be involved in that meeting. In August, Greg Dyke announced more resources would be thrown at the north-west to help Radio 4 in particular to reflect 'the culture, aspirations and interests' of the north'. Years later, huge swathes of BBC production were moved to Salford.

Before the riots, the Asian Network went to Bradford for a week in March. The Drive programme was broadcast from the BBC studio in the city with presenter Nasser Hanif, who co-hosted the last two hours with Mussy Abassi, the presenter of the Radio Leeds Asian programme 'Connections'. Sanjiv Buttoo had produced a series on the 50th anniversary of the Asian communities in Bradford, an event which had also been featured in a special television programme by BBC *Look North*. The same month, we took our Drive show to Blackburn with Sameena Ali-Khan presenting. The programme included reports from Nasser at Bury football ground where the Pakistan national side were playing for the first time outside of the sub-continent.

Asian Network was back in Bradford after the riots for the BBC's Music Live weekend. It staged a concert featuring Kavita Krishnamurthy at the St George's Concert Hall in Bradford and, earlier in the day, ran a three hour show from a stage in Centenary Square in Bradford.

Later in the year, Ted Cantle's report on the riots came out, having been commissioned by Home Secretary David Blunkett. It made 70 recommendations and introduced the concept of 'community cohesion' by promoting cross cultural contact, developing support for diversity, promoting unity and tackling inequality and prejudice. Ted Cantle concluded that the towns hit by the riots showed a 'depth of polarization' around segregated communities living 'a series of parallel lives'.

CHAPTER 12

dramatisAsian

T he Master of the Household was commanded by Her Majesty the Queen to invite Mr Mike Curtis to Windsor Castle in April. One of the events to mark the Queen's Golden Jubilee was a reception for Her Majesty's Media. Shoes polished and remaining hair trimmed, I duly presented myself at the Castle gates, joining a long line of newspaper, television, radio and magazine glitterati. There were a lot of people I recognised and a few BBC people I knew.

We did not get the little booklet listing all the attendees until we left. Like the Sony Awards judges list, I found myself alongside an awesome roll call of public figures. I never saw Jenny Bond, Alastair Campbell, Michael Gove, Max Hastings, Ian Hislop, Boris Johnson, Marie Colvin, Piers Morgan, Mathew Parris, Janet Street Porter and Nicholas Witchell but, according to the little white book, they were there too. I hesitated to introduce myself to Libby Purves, who had left Radio Oxford for the Today programme a short time before I arrived. I shared a rail carriage back to Waterloo with Simon Hoggart of The Guardian but he never knew.

I did fall into conversation with a convivial commercial radio journalist from Belfast. A few drinks in, he suddenly pointed and said; 'Let's go and meet the Queen!'. Her Majesty was making slow regal progress down the middle of the Great Hall, asking everyone who they wrote for and how far they had come in their careers. My new friend found a gap and lurched forward, bowed deeply, thrust out a hand and exclaimed; 'Your Majesty!'. This surely was outside Royal protocol. Over the bowed figure, the Queen looked at me hanging back with an expression that sighed: 'Is he with you?'. I smiled wanly and bowed slightly.

A few weeks earlier the Queen Mother had passed away. The news broke early on a Saturday evening when newsrooms outside of London were on minimal staffing. There was no one in the Asian Network newsroom so there followed a flurry of activity and frantic phone calls with a presenter and producers in Birmingham fronting an Asian Network programme before and after joining the special national show for all radio networks from London.

A few hours before Mr Ozzy Osbourne let rip with 'Paranoid' in the Monarch's back garden, the Asian Network had rocked Hyde Park as its contribution to the Golden Jubilee and the BBC's 'Music Live'. The Network hosted the Asia stage – one of five set up in the Park to celebrate music from across the Commonwealth. 'Music Live' was a huge enterprise for the BBC, led by people like Bill Morris, Mike Gibbons and Chris Lycett. All three were very supportive of the Asian Network over the years, with Mike, who was Programme Organiser at Radio Devon when I was down the A30 at Radio Cornwall, and Radio 1 veteran Chris Lycett helping us out on site on several ambitious enterprises in the following years.

The Hyde Park stage gave the Asian Network the taste for big music events that it got very good at over the years, such as the London Mela in Gunnersbury Park. Punjabi star Malkit Singh, tabla player Trilok Gurtu, Taz from Stereo Nation and classical saxophone player Kadri Golpanath were among the artists who performed on that June Bank Holiday Monday, introduced by our front-line presenters. The staff briefing warned: 'NB: 41 Gun Salute at 3pm in Hyde Park. Carry on as normal'.

—m—

The 2002 expansion of the Asian Network finally acknowledged that sport – mainly cricket – was important to the output. Up until then, sport had been handled by the newsdesk underpinned by the particular enthusiasm and knowledge of individual team members. I often felt moved to remind those without much interest in it that 'Sport is News' and could sometimes lead the hourly bulletins.

Looking back, amid all the expansion plans and associated costs, it was still surprising that we got funding for four sports journalists. Kamlesh Purohit, Sanjeet Saund, Deepak Patel and newcomer Lee James could now devote their time to the fixtures of the South Asian cricket teams, cover the Commonwealth Games in Manchester later that year and put an Asian 'spin' on general sports stories.

The MCC (Michael Colin Curtis) takes the wicket in June 1957. Teddy was a dire wicket-keeper, lacking agility and shouting 'What was that?' every time he was knocked into the tea chest.

The idea of an Asian Network tournament in the indoor cricket centre at Warwickshire's Edgbaston ground was explored – and got the support of Dennis Amiss, by then Chief Executive of the club. Eight teams (nearly all of them from the north and of Pakistani background) took part. They got the chance to meet Warwickshire's Alan Donald and the legendary West Indian captain Clive Lloyd, who was delayed on the journey from London and turned up right at the end. Unfortunately the tournament proved to be a one-off.

Like the sport initiative, we were upping our game across the board. A former Managing Editor of BBC television news, Phil Longman, was asked by Jenny to help reorganise our London operation. In the new national schedule, the phone-in would be broadcast from BBC Television Centre and the staff would sit alongside Five Live production staff. The logic behind this was that more 'big name' guests would be available in the capital, and that 'good practice' would rub off Five Live onto the new Asian Network.

The BBC is regularly criticised for being top heavy on managers and specifically having too many 'middle managers' floating around just above the production teams. Despite the extra help we were starting to get, the Asian Network was still being run day to day by only three people – and Vijay, Ishfaq and myself had no experience of running a national service. It took two years and a national review of digital radio to bring the Asian Network into line with other national networks.

Among those who came to talk to us in the Midlands in 2002 were two network radio Controllers, Bob Shennan from Five Live and Andy Parfitt from Radio 1. Little did we know how those two would loom large in our lives in later years.

Across the summer of 2002, the plan for the Asian Network to go national on DAB and to broadcast its phone-in from Television Centre in London created a firestorm of work for a small group of technical people at the top of Radio and Music and News. The Asian Network was eventually offered studio S2 in TVC but it was not equipped with the Radioman play out system used by the radio station in Birmingham and Leicester – and it would require a studio manager to operate the desk which was another new expense.

This studio was also used by Five Live and occasionally by some of the Radio 4 news programmes such as *Today*, *The World at One* and *PM*. Consequently the people responsible for the studio were nervous about a bunch of newcomers from the provinces asking for various modifications. To help smooth the process and chase the progress, Owen Bentley asked Dave Wilkinson, my former manager at BBC Radio Lincolnshire, to come on board as a technical project manager.

Dave had an engineering background but was, in his own word, 'bi-lingual', in that he understood production as well and could talk to programme makers and journalists in plain English. He was tasked to sort the London studio and office for the phone-in team, chase the right people to ensure that all the Asian Network's production centres were linked together and to the transmission system, and draw up emergency plans for line failures and major disasters. He also went with Owen and Vijay to speak practical engineering for them at meetings with the London technical teams.

Tim Locke, the production editor for Radio News, described the Asian Network's phone-in show as 'one of the most complex shows produced in Television Centre'. Certainly Radioman was complicating things and eventually the decision was taken to delay its installation until everything else was bedded in, not least the studio managers. It looked as though Radioman could not be delivered until a month or two after the DAB launch anyway, so the SMs would play in the music direct from a CD, and the jingles from a simple system called Cool Play. Without Radioman, the Asian Network show requirements were similar to the Nicky Campbell programme on Five Live although that had the luxury of two studio managers at the time.

The costs of the technical work associated with the Asian Network's launch on DAB and its London phone-in programme were also starting to cause concern. By the end of August, the overall bill was well over £120,000 – well above the initial estimates. Dave Wilkinson was still diplomatically chasing the work that still needed to be done before the launch, such as the back-up transmission connection between Leicester and Birmingham, and the permanent circuits from Television Centre to Leicester. He also flagged the point that staff needed to listen to the DAB output at their desks, which began a scramble for portable DAB radios which, at the time, had the cheapest option at £99 each.

In the middle of all this came another reminder of the fragility of the Asian Network's systems and the consequent risks to its output. A power failure in Epic House in Leicester lasted about 24 hours, leaving everything at the mercy of the emergency power generators. I came within 30 minutes of ordering an evacuation to Pebble Mill – both lifts were out of action, the emergency lighting batteries had run out and the water pump was not working which had led to rapidly deteriorating toilet facilities. Power was restored just as the evacuation plan was about to be activated.

'We can still make the launch date – but it is REALLY tight', wrote Tim Cowin, the Broadcast Projects manager, a few weeks before the agreed date of Monday 28th October. Certainly the relaunch timetable for the Asian Network was much shorter than the run-ins given to other digital stations which were starting from scratch. People like Tim Locke and Tim Cowin, Simon Tuff, the technology specialist at Radio and Music, and another projects manager Dave Seditas were working flat out to meet the deadline. Local support in the Midlands arrived in the form of Gareth Jones, who was appointed as the senior engineer for the Asian Network.

Gareth was good at his job but was not bi-lingual, sympathetically describing bewildered journalists who failed to understand technology as 'muppets'.

Elsewhere in the Midlands, Zab Khan was appointed Music Manager for the station and started to work on playlists for programmes across all the output. This came as a shock to the old timers who were used to playing whatever came to mind or tickled their fancy that day. Neerja Sood was appointed as the senior journalist in charge of weekend broadcasting. Among the newcomers who joined the news team were reporters like Shabnam Mahmood, Phil Churm and Dil Neiyyar. Others who passed through included Kasia Madera (who went on to be a presenter on the BBC News Channel), Priya Kaur Jones (also television-bound to BBC East Midlands Today and later GMTV) and Imtiaz Tyab (whose determination for a reporter job ultimately led him to the BBC News channel and then to be one of Al Jazeera's Pakistan correspondents).

Ian Wood, a freelance who had a legal background but yearned to present radio programmes, was another freelance who passed through the Asian Network newsroom around 2002. Ian's voice was similar to mine in that it was good for radio but not the one you expected to hear on a radio station for Asians. On one occasion after I had read a news bulletin, the programme presenter Shabina Akhtar buzzed through to me on the internal intercom: 'Did we just go to Radio 4 for the news?'. She were right cheeky, that Shabina.

One very hot day in the summer of 2002, Ian Wood rang me from his home in the Derbyshire Peaks and asked if it would be acceptable for him to wear shorts for his late news reading shift. I said ok as long as they were not 'budgie-smugglers' that might offend the more delicate of his colleagues or frighten the horses. Staff were duly warned and bets laid that the shorts would be voluminous and khaki. Ian did not disappoint.

Another journalist who spent some time at the Asian Network in Leicester was Parveen Ramchurn. Whenever a senior appointment was announced with an email to all 20,000 or so BBC staff, Parveen would be moved to send the individual a congratulatory note. So the new Director of Television or Controller of BBC2 would get this note from someone he or she had never heard of, exclaiming: 'This IS exciting news – well done!'.

After Windsor Castle, Spencer House in central London was a step down. However this fine 18th century private palace, built for an ancestor of Princess Diana, was the location for Jenny Abramsky's Summer Receptions for Radio and Music staff. A few Asian Network people got their first invite in 2002 and enjoyed this annual shindig for a few more years until Jenny left the BBC and parsimony prevailed. It was another 'spot the celebrity' opportunity, conducted ofcourse with dignity and insouciance. But I did fall into brief conversations with people like Bob Harris, who had an afternoon show at Radio Oxford when I was there, the admirable Barry Cryer, Lincolnshire-born Nicholas Parsons, and Russell Davies who had edited the wonderfully waspish Kenneth Williams diaries. If someone upset Williams, he would exclaim 'You'll be in my book!'. Now there's a thought.

Three months before the national launch, Jenny Abramsky announced a brand new daily soap opera for the Asian Network. Immediately dubbed the 'Asian Archers', the £1.2 million pound project would follow the lives and loves of a group of people of mainly Asian origin in an urban Midlands town. It mirrored *The Archers* in being broadcast every weekday with an omnibus on Sunday. It would be recorded and produced alongside *The Archers* in Pebble Mill.

Talking to The Guardian, Abramsky admitted the BBC had failed the Asian population and described the relaunch of the Asian Network as one of the most important things it had ever done. She felt the daily soap opera was an important part of the new service. 'Alan Yentob (BBC director of Drama and Entertainment) and I took the decision that a soap was what was needed in the long term on the Asian Network. They did n't ask for it. It was something we took to them as an extra on top of the relaunch. Hopefully it will become *The Archers* for the Asian population. It's a massive investment'.

Gordon House, the head of BBC Radio Drama, said: 'Some websites have been saying that this will be made by white middle class people who know nothing about Asian culture. But the production team we are going to recruit will very much NOT be like that. This soap is going to provide an excellent forum for Asian talent across the UK, if they are writers, directors, performers or technical staff. It's going to be realistic, entertaining with reflections on the challenges that face the British Asian community in their daily lives. It will also be a lot of fun'.

The Labour peer Baroness Uddin, who was heading a Home Office select committee on forced marriage at the time, hoped the BBC would put together a team which had an understanding of the Asian community. 'I hope the soap won't sensationalise Asian lives by concentrating on things like arranged marriages', she said. 'The BBC has a responsibility to the Asian licence payer to ensure that the community is presented in a sensitive and truthful way'.

Dr Ghayasuddin Siddiqui, leader of the Muslim Parliament of Great Britain, was positive about the soap and hoped it was an opportunity to portray Muslim families in a realistic manner. 'Now more than ever before do we need to discuss topics like Islamaphobia, discrimination and segregation, and why the race riots occurred in the North'.

Paresh Solanki, who ran the BBC Asian Programmes Unit in

Birmingham, said: 'Asian culture has now become hip. A confident British Asian identity is now emerging with programmes like *Goodness Gracious Me* and *The Kumars at No 42*'.

Those two television comedy shows and the new radio soap – eventually called 'Silver Street' – demonstrated how far the BBC had come in trying to cater for the growing Asian community and the success of Asians within the UK media. It was a far cry from the BBC's Immigrant Programmes Unit of the 1960s and '*Make yourself at Home*'.

James Peries, the literary manager at the Theatre Royal Stratford East in London, was appointed as the Editor of the new soap. Peries had developed plays from new and established writers at the Theatre Royal, and worked with playwrights, performance poets and rap artists.

The new editor was not short of advice about his new project. Focus groups were set up to get a feel of what the target audience wanted from their new drama. The team's Pebble Mill office walls were covered in post-it notes with ideas, scenarios, character profiles, location suggestions and plot-lines. As Gordon House firmly stated: 'We're certainly not just going to have an Asian corner shop owner whose daughter is having an arranged marriage'.

It took nearly two years to get 'Silver Street' on-air, with the first ten-minute episode being broadcast on 24th May 2004. Despite the quality of the writing, acting and production, it suffered from the constant changes around it and never found a true home amidst all the bhangra and Bollywood. Once the expansion plans were over and the Asian Network had to make cuts, it was inevitable that management turned to expensive drama for the first savings.

Silver Street started as a ten-minute daily episode but over the course of its five year run, those episodes became eight minutes then five. It started in Sonia Deol's morning programme then got moved to lunchtime. No-one was quite sure where to put the daily episode and its evening repeat. The Sunday omnibus also threw up a scheduling issue whatever length it was – 50 minutes, 40 minutes or 25 minutes. It became a popular download podcast in 2007.

The storylines remained strong and the cast sounded good. It won several awards including a top one in the Mental Health Media Honours in 2005. Saeed Jaffrey, Anita Dobson and Toyah Willcox were among well-known names that popped up in the cast – and Sonia, '*Countryfile*'s John Craven and singer Hard Kaur all put in cameos as themselves. Radio Leicester took '*Silver Street*' for 18 months but it was doomed to follow another BBC radio soap, '*Westway*', which lasted eight years up to 2005 on the World Service.

By the middle of 2009, the Asian Network was in trouble with its audience down by 20 per cent and an unwelcome status as the most expensive network radio station in terms of cost per hour. On 16th November that year, it was announced that '*Silver Street*' was to end the following March. Some money was left to fund ten 30 minutes dramas a year until 2012.

CHAPTER 13

nationalisAsian

Less than two months before the DAB launch, there was concern that BBC Marketing had completely missed the point. It seemed that the audience objectives had been misread and Marketing was positioning the Asian Network as a music station aimed at teenagers. This was despite meetings in which they had been told about the importance of speech and news, the 50/50 equal split of output between speech and music, and that the average age of the target audience was a 27 year old family man.

Ishfaq Ahmed, the Assistant Editor responsible for programmes, had come up with this mythical figure to personify the target audience in the minds of staff. Based on the audience research, the 15-34 age group was in our sights because of the UK Asian demographics. In an email to Jenny's 'gatekeeper' Amanda Ashton, Owen Bentley suggested revising this to 20-35 to take the teenagers out of the core audience but not out of the aspirations for late night programming. It put the 27 year old bang in the middle of the age group.

Ishfaq's fictitious 27 year old was named APS (Ali Patel Singh to cover the three main communities). He worked in IT for Nike, lived on a pleasant estate in the heart of a city and was married with a four year old girl. His background, education, interests and religion were all mapped out. He believed he lived in a racist society but he also loved the UK and would not want to live elsewhere. He believed that Britain had improved on race relations over the last ten years.

Elsewhere marketing came up with a list of 'buzzwords' that would define the new Asian Network. 'Dynamic, brave, credible, stylish, sharp, streetwise, passionate, in touch with its roots, articulate, funny, smart, confident, proactive and challenging' just about covered it. It would be truly interactive with its website, text messaging, telephone and other emerging technologies. In the studios, Asian Life's Dharmesh Rajput , who would later lead the radio station's interactive operation, was sorting out the webcams that would show the presenters at work, whether they liked it or not.

'A one-stop shop for Asian communities' was the strapline that Vijay Sharma gave to her revamped national outfit. 'A radio station where they can get national and international stories, music ranging from the latest Asian sounds to old favourites, gossip and debate, religion and South Asian languages. A radio station that will hold up a mirror to the communities. If there is a hot issue to be talked about, we will not shy away from it. In the process, we may annoy a few people but that is what debate is all about'.

Fronting the daily debate programme from the new London studio was Sonia Deol. Back from BBC London, 29 year old Sonia attracted most of the publicity. Described in BBC publicity as 'this chatty, vivacious young woman', she was also very photogenic and the media loved her. Asjad Nazir, a journalist on the west London-based *Eastern Eye* newspaper, was moved to write: 'Bright and bubbly, she has all the high-kicking presence of a Charlie's Angel with the beguiling looks and sultry presence of a silent era screen goddess. Tall, slender yet curvy with stunning skin and perfect hair, she is the personification of femininity. She is dressed in clothes that show off her stunning new figure'.

While the besotted Nazir continued to salivate over his double page spread with five photos, other plaudits rained down on Sonia. In a comment reminiscent of 'the future of rock and roll' line aimed

Sonia Deol

at a young Bruce Springsteen, the media correspondent for BBC News, Nick Higham, opened an article for *Broadcast* magazine with: 'I have heard the future of digital radio and she's called Sonia Deol'. Gathering his composure, he went on to point out that in 2002 only 85,000 digital radios had been sold and that the cheapest was just under £100. He hoped that the Asian Network – with Sonia ofcourse – would boost demand for digital radios to benefit all stations, including the 127 that were broadcasting solely on digital.

Much was made of the Asian communities being enthusiastic embracers of new technology and therefore they would all rush out and buy digital radios. Among questions anticipated by the BBC press office was one that, in view of the fact that few people owned digital radios, the Asian Network on DAB was just paying 'lip service' to these communities. We were told our answer should be that research shows that Asians are 'well disposed to adopting new technology and include more multi-channel households than on average. This, coupled with the decreasing price of digital radios, means we expect the national audience to build strongly'.

Jenny Abramsky asked for more detailed audience research ahead of the relaunch which was going to take the Asian Network's annual budget up by £900,000 to £2.7 million by the end of 2002. She wanted to be sure that the BBC was going for the right gap in the market. The station was going to pitch its core programmes at Asians aged between 25 and 35 but also aim, at various times in the schedule, to attract those over 45 and younger people down to age 15. Jenny wanted to be convinced that young Asians would listen in sufficient numbers to the music and speech mix, and was worried that the target audience was already hooked on commercial local stations and would not abandon them for the Asian Network.

There were also doubts about getting to more people in the heartland of the Midlands. Jenny wanted to know what the audience thought of the existing Asian Network in late 2001. Why did 80 per cent of the available audience here still not listen? There was a notable drop in the audience figures amongst the Pakistani community in the West Midlands at the end of 2001. Was this down to a problem with the sample of listeners chosen to take part or did people in that community just not bother to respond after the 9/11 attacks in the USA?

The worries about targeting the right age group were a recurring feature in the story of the Asian Network. One idea discussed before the DAB launch was splitting the Asian Network into two different services at certain times, making the digital platform the main station for the 25-35 age group and running programmes for the older listeners on the analogue AM frequencies. This plan did not stand up after a SWOT analysis – strengths, weaknesses, opportunities and threats – and it would have been too expensive.

While public awareness of the radio station and the ability to actually hear it were paramount, the success of the revamped Asian Network would lie with the presenter line-up. On weekdays, Gagan Grewal kept his slot on the weekday Breakfast Show. Aged 24, he was already a veteran radio performer having secured work at Sunrise in London. A two-week work placement when he was 15 ended up as a three year stint at Sunrise. Ray Khan moved to lunchtime, Navinder Bhogal and Sameena Ali Khan kept their afternoon and Drive time slots and the part-time language presenters just carried on. The decision was taken to retain the separate East Midlands language programmes which could only be heard on the Leicester medium wave transmitter (837 AM). The West Midlands language programmes went out on the national digital platforms.

Competing with Sonia for the star turn in the launch publicity was 28 year old Adil Ray. Coming from commercial music stations Choice FM in Birmingham and Galaxy 105 in Yorkshire, Adil had joined the Asian Network the previous year and decided, in his words, 'to nestle in with them as big plans were ahead'. For the publicity, he described his late weeknight show as 'young, irreverent, pioneering, bhangra and massive'. It aimed to showcase the latest music from British Asians, hosting live sessions and flagging up new talent.

Writing in the Sunday Express, critic Ken Garner waxed lyrical: 'I thought the BBC's new digital black music station 1Xtra was groovy. That was until I tuned into Adil Ray and his late night show of contemporary British Asian music. The styles of dance music he plays have the odd airing nationally (John Peel, Andy Kershaw, Pete Tong) but to have 150 minutes nightly is a revelation. It's like landing on another planet. Even if non-Asians are only passers-by, loving the music as a tourist might, what the BBC Asian Network does is make you see – or rather hear – another Britain. In some respects, it sounds a great Britain in which to live'.

One of the leading lights in the Asian music business, Rishi Rich, said the Network provided a credible outlet to showcase new British Asian talent. 'Whether they are a singer/songwriter, journalist, musician, radio presenter, DJ or basically anyone trying to break into a career in the media, they provide a very powerful platform for us'.

Mo Dutta, who had a weekend early show on Radio 2 and was well known on daytime TV, was recruited to front the weekend Breakfast Shows. Maz Khan (new to radio after working as entertainment correspondent for Sky News) and Rajni Sharma looked after Bollywood matters on Saturday and Sunday mornings. The new sports team got its own programme on Saturday afternoons, presented by Sanjeet Saund. Mike Allbut, Kanwal Qazi, Veronica, Najma Saeed, Anwarul Huq, Navid Akhtar and the internationally known DJ Ritu completed the weekend line-up.

Away from the presentation, my news operation was tasked with finding good exclusive stories for the launch week and beyond. Sanjiv Butto discovered a report from medical experts about disabilities attributed to inter-family marriages among the Pakistani community in Bradford. It claimed that up to 50 per cent faced some sort of disability as a result of people marrying their cousins. Other stories surrounded the growing number of young Asian millionaires, a shortage of Asian GPs, plans for Europe's largest Sikh temple in Southall, a look back at what if anything had changed six months on from the riots in Lancashire towns, and a series on the changing face of Asian London.

One of the first guests on Sonia's show was the Bollywood actor Aamir Khan, star of the hit film 'Lagaan'. Arriving in a hurry at Television Centre, he backed his car into one owned by a BBC employee. Khan claimed this individual threatened to punch him and, according to a BBC insider talking to *The Independent*, he asked for an escort off the premises after the interview in case the man was still waiting for him.

On more serious matters, the mother of Ricky Reel, a student from Kingston-upon-Thames who drowned after a racist attack in 1997, was another guest, as was Satpal Ram from Birmingham who served 16 years in prison for killing a man. He said he had been defending himself against a racist attack and wanted to clear his name.

The Guardian's Elizabeth Mahoney often wrote positively about the Asian Network. After the launch, she called it 'populist and passionate radio at its powerful best'. She said the output felt rather '5 Livey' but with plenty of good music, thus making the BBC Asian Network 'that most rare thing – an intelligent speech station that is also a smart place for music'.

'Immediately, it felt different. From the first moments of Sonia Deol's mid-morning show, BBC Asian Network felt vital in more ways than one. Yes, it was about time the BBC addressed its under-serving of the British Asian community, and you do wonder why they chose to begin their digital radio operations with the lumpen 6 Music, aimed at a rather more well-provided for audience. But just as importantly, BBC Asian Network is finally a new digital station with a bit of life about it'.

The commercial Asian radio stations had a different view, claiming the BBC was trying to muscle in on their lucrative market. 'The Asian commercial radio market has been around for 12 years and the BBC are taking the fruits when they have come up to ripe', said Shujat Ali, chief executive of Asian Sound Radio in Manchester. 'But the BBC have the funds and resources to railroad the commercial operators'. The BBC pointed out that no commercial enterprise had offered a national station for Asians. Apart from taking listeners, there would also be complaints about the BBC luring the best presenters from commercial stations over the years.

The Asian Network saw commercial television stations as serious competition, especially those a few clicks away on digital satellite. There were around 20 Asian channels on Sky Digital, including the big four with parent channels in India – Zee TV, B4U (specialising on Bollywood) , Sony TV Asia and Star TV.

Home Secretary David Blunkett was another early guest on Sonia's phone-in. He had agreed to take calls for about 20 minutes but stayed for an hour, speaking to mostly hostile callers. Blunkett had upset many Asians a month earlier by suggesting they should all learn and speak English in their own homes. He believed it would improve family relationships across the generations. Earlier in the year, he questioned arranged marriages back in the sub-continent and urged young people to find spouses in the UK. On both issues he was accused of trying to dictate the private lives of the UK Asians and many came on the phone-in to argue with him.

Another regular contributor to Asian Network debates over the years was Aki Nawaz, the Muslim front man of the band 'Fun-Da-Mental' and founder of Nation Records. He applauded the station for entertaining some very edgy subjects and 'creating a platform not only for Asians to air their view but also non-Asians to participate fully and unconditionally. The very unconservative attitude of their station is reassuring as it is much needed to represent the wider community and especially the young people'.

Aki Nawaz was always good value but he did occasionally give the phone-in production teams some heart-stopping moments with his passionately held views on life. He nearly got arrested in Bradford in 2001 for comments made on the Asian Network music stage about local policing in the riots. Shortly after his outburst, two of West Yorkshire's finest appeared backstage asking who was the most senior BBC person on site. 'Er, that will be me, then', I confessed, Vijay having gone walkabout. The constabulary were concerned about incitement in front of such a large crowd. I convinced them to leave it to me to have a word and there would be no repeat. We got away with it.

The BBC made quite a fuss about the new Asian Network on relaunch day. Sonia popped up on Breakfast TV, Five Live and the Today programme. World Service and the News Channel (then News 24) interviewed Vijay and there were features on BBC London, Midlands Today and the national One and Six O' Clock News. All the Asian MPs in the House of Commons, including Keith Vaz, Piara Khabra, Marsha Singh, Parmjit Dhanda and Khalid Mahmood, signed an Early Day Motion congratulating the station on its launch and welcoming the BBC's commitment to make the Network available across the UK. Fifty five other MPs also signed up.

Four days after the launch and just ahead of Ramadhan, Jenny hosted a big party at Zandra Rhodes' Fashion and Textile Museum in Bermondsey. Actors Saeed Jaffrey, Ameet Chana and Deepak Verma, MP Keith Vaz, Rishi Rich, comic Jeff Mirza and Radio 1 DJs Bobby Friction and Nihal were – according to the gushing *Asian Express* – 'among the Asian celebrities who turned up, tuned in and partied all night'. DG Greg Dyke put in an appearance and live music was provided by Rahat Fateh Ali Khan, nephew of the Qawwali legend Nusrat. A few years later, Saeed was on '*Silver Street*', Ameet , Bobby and Nihal were all presenting on the Network and Rahat was being introduced on his sell-out tours of the UK by Asian Network presenters.

CHAPTER 14

invAsian

The second Iraq war dominated the news agenda in 2003 but six weeks before it started, the Asian Network had a poignantly sad angle on another major story. On a Saturday afternoon at the beginning of February, reports started to come in that the American space shuttle Columbia was in trouble as it returned from space. One of the astronauts on board was an Indian-born Mission Specialist called Kalpana Chawla.

India was justifiably proud of Kalpana Chawla, who was the first Indian woman in space. Her success highlighted its own sometimes controversial space programme and had been an encouragement to many aspiring female astronauts around the world. On her second space flight, she died with the rest of the Columbia crew after the shuttle broke up as it re-entered the earth's atmosphere. The Asian Network extended its bulletins that afternoon and reported the many tributes in the following days, but no radio could match the chilling film of the trails across the Texan and Louisiana skies as Columbia disintegrated.

After her first launch, Kalpana Chawla said from space: 'When you look at the stars and the galaxy, you feel that you are not just from any particular piece of land but from the solar system'.

On 19th March 2003, the first air strikes were launched against Iraq and the second invasion of that country in just over a decade was underway. Since the beginning of the year, BBC editors had been summoned to briefings and meetings about the likelihood of this conflict following the military campaign in Afghanistan after 9/11. *Ariel*, the BBC's in-house newspaper, ran a story on how BBC4 and the Asian Network were preparing and quoted me thus: 'We have a large Muslim audience and our messageboards and phone-in have shown an overwhelming opposition to any war'.

Jenny Abramsky decided that we should have some senior editorial support for the first few weeks of the Iraq war and suggested two very experienced former colleagues. Sue Bonner had worked for the main Radio 4 news sequence programmes *Today* and *The World at One*. Bob Simpson had retired five years earlier after a career as one of the BBC's most travelled and trusted foreign correspondents. The plan was for them to primarily take turns to sit alongside Sonia on the phone-in show and explain developments and put breaking news into context. I was asked to contact them both and sound them out.

Bob Simpson had also started his career in local newspapers and BBC local radio (at Brighton and Sheffield). But while I sat out the first Gulf War in 1991 in the newsroom at BBC Radio Lincolnshire, Bob was on the front line, defying his bosses back home by refusing to leave Baghdad when the allied attacks intensified. He was working alongside his namesake John Simpson and was with him when their cameraman got footage out of their hotel window of a cruise missile whizzing down the street and apparently turning left at the traffic lights.

Bob related this story and many other reporter tales over lunchtime pints in a pub near Shepherds Bush after the show. He needed reassurance that his contribution was working – why would an Asian audience wanted to hear an old white journalist sitting in London telling them what was going on in a war in a Muslim country? The production team of George Mann, Rabiya Parekh, Sheetal Parmar and Bill Mostyn assured both Bob and Sue that it was working well. Although he had a newsroom reputation for being grumpy over the years, Bob worked well with us and we all enjoyed having him on board. I liked him enormously, enjoyed his company and was in awe of his experience. He died three years later at the age of 61.

That spring the Sonia show got another Sony radio awards nomination in the Interaction category for its work the year before. The coverage across 2002 of the aftermath of 9/11, led by Harjinder Mann, also got us a nomination at the Race in the Media Awards. Another nomination at RIMA was for '*Any Sporting Questions*', a Five Live sports panel programme which concentrated on Asian sports in the UK for one edition. At its recording in Leicester, presenter John Inverdale, who had worked with me at Lincolnshire, said in the warm-up that he had been talking earlier to 'the boss of the Asian Network Mike Curtis'. My colleagues all turned round and grinned at my apparent elevation. Mercifully Vijay was not there.

Five Live poached our most pro-active reporter in July when Rahul Tandon was given a six month attachment as the station's Birmingham regional journalist. But to compensate, the Asian Network benefitted from a Community Affairs journalist, Helen Dafedjaiye, who was given a six month attachment by Five Live to work out of Leicester.

The Gujarati speakers of Leicester and beyond were not happy with us at the beginning of the year. Just before Christmas 2002, a 45 page petition had arrived at the offices of the BBC Governors in Broadcasting House. Signed by around 1000 people from the East Midlands, it highlighted complaints about the way in which Gujarati listeners were being treated by the Asian Network. Specifically they were angry that they had to stay up late on a Saturday night to hear Mira Trevedi's two hour show.

In the schedule shuffle-round, the weekend language shows in Gujarati in the East Midlands and Mirpuri in the West Midlands lost their cosy 6pm-9pm slot on a Sunday evening. Instead they were replaced by four separate shows for the new national audience on Saturday and Sunday late nights. Punjabi and Gujarati ran on Saturdays and Mirpuri and Bengali on Sundays.

The petitioners said the presentation and content had not been reviewed for a long time and as a result, the programme was becoming less appealing to ardent Gujarati speakers. Such was the low esteem in which it was now held by the Asian Network, it had been moved to the 'unearthly' time of 10pm to midnight which 'was an insult to younger listeners and older mature listeners from whom it is bedtime by then'.

The BBC met a delegation but held the line. It pointed out that the Gujarati-speaking community was super-served in the East Midlands with a weekday regional programme as well as the two national ones. It also said that initial audience research since the changes showed a modest growth in listening. Nearly two years later (in September 2004) the dispute was still rumbling on with letters of complaint from a Gujarati association in Nottingham, The Swaminarayan Hindu Mission in Leicester and the Hindu Council of Birmingham.

Over the years, the weekend language programmes were shuffled around but the last programme on the Sunday night was usually deemed too late by its listeners even after the introduction of the 'listen again' option on-line. It was the same with the weekend devotional music shows which, at an hour long for each religion, meant someone had to set a 4am alarm to hear their bit.

—ᴧᴧ—

In five years at the Asian Network, I had never actually met a Bollywood star. Not quite on my list of 100 things to do before I die, but nevertheless my chance came at the next Mega Mela which this time was held at Wembley Exhibition Halls in London. Another three days of wall to wall bhangra at high volume, it was an opportunity to meet our audience a year after the digital launch and push our presence in London in particular. Marketing put an advert in the Mela programme which had the slogan 'Have you heard yourself lately?' which I thought was somewhat ambiguous. Rather like the old slogan of one BBC local radio station which proclaimed 'We'll let you know.'

The star attraction was Karisma Kapoor from one of Bollywood's most famous dynasties. Karisma, sister of Kareema and married only the week before, glided around backstage, nodding serenely as people like me were introduced to her. She appeared on the main stage for what was described as an 'intimate' one-to-one with Asian Network presenters, talking about her career, her fantastic family and her plans for the future. It was my first experience of the circus surrounding Bollywood – not just the devotion of the fans but also the shenanigans around the agents, hangers-on, the travel arrangements, the hotels , the dressing room 'riders' and the money.

Celebrities usually travel with an entourage but one occasion back in Birmingham in 2006, the star and his team were overwhelmed by Asian Network staff and their friends and relatives. The cause of the excitement was actor, producer and former model John Abraham who came to the studio for an interview one evening. These friends and relative were let in through a fire exit, by-passing the main reception, and then crammed into the studio areas, taking photographs, tripping over cables, squealing for autographs and talking loudly – basically breaking every radio studio rule with a colossal disregard for health and safety. The BBC security team were apoplectic, saying it could only happen at the Asian Network. There was no forward planning or managerial co-ordination on the night – time for another inquest and stricter guidelines.

The Wembley Mega Mela also featured many of the bands and musicians which were now on the Asian Network playlist. Apache Indian, Juggy D, Sean Paul, Hunterz, NRG, Dalvinder Singh, Rishi Rich and the up and coming Jay Sean were all on the Asian Network stage that weekend. It all helped the Asian Network to be judged Station of the Year in the Asian Music Awards. Jay Sean, speaking on the night, said 'he would not be where he was without the support of the BBC Asian Network'. Recently signed to Virgin Records, Jay Sean went onto have solo hit singles the following year and huge success in the United States.

The playlist was put together each week by six of the Asian Network team under music manager Zab Khan. The in-house newspaper Ariel ran a feature on the playlist team in March 2003, describing the group cringing at an MC rapping in Punjabi. The week had an eclectic mix of Bollywood, Lollywood, bhangra, pop and dance music. They added Gareth Gates and former Miss World Priyanka Chapra to the list. A schmaltzy balled by Sukhdev – a sort of Asian Enrique Iglesias – was driving them all insane but it made the cut because of the relentless requests from listeners. A weekly chart was compiled based on audience feedback, requests noted on Asian TV channels, votes on-line and sales in selected shops.

The new sports team was proving its worth. Three of them went to the Cricket World Cup in South Africa to follow the South Asian sides. India made the Final but were beaten by Australia by 125 runs. There was live commentary on fights by Jawaid Khaliq, the World IBO welterweight champion from Derby who thanked the sports team 'for the brilliant coverage of my fights'. Asian Network reporters got to Wimbledon for the first time to follow the British Asian player Arvind Parmar and two top Indian stars, Mahesh Bhupathi and Leander Paes.

John Read, the Director of Corporate Affairs at the England and Wales Cricket Board, wrote to us: 'There is no doubt that the Asian

Network has made a significant and very important contribution in helping the EWB to promote cricket to the various Asian communities around England. We are very grateful for your help in doing this and value the close working relationship that we have established with your organisation'.

Fulham football club and the Asian Network worked together to arrange interviews with their Asian player Zesh Rehman. The club wrote; 'We are sure your overall coverage will help tremendously in promoting the game of football within the Asian communities'.

When Tessa Jowell, Secretary of State at the Department of Culture, Media and Sport, gave the BBC the go-ahead to launch the national Asian Network back in 2001, she imposed several conditions. These included speech content of 50 per cent, a strong focus on news and sport, the broadcast of a range of South Asian languages, and a serious reflection of Asian communities across the UK. She also wanted an independent review of the station in 2004.

In the final months of 2003, work began on compiling a submission to the DCMS outlining what had been achieved and assessing if the conditions had been met. Many management hours were spent compiling statistics and trawling back through old programmes and bulletins to prove that we were ticking all the boxes. An independent company was hired to go back through tapes of programmes and work out how many minutes per year were devoted to news and current affairs (112,632 in the 12 months up to October 2003 since you ask).

A snap shot week showed that music accounted for 55 per cent of the output – and speech 45 per cent – so that we were roughly in line with the first condition. The news, sport and language conditions were all met.

The weekly audience figure had shot up to 495,000 since the national launch (Rajar October 2003). More than 61 per cent were aged under 35. Figures for London showed 120,000 listeners which could only be attributable to the digital take-up. It seemed that one fifth of the UK Asian population was now tuning in.

On the messageboards, there was evidence of the impact on people's lives. 'I am a second generation Bangladeshi living in Portsmouth, trying to positively integrate and live with the changes that my parents are so afraid of', wrote Raja. 'It is difficult sometimes to accept how different we are from our parents but it is wonderful when we can share the more colourful parts of a heritage such as arts and music. I find your show a truly positive achievement for our community, creating a common ground for us all.'

29 year old Hardip wrote; 'It's the only place where I can meet like-minded individuals and share experiences. I live in a small town with few Asians. The Asian Network is my saving grace in an ordinary and incredibly boring working life'.

The annual budgets in the three financial years up to March 2004 were £1.7 million, £3.4 million and £4.1 million. A further million pounds was being invested in the new soap before March 2005. Everyone seemed happy that the money was being well-spent. Now we had to face that independent review.

CHAPTER 15

examinAsian

When Greg Dyke took over as Director General in January 2000, he spent several weeks travelling around the country to meet his staff. One of his early conclusions was that the BBC was being strangled by the bureaucracy of the internal market introduced by John Birt. He wanted to 'cut the crap' and 'make things happen'. He said the Corporation was over-managed and under-led, and the whole culture had to change.

To that end, hundreds of BBC people from Controllers down to senior producers found themselves in the Hertfordshire countryside learning to be better leaders. We were all sent to the Ashridge Business School for a total of five days to brainstorm each other, role-play, agonise over our individual strengths and weaknesses, build bridges across a stream, come up with an animal or a vegetable that best defined the BBC, and audition for the percussion section of Santana. The drumming workshop – aimed at collaboration and unity – was one of my over-riding memories of Ashridge, along with trying to work out how to cross a stream with rope and planks (also aimed at collaboration and unity). My group on this exercise included the then Controller of BBC Northern Ireland Anna Carragher and Peter Salmon, then Director of BBC Sport. Deep in the Ashridge woods, it was a strange place to meet such people but frankly better than having them on a stage 'sharing their vision'. As a group, we achieved our objective, kept our feet dry and our dignity intact.

Lots of companies indulge in these team bonding scenarios and it is easy to be dismissive of them. I am not sure if they worked for me but it was good to meet people from all over the BBC and share experiences, highs and lows. The 'crossing the stream' saga always reminded me of an episode of the wonderful *'Drop the Dead Donkey'*, the 1990s newsroom television sit-com written by Andy Hamilton and Guy Jenkin that everyone in the broadcast media of every generation should watch. Crossing that stream, we could not afford any 'slight togetherness shortfall ' as the show's Gus Hedges character memorably said. Another sight to behold on the Ashridge horizon was that of senior BBC executives wandering around the grounds with an arm in the air trying to get a mobile phone signal. (A scriptwriter for the last series of *'The Thick of It'* must have been on the course).

Despite my personal reservations about such bonding exercises, I counted myself among the many staff who believed that Greg Dyke genuinely had the welfare of his workforce at heart and wanted to make things better. I joined thousands of others to help pay for a full page advert in the Daily Telegraph to express 'dismay' after he resigned in January 2004 (thus being deprived of the opportunity to formally open the new BBC building in Leicester a year later). He went after the fallout from the Hutton inquiry into the death of the scientist David Kelly and Labour claims about Iraq's weapons of mass destruction. Apparently 10,000 staff signed up to contribute to the Telegraph advert but there was only room on the page for 4000 names – inexplicably my name appeared twice although I only paid once. There was only one 'Mike Curtis' on the BBC email list throughout my career until, strangely, another appeared in BBC Wales just a few weeks before I finally departed in 2012. I imagined this new MC getting complaints about playing too much Punjabi music and not giving enough prominence to the festival of Krishna Janmashtami – and wondering if he had actually got the job that he'd originally applied for.

—⟋⟍⟍⟍—

Mark Byford was asked to be acting Director General for five months between February and June 2004 before Mark Thompson was appointed as the new DG, coming back from two years as Chief Executive of Channel 4 from where he had described the BBC as 'basking in a Jacuzzi of public cash'.

Back in the Midlands hot-tub, the BBC was getting out of one of its most iconic buildings – Pebble Mill in Birmingham. We moved the Drive show to Leicester for a week at the end of June 2004 while the Birmingham operation moved to the Mailbox building in the centre of the city. This was a real culture change for everyone as the Mailbox production area was 'open plan'. Everyone had been used to their own team or individual offices in the rabbit warren of corridors in Pebble Mill. In the Mailbox, there was no hiding place – and you had to keep to the blue carpet corridors and not cut through another team's space or else they shouted at you.

'Silver Street' and Radio 3's 'Flashmob the Opera' were joint winners of the Team of the Year category at the 2004 BBC Radio and Music Awards, held in the imposing surroundings of the Royal Courts of Justice. Accepting the award, the Silver Street editor James Peries said it had been a privilege to create a soap from scratch with a new team. 'And it was great to hear Jenny Abramsky say it sounds like it's been running for ever', he added.

It was a good night for the Asian Network with Sonia Deol and her team winning the 'Connecting to Communities' category. The citation quoted 'original, fearless, broadcasting – Deol's show challenged people to think and provided a platform for people whose first language is not English'. Collecting the award – like all on the night, made of grey slate off the roof of Broadcasting House – Sonia told the audience: 'Asian is an umbrella term that encompasses a big community – what pleases one person won't please another. We relate to their issues and give them a voice – that's the magic formula'.

Six months earlier, the show found itself in a firestorm of controversy after upsetting the Sikh community. The topic of the day was 'Do inter-religious marriages work?'. One of the guests was a 22 year old student whose father was a Sikh and whose mother was a Muslim, and she felt under pressure from both parents to follow their respective religion. The student had emailed the show asking for advice on how to break the news to her father that she had chosen Islam over Sikhism. Although the debate was going off at a tangent from marriage, Sonia was obviously interested in why her guest had chosen Islam.

The student's reply was that she did not want to 'burn in the fires of hell' and referred to one of the most revered of the ten Sikh gurus as a 'Shaytan' (Devil). All of this was extremely offensive to Sikhs, and Sonia cut across her guest immediately. She made it clear several times that the remarks were unacceptable but the damage was done. Complaints flooded in and *The Sikh Times* newspaper, published in Birmingham, launched a campaign to get Sonia's show taken off air. With a picture of Sonia filling its front page, the headline screamed (as they do):'We are not powerless. You DO have a voice. TAKE HER SHOW OFF' and invited readers to sign the page and send it back to them.

The following week, *The Sikh Times* led with the story again, devoting a double page spread inside to the row. Many of the complainants felt the guest got the opportunity to be offensive because the discussion went away from the central theme of inter-religious marriages. They also accused the production team of not understanding more about the guest and her views before allowing her on air. Others wondered why the Asian Network did not censor the remarks before they went to air but, unlike commercial stations, the BBC did not operate a ten second delay mechanism. 'Live' really meant 'live'.

Jenny Abramsky got pulled into the controversy and agreed to meet a delegation of Sikhs, with Vijay and Stephen Whittle, the BBC's Controller of Editorial Policy, also present. The BBC stressed that Sonia had apologised immediately and that Vijay had apologised for the offensive remarks in a news release and on-air. All the complaints that the BBC had received had been sent to the BBC's Complaints Unit which would investigate them and publish the findings.

An article in *The Sikh Times* of 10th June 2004 claimed the BBC was prepared to look at the production processes but not at the personnel at the Asian Network. It claimed the BBC was afraid that it might discover that not only was there a disproportionately high number of non-Sikhs but also that the Network might have been hijacked by those who had an agenda to promote their Faith or politics at the expense of others. It also claimed it would show that the team was inexperienced and incompetent, and that many were working at the Network due to nepotism rather than qualification and ability.

The BBC denied these spurious claims, adding that the religious conviction of its staff was a private matter. Once some people actually heard the recording, they retracted their complaints. The secretary of the British Sikh Consultative Forum at the time withdraw his complaint to the BBC because he thought Sonia Deol had in fact managed the debate extremely well and it was the caller that had made a complete fool of herself. He said he regretted that he was misled into believing otherwise.

The prompt on-air apology took most of the sting out of the issue as far as the BBC Complaints Unit and indeed Ofcom were concerned. Jenny ordered better editorial support for the phone-in – effectively ensuring that there was always a senior producer running the show (the team only had one and thus no cover for his sickness or leave). Editorial Policy arranged a seminar for staff on religious sensitivities.

The only time when the religious background of people at the Asian Network was ever considered was in the presenter line-up. If the Network was reflecting the whole diverse Asian population in the UK, then the presenters should reflect that audience in some way. Having a line-up of all Muslim or all Hindu presenters would be difficult to defend but it was never the over-riding reason for hiring someone – you still wanted the best available regardless of background. It was the same with sex – ideally you wanted a balance between male and female presenters.

Religion and gender were never considered in recruiting production staff. Authenticity was a consideration for presenting the devotional programmes – obviously it made sense for a Hindu to present the Hindu religious music show but the producers could have any religious background. Similarly you really did need someone fluent in Mirpuri to front the Mirpuri programmes and so on.

One of the most baffling complaints around religion came from a listener who accused the Asian Network of branding all Sikh men as smelly. A weekend presenter called Murtz told a story about getting on the London Underground at rush hour, finding himself a rare spare seat and ending up sitting next to a gentleman who clearly had body odour issues. It was an unnecessarily long and somewhat inelegant rant but, listening back, there was no reference to any religion.

And then it clicked. The presenter had got on the tube and said to himself 'There's a seat!'. The listener had obviously misheard the word 'seat' as 'Sikh' and, from that initial misunderstanding, the whole sorry tale had taken on a completely different aspect. I gently replied that she had misheard – and we heard no more.

—⁂—

Tim Gardam came to Leicester to talk to the Asian Network management team on 12th July 2004. A former editor of BBC's

Newsnight and Director of Programmes at Channel 4, Gardam had been tasked by the Department of Culture, Media and Sport (DCMS) to undertake the independent review of the BBC's digital radio services. A separate review of the digital television services was also underway by a Professor Patrick Barwise.

The senior managers and Tim Gardam gathered in the tenth floor conference room for a discussion about where the Asian Network was and where it was hopefully heading. It was a bit like a BBC 'board' and I felt nervous for myself and the wider station. I jokingly conceded that the news team had its moments but had hardly broken stories of the magnitude of Watergate. Tim Gardam responded, a suggestion of a smile across his face, that the example rather showed my age.

It was important to put up a strong case for the Asian Network in front of Gardam as we knew his report could cause trouble for us. While Gardam and Samir Shah, a former BBC current affairs executive and now a non-executive director of the Corporation, were pulling together their report, Avtar Lit at Sunrise was sniping away at the Asian Network. He accused the BBC of poaching his best presenters (who were attracted by the better pay at the BBC anyway) and he was also obviously opposed to any changes which would allow the Asian Network to better serve the huge Asian population in the London area which was Sunrise's heartland.

The two reports from Professor Barwise and Tim Gardam went to Tessa Jowell, Secretary of State at the DCMS, in November and she in turn asked Michael Grade, the Chairman of the Governors, for the BBC's response. Apart from a few concerns around the television ideas, the reports were broadly welcomed and the recommendations were fed into the latest BBC internal review – this one called 'Building Public Values'.

British Asians had always been early adopters of new technology such as cable and satellite services, usually to get old Bollywood films, music and programmes produced in South Asia. It was therefore hoped that they would take DAB radio to their hearts but Tim Gardam noted in his report that, of the new BBC digital stations, only BBC7 (the offshoot of Radio 4) had prompted an increase in DAB radios. Radio 1Xtra and the Asian Network had not increased the overall BBC reach on DAB, with Asian Network listeners sticking doggedly to the creaking AM signal in the Midlands.

There were six recommendations about the Asian Network. The central theme was that the Network should 'up its game' by being more ambitious in its programming, including commissioning documentaries and looking at broadcasting other languages. It also needed to be better integrated into BBC radio management, should be based on a single site (probably Birmingham) and minimise any disadvantages that it may present to Asian commercial stations.

The BBC agreed that, given the Network's success to date, it could develop a more ambitious editorial proposition. Gardam had said that 'its editorial standards do not always match the audience's expectation of the BBC' and that 'there is a lack of ambition in the programming genres'. He noted that the Asian Network's remit focused on its target audience rather than the distinctiveness of its content. That was true – the Asian Network was aimed at the Asian population whereas Radio 1Xtra, for example, was not specifically targeting the African-Caribbean communities but anyone who liked its black music output.

Gardam found the Asian Network to be of superior quality and more editorially diverse than similar commercial stations but asked the BBC to ensure that it did not disadvantage the commercial sector by effectively dumbing down and playing more music. Documentaries would be one good way to emphasize the difference between the BBC and commercial offerings. Specialist correspondents for Health and Education were another option although all of these ideas were expensive. Ultimately the Network only got a political correspondent who was based alongside the mainstream Parliamentary Unit at Millbank near Parliament.

Every so often, the Network was asked why it only broadcast in five South Asian languages of Mirpuri, Punjabi, Hindi-Urdu, Gujarati and Bengali. It also got requests and indeed demands that it should do shows in other languages such as Tamil (South India and Sri Lanka), Sinhala (Sri Lankan), Sylheti (considered by many as a more relevant dialect of Bengali) and Pashto, a language spoken by Afghans. The BBC agreed to keep the demand for other languages under review but in fact nothing changed. Every so often, we were asked why – as the Asian Network – we were not covering South East Asia as well (Thailand, Malaysia, Indonesia etc).

Gardam's recommendation that the BBC should consider relocating the Asian Network's operation to a single site was sensible but the timing was unfortunate. He suggested Birmingham where the BBC had just made the move from Pebble Mill to the Mailbox. But in Leicester, we had the 'topping out' ceremony at the new building six months earlier and the Asian Network team, along with Radio Leicester, were on the verge of moving into the brand new, specially designed new premises. To abandon Leicester so far down the line would have looked somewhat irresponsible – both in terms of money wasted and bad publicity. And additionally we had started using yet another base with the phone-in coming out of Television Centre in London.

The suggestion that the Asian Network should get out of Leicester was disheartening for people like Owen Bentley who had deliberately carved their BBC careers away from London. 'The BBC should have been proud that it had a national radio station whose headquarters was in a medium-sized East Midlands city', said Owen years later. 'It should have shouted its virtues from the rooftops. It was a typical centralist approach to close it (Leicester) down. It is the British Broadcasting Corporation for heaven's sake, not the London Broadcasting Corporation'.

Nevertheless it took another five years before the Asian Network abandoned Leicester completely with the move of the newsroom to the new Broadcasting House. Jenny Abramsky and others were understandably nervous about centralising everything in Birmingham or London – and thus leaving a brand new building in Leicester half-empty with just BBC Radio Leicester. The line was that the Asian Network could only leave if another department was prepared to move in – and there were no takers. Mischievous suggestions that The Archers might like to move their Midlands base from the west to the east fell on deaf ears in the snug of The Bull at Ambridge.

The most significant recommendation from Tim Gardam was that the Asian Network should be better integrated into BBC radio management in order to get more support in its editorial development. His report noted that 'the commitment and seriousness of purpose of the more experienced editorial managers was clear' and he also added that 'the news management was clearly responsible and reliable'. Mr Gardam was indeed a wise and perceptive man.

However we were often forgotten at Radio and Music headquarters. The other new digital networks all had a Controller fighting their battles and waving their flags at the top table of network radio. 1Xtra was under Andy Parfitt at Radio 1, 6Music under Lesley Douglas at Radio 2, BBC7 under Radio 4's Mark Damazer and Five Live Sports Extra under Bob Shennan at Five Live. It was clear that not everything that was discussed or decided at headquarters was getting back to Vijay.

Despite all the strategic support and money that Jenny Abramsky had given to the Asian Network, the day to day stuff was getting overlooked. With Vijay, Ishfaq and myself being out of London most of the time, we were out of sight and thus out of mind. So it was that Bob Shennan, former Head of BBC Sport, and Controller of Five Live since 2000, was given the job of strategic direction of the BBC Asian Network and became its first Controller.

CHAPTER 16

humiliAsian

In the early hours of Boxing Day morning 2004, reports began to come in to the BBC of an earthquake on the other side of the world. Its epicentre was under the sea off Sumatra in Indonesia. The earthquake triggered one of the worst tsunamis that the world has ever experienced and claimed 230,000 lives in 14 countries.

In the Asian Network newsroom in Leicester, the lone early newsreader was preparing the first bulletin of the day. Like BBC newsrooms across the corporation, particularly outside London, the staffing was down to a bare minimum for the Christmas holiday. The earthquake was looking like the lead story on what was usually a quiet news day.

One hundred miles away, I was in London with relatives for Christmas. I was not the on-call assistant editor – Ishfaq Ahmed had drawn the short straw for Christmas and Vijay was on holiday in India. But I was the news editor and anyone on duty in the newsroom could call me at any time if something big was breaking. I heard an early bulletin on Five Live and clocked an earthquake under the sea off Indonesia and thought no more about it in terms of Asian Network news.

A couple of hours later I heard another bulletin which talked about a huge tidal wave hitting Indonesia and Sri Lanka. This made the story an Asian Network one and I rang the newsroom. The journalist on duty was relatively inexperienced but believed she was coping. The story was leading the bulletin but it was not reflecting the unfolding enormity of what was happening. And not only had Sri Lanka been badly hit but the tsunami had rolled on towards the east coast of India.

I asked her to extend the bulletins and tell the programme presenters in Birmingham to watch their tone – it was obvious that people were dying. She needed help and I asked her to ring a couple of people who were around and said they were happy to be on call. I switched on the BBC television news channel and realised how serious this was. The journalists supposed to be available were not answering and I could not raise Ishfaq. I decided to head back to Leicester.

Driving back up the M1 listening to Five Live, the devastating effects of the tsunami on Sri Lanka and eastern India was becoming horribly apparent. Asian Network listeners would be turning to us for information and getting very little. Five Live and the television news channels were now in 'rolling news' mode and they were the places to go to for the latest information.

The tsunami claimed the lives of 130,000 people in Indonesia. 35,000 died and 21,000 were injured in Sri Lanka. Twelve thousand died in India. People in the Asian communities in the UK lost many relatives and friends. They were desperate for information. By the time I got to the Leicester newsroom, a couple more journalists had been raised but they were now having problems trying to get 'slots' (interviews) with BBC correspondents covering the tragedy.

We recovered our poise over the next few days. The programme schedule was almost back to normal, more people were available and presenters who could handle news were on hand rather than relying on holiday stand-ins whose talents were fronting music and light entertainment shows. But the Asian Network coverage in the first hours after the tsunami hit on Boxing Day was inadequate and, as news editor, I felt ashamed that we had let down our audience.

There was some wider criticism of BBC coverage of the tsunami, mainly around how long it took to send high profile correspondents to the region compared to Sky News. Helen Boaden, the Director of News, and Roger Mosey, Head of Television News, defended their decisions but the DG Mark Thompson did eventually acknowledge the slow response, kindly highlighting the Asian Network's initial shortcomings in the same breath. The extra support that we had in preceding months from senior news executives in London did not help us on that Boxing Day morning. We were short on bodies and experience, and no one in the central BBC newsroom really wanted to help us due to the demands of Five Live, rolling television news and World Service.

The Gardam report had argued for better integration of the Asian Network into network radio management. The tsunami coverage underlined the need for better integration in to BBC News as well. As part of the process of coming under the Controller of Five Live, it was not a big leap of imagination to suggest that, like Five Live, the Asian Network should commission its news service from BBC News. But it would be another year before that actually happened.

Asian Network 'Unsung' set out to find new talent from the Asian communities across the UK. The finals were held at the Symphony Hall in Birmingham on 31st March and featured a line-up of established Asian music stars as judges or performers – people like Gurdas Maan, Swami, Juggy D, Sukshinder Shinda, Jassi Sidhu, Taz of Stereo Nation and Shin of DCS. The winner was 20 year old Navin Kishore Kundra from Coventry who did his version of Robbie William's 'Feel'. I was in and out of the auditorium all evening on 'Pope-watch'. Pope John Paul was on his death-bed and, once he died, all BBC output would have to change its tone, watch out for inappropriate song titles and extend its bulletins. He died two days later.

At the beginning of June, the Asian Network, and the BBC, finally got out of Epic House in Leicester. Two months earlier, Radio Leicester had moved to the new building across the city centre and flushed out the initial teething problems.

The last voice heard on-air from Epic House was Mira Trivedi as she wrapped up her Gujarati programme late on the Friday night, almost 29 years after she first started presenting Asian programmes on Radio Leicester. The first Asian Network voice from the new building at St Nicholas Place was Tamasin Ford, reading the 7am news on Saturday 4th June. 'The smooth changeover was a tribute to the regional project and technical teams', according to assistant editor Mike Curtis who was asked for a quote by the BBC staff newspaper Ariel. In fact most of the credit went to the project manager and Leonard Cohen fan Roger Francis.

One sunny morning a month or so after the move, BBC News and Sky News were reporting what appeared to be some power surge bangs on the London Underground. Several trains were stuck in tunnels. Very soon the power surge explanation was replaced by explosions – at least three of them. It suddenly looked very serious. It was Thursday 7th July 2005 – the day after the UK bid had won the Olympics for 2012.

One of the first tasks was to account for our staff. One senior producer Anne Reeves was on a train from Leicester which was just about to pull into St Pancras. We phoned her to tell her to get on the first train back. The Sonia Deol team were all at Television Centre apart from one who was stranded on a tube above ground but she was safe. An hour after the bombs on the Underground went off, another was exploded on a bus.

As more details emerged of the atrocity and the number of casualties rose steadily, the extended bulletins and news flashes were proving inadequate. This time we did throw out the schedule and go for an 'all speech' news hour between 12 noon and 1pm. We took Five Live for a short period while Asian Network journalists were tasked to chase people for interview and gather material from Five Live and the circuits from the central London newsroom.

All the Controllers were on standby to go to the BBC's emergency broadcasting centre near Evesham. For Bob Shennan, that would mean going from Leicester as he was in town for another visit to his new charges. Once again my old AA handbook proved its value as I explained the quickest way from Leicester to Evesham. I always kept the handbook on my desk if only to illustrate my answers to maddening questions from normally intelligent colleagues like 'Is East Anglia near Dorset?'. In the end Bob stayed in Leicester until lunchtime – on the phone to London most of the time – and then went to our Birmingham studios.

In contrast to the initial tsunami coverage, the Asian Network output on the day of the London bombs was described as 'outstanding' by Bob Shennan, who felt it was an advantage to be with us on such a big news day. In a note to staff the following day, he wrote: 'I think the right set of decisions was taken to pull programmes, to simulcast and to put effort into all-speech specials. If we ever wanted to articulate our ambition for news coverage, it was delivered in buckets yesterday'.

The aftermath of the London bombs presented many challenges to the Asian Network in the following days. It echoed the aftermath of 9/11 except that the terrorism was home grown. The four suicide bombers with bombs in their rucksacks lived in Leeds and High Wycombe. 52 people had been killed and more than 700 injured, including people from the Asian communities – some of them Muslims.

A month after the bombs, we took Sonia Deol's programme into the heart of the London Muslim communities in Bethnal Green. Another programme came from Paris, marking the first anniversary of the French ban on religious symbols being worn in schools (ie: turbans, hijabs). In the UK, a senior cleric suggested that Muslim women stopped covering their faces for a while to deflect racist abuse. The Asian Network's soap 'Silver Street' had its scripts updated and the audio was edited to reflect the story and the mood in the Asian communities.

Asian taxi drivers in Leicester spoke of a surge in racist abuse. Race hate crime figures confirmed that all Asians were being targeted, not just Muslims. A pig's head was left outside a mosque in Cardiff. I sent a reporter to Newport in south Wales, a town not normally associated with Asian communities but where the Pakistani population (2.4 per cent of the town's total) told us they had faced an increase in racism, hate mail and offensive graffiti. Two Asian Network colleagues told me that they had stopped using rucksacks on public transport because of the looks of suspicion they were getting.

Amidst all this, the Asian Network led the way in finding positive stories about UK Muslims. In a note to the BBC's Director of News Helen Boaden, who had asked what we were doing in the aftermath of 7/7, I was able to flag up good news stories, especially in sport. The England badminton champion was Aamir Ghaffar, a Pakistani Muslim living in Southall. He was about to compete for the World Championship. The country had warmed to the young Bolton boxer Amir Khan at the Olympics the previous year and we were sticking with him, covering every fight. We found two Cardiff faith schools (one Christian, one Muslim) whose teachers had taught in each other's classrooms to foster understanding between the two religions.

Earlier in the year, we got a nomination in the Radio News category at the Race in the Media Awards for our coverage of India's cricket tour of Pakistan in 2004. Two years earlier, both countries had been on the verge of nuclear war. Now they were playing cricket again. We called it 'Red Button to Red Ball'.

CHAPTER 17

excitAsian

B ob Shennan said he was 'bursting' to tell us what plans were in store for the latest version of Asian Network. We were now more involved with his main station Five Live and were gradually 'upping our game' as recommended by the Gardam report. We had done our first simulcasts with Five Live as part of both stations' coverage of the 2005 General Election campaign. Simon Mayo and Sonia Deol co-headed a programme from Warwick, and Peter Allen and Nikki Bedi, who had joined the Network as the weekend's 'Hot Breakfast' presenter the year before, did another election special from Blackburn. The overnight results programme on 5th May used Sonia Deol for a while early on but it was a token gesture.

Bob started the 'Evolution' process with team meetings in Leicester and Birmingham on Thursday 22nd September. The Director General Mark Thompson had confirmed to Jenny and Bob that he was authorising new investment in the Asian Network. Bob said that Thompson was 'very excited by our plans and recognises that the Asian Network is a crucial part of the BBC's future'. Five years later Mark Thompson announced its closure. But for now, Bob was sure the Network could live up to Thompson's expectations and 'turn it into one of the BBC's most significant success stories in years'.

Tim Gardam had urged the Asian Network to 'break free of its roots in local radio to become a fully fledged national service'. To do that, it had to 'get a vision' as it was still defined by its target audience and not by what was coming out of the speakers. It needed closer links with BBC Drama to make '*Silver Street*' feel more at home. It needed to strengthen the languages output and make big improvements in its station sound (jingles and trails) and forward-planning. And it needed to invest in its music and journalism.

The aspirations for improving the news coverage were both ambitious and unrealistic. I was asked to draw up a 'wish list' of reporters and specialist correspondents. The radio station already had reporters in London, Bradford, Manchester, Birmingham and Leicester but I suggested one to cover north of London (Luton, Watford, Bedford area), another for the north east based in Newcastle, another in Peterborough where the Asian Network was available 24 hours on the AM frequency, and a couple of others to cover Glasgow/Belfast and Bristol/Cardiff.

I was equally 'over the top' in suggesting specialists. You could make a case for a social affairs correspondent who would cover health and education, and a business and finance correspondent. Sport would benefit from cricket and football specialists – and ofcourse we should have our own man or woman out in South Asia.

In the end, the number of reporters on the ground did not change and the list of specialists came down to just one – Joanna Shinn became the Network's Political correspondent with a brief to reflect Asian angles from the world of Westminster. The previous autumn, we had sent our own regional reporters to the three main party conferences for the first time. Now we had someone to specialise in politics – another indication of chasing the ambition flagged in the Gardam report.

Vijay would keep her job as Managing Editor of the Asian Network but she did have doubts. She was used to being the most senior person on the Network but now she would have to answer to a Controller. Crucially she needed to be sure she could work with

Bob and she did spend a few thoughtful days contemplating the options with her husband Surinder before finally committing. Owen Bentley remained on board as a consultant to help with the changes and was then persuaded to hang on for a further year before being released back into the community.

Underneath Vijay, there would be three new senior posts – a Head of News (who would actually report to the Head of BBC Radio News), a Head of Music and a Network Co-ordinator, a sort of business manager. Ishfaq and I would keep our Assistant Editor posts alongside the seven new ones but we could apply for any of the jobs that were going. As soon as the announcement about this new structure was made at a staff meeting, I rang Susi Sadeghi in HR and asked her to email me Michael Hill's job description.

Michael Hill was the Network Manager for Five Live and was thus the Controller's representative on earth. He had been running the interactive bits of Radio 1 before moving across to Five Live. Michael would figure heavily in the evolution of the Network which was looking like a very complex project. His role at Five Live covered strategy, budgets, transmission, digital issues, performance review, the Royal Death procedures, HR and training, and a host of other things. He seemed to relax by going home to Kent and building a new house with parts imported from Germany.

For the past few years, the number of extra duties I had inherited or volunteered for had grown. Some of these, like being the station's main link with the team working on the new building in Leicester, undoubtedly interfered with my core role as News Editor but it made the job more interesting. But with the management team going up from three to ten, and the involvement of the Five Live hierarchy, it was clear that anyone running News would no longer get side-tracked by back office duties.

I reasoned to myself that the Head of Radio News Steve Mitchell would want to put his own man or woman in as Head of

News on the Asian Network. But I also felt it would be dishonest to apply because I did not really want to do it. I had set the newsroom up and had run it for seven years. It was a big responsibility and getting bigger as the news agenda changed and hardened in the light of events like 9/11 and the London bombs. As much as I still loved news and sport, I did not want to be in charge of it all anymore.

Instead I went all out for the Network Co-ordinator, convincing myself they really needed me in that role. I knew the place inside out, where the bodies were buried and I was already involved in a lot of what this person was expected to do. I already had contacts across Radio and Music headquarters and at Five Live, and in English Regions and in local radio. I was comfortable with the 'dark arts' of the engineering and IT worlds. It would also elegantly move me out of the way of the new Head of News. He or she would not want the old news editor grumbling about the good old days being better and reminding everyone that we'd already done a particular story to death dozens of times.

Each week we got an email newsletter called 'Evolution' updating us on developments and progress. There was a sense of excitement and trepidation. People were facing more dreaded BBC 'boards' and could end up in places or programmes where they did not want to be. We were invited by the Controller to complete the sentence: 'We'll know we've succeeded in evolving the Asian Network when...'

According to the responses sent into Michael Hill, some of the team would deem success as defining the station and purpose, attracting a more diverse audience, sounding and acting like one station, and when the programmes were consistently excellent.

Actually, how individuals would really define success though was staying in work or evolving into a better job at the end of the whole process.

Seminars for staff – called 'Just imagine the Asian Network'- were arranged to find out what everybody really felt about the way forward and how they might benefit from being under Five Live . There were held in places like Aston University, the International Conference Centre in Birmingham and the new Leicester City football stadium and discussed news, sport, music, marketing and interactivity. The Controllers of Radio 1 and Radio 2, Andy Parfitt and Lesley Douglas, came to talk to us about music policies and strategies. Steve Mitchell and Stewart Lansley, from the Current Affairs unit, addressed us in a freezing Leicester Guildhall about news and documentaries.

The BBC governors, meeting in Glasgow on 24 November, endorsed all the Asian Network plans including ideas for its revised programme schedule. Jenny Abramsky was at the meeting and said she had never seen them as enthusiastic as they were about the proposals. Five years later, as the reconfigured BBC Trust, they agreed to Mark Thompson's plan to close the Asian Network as a national enterprise.

Someone from Radio News in London did indeed get the Head of News job – Husain Husaini, who had been producer of the Victoria Derbyshire show on Five Live. Punjabi Hit Squad's Markie Mark , already presenting a Saturday show for the Asian Network and DJing at Radio 1Xtra, was made Head of Music. His real name was Mark Strippel and he had grown up in Hounslow, immersed and enthused by Asian music. And after one of the more convincing performances of my career, I secured the Network Co-ordinator role and felt liberated by leaving the responsibility of news behind me after more than 30 years. Telling a friend outside the BBC that I had been appointed Network Co-ordinator, she said; 'Oh, so you look after the computers do you?'. Which in a roundabout sort of way, I would.

Ishfaq Ahmed, the other Assistant Editor before 'Evolution', was given the task of running the Drive programme. The two Assistant Editors in the newsroom were Neerja Sood, who was already with the Network, and Louise Cotton from Five Live on a six month attachment. Three of the other Assistant Editors also came from Five Live backgrounds. Jonathan Aspinwall took on Sonia at Breakfast, George Mann was back on familiar territory with the phone-in show, and football executive Caj Sohal got Sport.

Khaliq Meer, a former BBC local radio producer who was currently working in Hong Kong, was brought in as the music assistant editor working to Mark Strippel. A producer already with the Asian Network, Kuljinder Singh, was asked to oversee the afternoons with Nikki Bedi's arts and entertainment programme, and Rifat Jawaid was appointed to run the language strand. Needless to say, there were some disappointed people among the internal candidates, some of whom were sent off on 'development attachments' to broaden their experience.

The new 'buzz phrase' for the Network, to be repeated parrot-fashion at every 'board', was 'Celebrate, Challenge, Connect'. We were told that is what the new Asian Network would be doing with its new schedule. More all-staff meetings were planned, including one which finished with the Christmas party at a Birmingham bar. This was a rare opportunity for everyone from the three cities and across the current schedule to celebrate and connect. It was my chance to meet the magnificently named Orifice Vulgatron, one of the Foreign Beggars musical group, two of whom fronted one of our Saturday night specialist music programmes.

Across January and February 2006, the recruitment and the shuffling of staff continued apace. The mixture of skill levels, the location of programmes, the knock-on effects of recruitment, the preferences of individuals and the fair distribution of experience all had to be taken into account. And while this was going on, there was still a radio station to run and programmes to broadcast. It was an immediate opportunity for the new managers and assistant editors to prove themselves.

The latest audience figures (Q3 2005) were up again to 524,000 a week – a year before what the marketing team said would now be called 'transformAsian'.

Engaging the presenters for the relaunched schedule caused one early stand-off between Bob and Vijay. Bob dealt alone with the discussions with Sonia, Nikki Bedi and Anita Rani – and Vijay felt out of that loop. She was afraid that, because she had not been present when they were booked to do new shows, they did not see her as their line manager.

Sonia consequently felt that Vijay did not want her to move to the Breakfast show which prompted her to have a public 'go' at Vijay in a staff meeting in London about the alleged lack of feedback. After the meeting, Bob said Sonia was upset and felt slighted because Vijay had not spoken to her about doing the Breakfast show. Bob said it was all his fault and that Vijay should have been with him when he spoke to all three presenters. He apologised to Vijay and they were back on course.

The new presenter line-up and their production teams had to come up with a programme description – what it was all about and how it would celebrate, challenge and connect. They did off-air pilot shows to settle the sound and 'feel' ahead of the first phase of the relaunch on 24th April 2006. On the weekdays, the hour of devotional music would start the day followed by Sonia on Breakfast and Anita Rani, another weekend 'Hot Breakfast' recruit the previous year from television, in the mid-morning phone-in slot.

Three weeks later – on 15th May – the rest of the weekday schedule would follow on. The two 30 minutes news bulletins had an early identity crisis with the first name The Wrap being thrown out and replaced with Asian Network Update. It eventually stayed as the Wrap before becoming 'Asian Network Reports' a few years later. After piloting The Wrap with a handful of people outside of the Asian Network, the 'anchor' for the programme in the end was our own Rozina Sini, who had been on the 2002 training course under her maiden name of Iqbal. Rozi, who had impressed with her news presentation around 9/11 and the London bombs stories, stayed as the main news anchor for another six years.

The presentation style of Navinder Bhogal, the long time weekday afternoon host of the Hindi-Urdu show, was deemed too old fashioned for the new look 'whizz-bang young' Asian Network. Navinder was popular with older listeners but Bob felt her style was one of the factors which made the Network sound like different radio stations across the day. Her show reminded me of an old East Midlands afternoon programme that was broadcast on BBC Radios Nottingham, Leicester, Derby and Lincolnshire. It was presented by Dennis McCarthy and sounded completely different and much older than all the local radio shows around it. But Dennis was phenomenally popular, getting vast audiences for that time of the day. The size of the crowds that turned out to witness his funeral cortege in Nottingham in 1996 astonished people like Nigel Chapman (then Head of BBC English Regions) and the youngsters in the radio stations who turned down the speakers when the show was on. Many said there would be only one bigger funeral in Nottingham and they were right – there was a massive turnout for Brian Clough.

Navinder was eased out with warm words of praise ringing in her ears but, although she departed with dignity, she was not happy. Her name came up again six years later as the Network repositioned itself for the family audience but friends said she did n't want to return after her previous experience of being dropped.

134

Niki Bedi took Navinder's mid-afternoon slot, with Adil Ray picking up the Drive programme, Sameena Ali Khan having departed in May 2005 to make her name in commercial regional television. An early evening languages programme started life as 'Salaam Namaste' (a common respectful greeting) but by the time it went to air it was named after its presenter, the former Breakfast host Gagan Grewal. Bobby Friction was the new late night host but kept his Radio 1 gigs.

'Jump Off' kicked off the Saturday evening shows featuring 'a strictly Desi-agenda from urban bhangra to Bollywood bangers' and fronted by three djs who called themselves Mentor Kolektiv. Electro East followed with dj Nerm playing 'leftfield, drum and bass, Asian electronic – in fact anything mashed-up, crossover, sampled or fused'. Then came *Mic Check*, with the aforementioned Mr Vulgatron and another Foreign Beggar, steaming in with grime, rap, hip-hop and anything urban.

Pathaan's Musical Rickshaw slipped in at midnight, moving Michael Hill to write: 'It will take us to a chilled out terrace where we can look at the stars and contemplate our place in infinity'. Actually that was the only Saturday evening programme description I understood.

For six nights a week, we pushed the button for World Service South Asian to keep the transmitter humming through the early hours. Bob Shennan, being the Controller of Five Live, unsurprisingly decided that the Asian Network should carry another of his networks overnight instead of the World Service South Asian programmes. Consequently Asian Network nighthawks were '*Up all Night*' with Five Live from then on.

transformAsian

'If ever a station has decided to revitalise its output by chucking youth at it, it's this and one can only wish them well. Nothing in the schedule looks terribly original – perhaps it really is true that all the unused ideas are gone – but there is something exciting about a list of programmes with 'New' written in the margin against the titles'.

The Times review, written by radio critic Chris Campling, was part of the blizzard of publicity about the new look Asian Network. The photogenic Sonia Deol dominated both the mainstream and the Asian media, looking sassy and sultry as she leaned against walls with her head on one side. Adil Ray, standing or squatting, alternated between cheeky and puzzled as he gazed out from *DesiXpress* and the Punjab 2000 website. Bobby Friction pulled faces and pointed a lot.

Asian Life asked Markie Mark if he had more to prove in his new post as Head of Music because he was white. He said he did not feel that pressure – he had proved he knew what he was talking about back in 1992 when he jumped on stage to dj for the first time in front of 3000 people at a west London bhangra gig. He dismissed fears that his appointment would mean that bhangra would dominate the station playlists at the expense of other forms of Asian music. He was pictured looking thoughtful with fingers pressed together, probably praying that people would now address him as Mark Strippel instead of Markie Mark.

Anita Rani told *Eastern Eye* that her style icon was Una Stubbs and her top fashion tip was to 'shave your legs before venturing out in daylight in a short skirt'. Caj Sohal, the new Head of Sport, confessed to *The Sikh Times* that as a small boy, he and some friends had sneaked under a gate to get into Nottingham Forest's ground to watch a midweek European Cup game.

The Observer compared the Asian Network to the old GLR (BBC's Greater London Radio) 'only with bushy-tailed young Asians hosting as opposed to cynical, old, white comedians'.

Elizabeth Mahoney in *The Guardian* concentrated on Sonia, now fronting the breakfast show. 'It gives some sense of the scope and mood swings of Sonia Deol at Breakfast that yesterday's show began with a report about the firebombing of Asian shopkeepers and ended with Deol seeing how long she could gurgle for on-air. Both items, in their own way, were impressive. Deol is chummy and likeable, breathless and a bit gauche: it's hard to imagine any of the Today team engaged in competitive gurgling'.

Sonia said that she was delighted that there were three female presenters in the core hours of the weekday schedule – Anita Rani, Nikki Bedi and herself. 'I'm no feminist but there is something quite liberating about the way the tables have turned. I'd question why the other networks are so male dominated. They have female sidekicks, don't they, on breakfast?'

Her unfulfilled ambition was to interview Prince Philip. 'There is so much to talk to him about – his position in the Royal family, what kind of husband he has been, what kind of father he was, what did he really think of Diana and what was his advice to Charles when all that was going on? And the gaffes that he's made. Were they meant? You could take him on a tour of the Far East!', she said, mischievously referencing the Prince's well-publicised remarks about Indian engineers and Chinese physiognomy.

The new programme rang up Asian newsagents around the country to ensure they were listening. It introduced listeners-turned-agony aunts Auntie Hazel and Uncle Tony who advised celebrities in the news – Michael Jackson's financial woes at the time could be solved by setting up a direct debit apparently. Edited by former Five Live journalist Jonathan Aspinwall, the show also handled news stories from an Asian contestant being dumped from The Apprentice television show to whether a 10 year old should be prosecuted for racism.

A few days before the relaunch in April, Sonia was the Asian Network's representative in a line-up of radio personalities to meet the Queen who was visiting Broadcasting House. She asked the Queen what she would like for her 80th birthday. The Monarch replied: 'A nice sunny day'. The exchange made national news.

'TransformAsian' created a huge amount of publicity across the mainstream and the Asian media. The press office put together a booklet of examples of the coverage which ran to 113 pages. Virtually all of it was positive although there were complaints in the Asian media that the BBC had only looked internally for talent – Bobby Friction, Anita Rani, and Mark Strippel. No one seemed to question the extra one million pounds being thrown at it when other areas of the BBC were facing cuts. Bob Shennan insisted the Asian Network had been under-resourced for too long and that the total budget of £6.4 million was justified.

Another major national marketing push was secured – a so-called 'Top 40' campaign which gave the Asian Network publicity trails or slides after popular BBC TV programmes such as *Eastenders*.

—ᔓ—

Bob Shennan had a photograph in his office of the 'Punjabi Army', a group of Sikhs who followed Sunderland football club and who would therefore make an obvious radio feature for the Asian Network. My mother, who died in April 2003, had been Sunderland born and bred and I had followed the team, mainly as an armchair supporter, ever since I was taken to Roker Park when I was eight. But I had not heard of this particular group of fans until I started visiting Five Live headquarters. Their exuberant faces beaming down off the wall of the office made me smile at every meeting, despite Sunderland being relegated (again) from the Premiership in 2006.

There was a perception that most Asians who liked UK football followed Liverpool. Certainly it was something that Nihal Arthanayake, a devoted Spurs fan who later took over the phone-in after Anita left, picked up on whenever football got discussed on his programme. Some say it was because Bill Shankly was manager of Liverpool across the period when so many Asians came to the UK – 1959 to 1974 – and they related to his down-to-earth, family orientated approach to life. Liverpool was also the dominant club across much of that period after Shankly got them back into the top division.

Others will say that Asians were drawn to Liverpool by John Barnes who signed in 1987 and stayed for ten years. Barnes was the first high-profile black player to join the club in the 1980s when racial abuse was regularly spewed off the terraces across the UK, and he was regarded as a role model by many black and Asian football fans. The appeal of Anfield also extended to Asians across the Indian sub-continent and beyond. And the Asian Network's first Controller Mr Shennan also happened to be a Reds fan.

Even before the appointment of an Assistant Editor for Sport and the closer links with Five Live, sports coverage on the Asian Network was relatively ambitious for a small outfit. With the extra support from Five Live and more money, it was easier to keep those aspirations high, sending people to cover the England Test matches in India and follow Asian athletes in the Commonwealth Games in Australia. Former England captain Mike Gatting agreed to front a series looking at Asian aspects of cricket for a paltry sum, and the team followed the progress of India's first Formula One driver Narain Karthikeyan who made his Grand Prix debut in 2005. The Network sent a reporter to every fight by Amir Khan after his Olympics Silver in 2004 – usually boxing fan Ade Adedoyin before he departed for World Service Sport.

Lee James was another recruit who won promotion to the World Service sports team. Alison Mitchell, who joined in 2002, moved on three years later just ahead of 'TransformAsian'. Alison was an expert in the male-dominated world of cricket and became the UK's only female cricket commentator, following the England team around every Test playing country for the BBC. Long-time Radio Leicester and Asian Network sports journalists Kamlesh Purohit and Deepak Patel were both accepted as members of the Cricket Writers Club in 2007.

The Saturday afternoon sports show was called 'Kickin' off' and mixed sports news and music. It was presented by the aforementioned Spurs fan Nihal , who co-hosted a Wednesday night show on Radio 1 with Bobby Friction. Kulvinder Ghir, of 'Goodness Gracious Me' fame, was an occasional stand-in for Nihal, and the ebullient actor Brian Blessed was booked as a summariser for one match in 2008 – to the apparent consternation of real football correspondents and commentators in the Emirates stadium press box. One contributor to an on-line football forum wrote that he had heard 'the greatest sentence ever uttered on national radio'. It went: 'And reporting for the BBC Asian Network on Arsenal v Newcastle is the actor Brian Blessed'.

In November, the music team hit the road with the Asian Network's 'Uni Tour'. Bobby Friction, Mentor Kolektiv and DJ Kayper (another big name addition to the late night line-up) hosted shows at universities and colleges in Nottingham, Leicester, Essex, Birmingham, Surrey and London. The aim was to introduce students and clubbers to the new wave of British Asian music and also to the Asian Network itself. Mark and his team also organised an Asian contribution to the Electric Proms, a BBC music festival based around the Roundhouse in north London. Nitin Sawney, Tigerstyle and a couple of other acts provided the music from the Asian angle. And Mark got me tickets to see the mainstream headliners The Who.

Bobby Friction was wearing a Rolling Stones T-shirt under his jacket when we had a group photo-shoot on the spiral stairwells at Television Centre. It was the first time that I had met him and he seemed relieved to find someone else in the group who actually recognised the Stones' tongue logo.

Bobby had first broadcast on the Asian Network on Sunday afternoons the year before the 2006 relaunch. He had an international reputation as a DJ in the world of Asian music but he had also won a Sony award in 2005 for a documentary on the General Election. He was largely responsible for getting music by UK Asian artists played back in India. Under the strapline 'Friction Introducing', Bobby encouraged aspiring artists to email him MP3s of their music recorded in bedrooms or garages and he highlighted a new one every week. With this support for new artists, he got himself a reputation as the 'Asian John Peel'. It was a tag he was happy with – he had sat next to Peel at Radio 1 for two years and learnt a lot from him, including dealing with the management.

At the Radio and Music Festival in March 2006, the Asian Network hosted a session which Mark Strippel called 'Break on Through' and which discussed if and how Asian music artists could break into the mainstream. Quoting The Doors song of (coincidently) the same name that had launched me on a musical journey in my early teens, I introduced the panel of Bobby, Mark and Paul Gambaccini, who had to rush off straight afterwards as he had an invitation to the 60th birthday party of the Pink Floyd's David

Gilmour. I had n't got an invite but could, if pushed, reveal that the Floyd's drummer Nick Mason was apparently my Auntie Mary's landlord when she was living in Crouch End in the early 1970s.

—ᴍᴍ—

While Bobby and Nihal were on Radio 1 on Wednesday nights (a show which was eventually also simulcast on the Asian Network), their slot was filled by DJ Kayper. The programme was called The Hype and featured the dynamic Miss Kayper scratching and mixing with her turntables. It was extraordinary to watch, let alone listen to.

Raj Dhanda and Pablo Sat-Bhambra were a double act of Bollywood broadcasters who had been invited to host the weekday lunchtime show from Leicester after the incumbent was arrested in a police raid actually filmed by our colleagues from BBC Midlands Today. The presenter, who was taken off air immediately, was found guilty a year later of nine charges of receiving stolen computer equipment. The defence said that the individual, apart from being a radio presenter, had a business buying and selling computers and had bought them all in good faith.

In the new world, Raj and Pablo looked after *Film Café*, a Saturday morning show devoted to the music, interviews and gossip of the Indian film industry. Raj wore sunglasses all the time to protect his forehead – I never saw them over his eyes. I discovered there were numerous messageboards devoted to why men sport this fashion accessory but I am none the wiser. *Film Café* was later to share the wrong sort of headlines with television's '*Blue Peter*' due to a producer malfunction and was later relaunched as '*Love Bollywood*'.

Another weekend presenter was Ravi Sagoo who counted down the most popular Asian hits on a Saturday afternoon. Ravi was the winner of an Asian Network talent search in the summer of 2005 and later went onto present programmes on Radio Scotland.

Tim Gardam's report said the Asian Network should feature regular current affairs documentaries as part of the plans to enhance editorial ambition. Initially these documentaries came from its own reporters or from the Radio 4 Factual unit based alongside the Asian Network in Birmingham but plans were in hand to commission from the independent sector. It had run three documentaries at the end of 2005 as a trial run. One featured a Bradford woman's personal story about her relatives caught up in the Pakistan earthquake and another, called '*Chicken or Fish*', featured the Asians who worked at companies near Heathrow preparing airline food.

The first documentary in the first proper series was about honour killings and was broadcast in Adil's Drive programme on Monday 4th September 2006. It was presented by Konnie Huq, well known for her work with BBC1's '*Blue Peter*' and who also was an occasional guest presenter on the Network's weekend breakfast programmes. Munazza Khan and Nicola Humphries were the Radio 4 Factual producers, with some Asian Network reporters and producers joining them for particular subjects.

The first series looked at Asians in the British Army, '*The Real Brick Lane*' with Konnie Huq examined the Bangladeshi area of east London highlighted by Monica Ali's book, and '*Trouble Abroad*' with the Network's Bradford reporter Sanjiv Buttoo unpicked the case of a British man, Mirza Tahir Hussain, who had been detained on death row for 18 years in Pakistan. Others had titles like '*Don't call me Asian*', '*Young and Minted*' (rich Asians), '*Pimped and Lethal*' (cars), '*Raggastani*' (someone of Asian origin with a Jamaican/African accent) and '*Brothers Gonna work it Out*', a Bobby Friction documentary originally done for Radio One on the hip hop community in New York. Another programme looked at racist attitudes within the Asian communities and talked to Asian people who supported calls for restraints on further immigration into the UK.

'*Sex, Lies and Culture*' attracted a lot of publicity after someone on BBC television's 'Six O' Clock News' saw a line about the Asian Network's pending investigation into the sex lives of young Asians. The idea for the programme had come from Munazza Khan after a conversation with a Glasgow doctor. He had said that the stress of keeping their sexual relationships secret from their parents was leading to medical and psychological problems among Asian youngsters. The 'Six O' Clock' team came on board with the project which was enhanced by some strong unpublished data from a clinic in Birmingham about the secret sex lives of young Asians.

Terry Jones of the *Monty Python* team passed through BBC Birmingham in June 2006, pushing his book '*Barbarians*' which was published alongside his BBC2 series of the same name. I was away that day but had mentioned in passing to one of the Assistant Editors, Kully Singh, that I had interviewed the said Mr Jones more than 25 years earlier when he was invited to open a student beer festival in Oxford. Then, as two sort of BBC kindred spirits (at opposite ends of the fame game), we had passed among the star-struck students, introducing each other to brews that we knew. Kully related this to the passing Python, who signed a copy of his book with the inscription: 'To Mike Curtis – Still at it!'. My whole career to date summed up in six words by a comedy icon – marvellous!

CHAPTER 19

mobilisAsian

T he new Asian Network Leadership Group regularly had meetings away from BBC premises – a practice that was banned across BBC radio in later years to save money. We were called to places with names like the Orange Space, the Wallace Space and Browns to take stock of where we were in the 'TransformAsian' process.

Michael Hill invariably started these sessions with a simple question for everyone. One was 'Tell us about the best meal you have ever had? '. I let rip about a fantastic fish restaurant overlooking the Puget Sound in Seattle with a waitress who really was called Peggy Sue and which was all paid for by Boeing (a media trip in my local radio life). Bob nominated his breakfast that morning which really was n't entering into the spirit of it at all. On another occasion, Michael said we should all talk about something that we had grown and nurtured and were very proud of. His example was a tub of garden cress. Dharmesh Rajput, the interactive editor, was next but asked for more time. Following on, I volunteered my two sons which I thought trumped the bloody cress.

Three months after the relaunch, the Heads group (Vijay, Husain, Bob, Mark, Michael and me) convened to discuss the Asian Network's Service Strategy. The DG had asked all divisions to come up with ambitious plans under the latest internal initiative – this one called 'Creative Futures'. Staff would get used to collecting battle honours in the BBC's internal navel-gazing campaigns which all had names like Building Public Values, Step Change, Going Digital, Creative Futures, Continuous Improvement, Putting Quality First which morphed into Delivering Quality First (or Destroying Quality Fast as the wags named it).

Creative Futures looked as though budgets would be based on the ideas that it threw up. Michael Hill was very good at this sort of thing and had written up a draft of the plans for Bob to send to Jenny Abramsky. Although the new money for the Asian Network was protected and another £3.9 million was earmarked over the next two years, everyone in Radio and Music had been asked to identify 25 per cent cuts that, if pushed, they reckoned they could offer up.

The extra money would go towards the journalism and language teams and also address the infrastructure issues like coping with studios in three cities and the shaky local radio playout system. There were plans to originate 24 hours of Asian Network programming instead of pumping out Five Live overnight, and ten per cent of the programmes would go out to the independent sector to bring the Network into line with other national stations. One of these programmes would be a new debate show at the weekend with the working title of '*Asian Provocateur*'.

Despite the recent investment, the Asian Network was still perceived as a local radio station at the centre. It had a complicated and unreliable technical base and, no matter how good the programmes were, the actual sound quality was poor with the DAB bit-rate (basically the speed and strength of the signal) being low and in mono. It was the same bit-rate as the Birdsong service which had temporarily twittered along on DAB for a couple of years.

Nevertheless, Bob Shennan was to recommend the creation of 'Asian Network TV'. This ambitious adventure would cover a central online portal for all things Asian and would pitch for television programmes on mainstream BBC channels, working with the Asian Programmes Unit in Birmingham. 'Red Button' video feeds from Melas and concerts would be on offer, along with mobile blogs from the audience and video blogs from the presenters. The creativity continued with grass-roots workshops in cities where there were under-served Asian communities such as the Bangladeshis in east London. All of these would be underpinned by partnerships across the BBC, be it BBC Blast (a short lived project to inspire and motivate young people to develop their creative talents), Big Screens, Electric Proms and other radio stations like 1Xtra.

A big part of the plan of getting out to the communities was a good one which unfortunately never happened. This was to set up a small network of 'open centres' in High Streets in places like Slough or the Manningham Road in Bradford or the 'Curry Mile' bit of the Wilmslow Road in Manchester. Using vacant shops at a hopefully small rent, the BBC would move in and set up a broadcast studio which could be used for broadcasting direct into the Asian Network and for allowing the audience to make their own content – be it audio, video or blogs. All in all, it would bring the BBC closer to the Asian communities and hopefully root out new talent. Husain Husaini, the Head of News, said he wanted to see all his journalists out in the communities rather than sitting behind their desks. His vision of the future was 'the empty newsroom'.

The radio station was not going to stop at Hounslow High Street though. The proposal would take in the Indian sub-continent. The logic was that the Asian Network was the leader in new British Asian music and, as Bobby Friction had proved, there was a huge appetite for that music in India. With the new line-up of top Asian presenters, why not take those shows and all the British Asian music within out to the Asian communities across the world? Indeed the BBC had recently been involved in a partnership which had won FM licences in seven Indian cities.

Weeks later Bob Shennan chaired a discussion with the music

team about this idea. At one point, an Asian Network roadshow was envisaged trailing round India giving out memory sticks and whistles. As the meeting broke up, Bob and I continued briefly on this wild hallucinogenic roll until his mobile phone rang. It soon became apparent to me that it was football legend and Five Live match summariser Jimmy Armfield. It was obviously the end of my conversation with Bob and there would be no extra time. I slipped out the room and I never heard any more about that sub-continental music extravaganza.

Every so often, the BBC did a staff survey to find out how the 'officer class' (to coin a phrase from a later DG) was perceived by the poor bloody infantry. At the end of 2005 just ahead of the'TransformAsian' recruitment process, one such survey was done in Radio and Music. Asian Network staff felt positive about change and having a vision but felt they were not involved or consulted – something that would change with further team meetings and specific seminars. They also said management did not address unacceptable behaviour or poor performance properly, and they had doubts about the way some people were recruited.

Towards the end of 2006, the results of another survey gave the first indications of what people thought of the new management structure. Despite the pleas for a 'one station' attitude, some of the new Assistant Editors were accused of setting up their own fiefdoms and only caring about their own programmes. Staff called for some of them to be more constructive and polite, better organised, and to work across the whole station. There was a suggestion that people be moved around different teams to try and break down this territorial attitude but not all of them had transferrable skills. Others bemoaned the unseemly scramble to secure top name guests for their own programme, bypassing a computer-based system called Offbid designed to ensure that interviewees were lined up for the most appropriate outlet and presenter.

There was evidence of this territorial blight during sessions with the Asian Network leadership group. Individual assistant editors would understandably fight their corner but this occasionally spilled over into 'handbags'. After one session up the road from Broadcasting House, Bob and Vijay kept two of the clashing male combatants back 'after school' to figuratively bang their heads together. At another session in April 2007, one openly questioned why the Network was spending so much money on Sport and on *Silver Street*, and he added that some of the staff were 'spare parts' and should be 'managed out'.

—⟶⟿—

The Asian Network started to use the Birmingham Mailbox network radio studios without paying for them – what Bob Shennan called the currency of 'wooden dollars'. It was an expression for trading between internal budgets that did n't actually make anyone any money or incur any real costs. Radio 2 was gradually pulling out of the Mailbox with its overnight programmes returning to the London studios, leaving only a handful of pre-recordings each week with presenters like Stuart Maconie and Bob Harris.

The actual name of the BBC Asian Network was regularly raised in staff surveys and those dreaded brainstorms – or when the logo was updated. It was a well established brand name but there were those who felt it was too old fashioned for the digital age. They felt the word 'Network' implied old steam radio rather than modern multi-media. The title 'BBC Asian Radio' was considered strong enough for some mock-ups of a logo to be drawn up. Some wondered about Radio 8 – 'Eight Asian' had a certain ring to it. But even Radio 7 eventually got rebranded as Radio 4Extra – and the Asian Network branding was retained. The Radio and Music division got rebranded though as *Audio* and Music to reflect its growing digital and interactive aspects. Years later, it was rebranded back as Radio again.

At a time when everyone was trying give the Asian Network a bigger profile both in and out of the BBC, it made sense not to change its name. One opportunity to shout about it was in the 2006 entries for the Sony Radio Awards. It was one of three shortlisted in the Digital Station of the Year category but failed to win at the awards night the following May. However two other entries fared better. An Asian Network documentary by Poonam Taneja on honour killings called '*Love, Honour and Obey*' got the silver in the News Feature category, and Bobby Friction won Gold in the Specialist Music Section. Mr Friction arrived on stage dressed somewhat informally for the occasion, topped off with a large black hat and launched into a long thank you speech that seemed to name-check most of the Network staff – even me.

CHAPTER 20

Asian Nation

'Is Big Brother a mirror on the nation? A lot of British Asians seem to think so. The BBC Asian Network calls the BB imbroglio its biggest story ever, with more audience response than Kashmir, the rise of the BNP, the Pakistani nuclear bomb and other ephemera'. An article by David Aaronovitch, writing in *The Times*, was one of more than 300 newspaper stories in Britain about the racism row that overwhelmed Channel 4's *'Celebrity Big Brother'* in January 2007. It was a story that attracted global interest, not least in India where there was particular outrage at the treatment of a Bollywood actress.

Shilpa Shetty was one of 11 housemates who entered the Big Brother house for the fifth series. Three days in, they were joined by Jade Goody, her boyfriend Jack Tweed and Goody's mother Jackiey Budden. Almost immediately, Shilpa Shetty was subjected to disrespect with Budden claiming she could not pronounce 'Shilpa' and so calling her just 'the Indian'. Soon the other housemates, particularly Goody, were verbally abusing the actress, swearing at her, bullying her and calling her racist names.

More than two weeks into the series, Ofcom had received 44,500 complaints and Channel 4, which had initially described the clashes as 'girlish rivalry', had got 3,000. Management finally agreed that there had been a cultural clash between them. Senior politicians got involved in the row with Chancellor of the Exchequer Gordon Brown and London Mayor Ken Livingstone condemning the behaviour. Leicester East MP Keith Vaz tabled an Early Day Motion in the Commons, the Indian government said it would take 'action as required', and Hertfordshire police, in whose area the programme was filmed, started an investigation into racial hatred.

All of this kept the Asian Network newsroom extremely busy, along with the phone-in show which attracted more than 800 calls on the subject. With its contacts, it was able to find fresh interviewees for every twist and turn. Shilpa's mother Sunanda told the Network that her daughter was tough. 'I hope she will be able to handle the situation. It is a game and there is a life beyond that. I understand her emotions but I really hope that she is not going to get too affected by this treatment that is being meted out to her'.

One of the housemates, newspaper columnist Carole Malone, told the Asian Network that she believed the incidents were motivated by jealousy. 'Shilpa is too good-looking for her own good. She's an incredibly powerful and beautiful woman. She is very strong woman and can handle it. Shilpa feels that she represents the Indian/Asian community and does n't want to let them or herself down by retaliating'.

The writer and comedian Meera Syal also appeared on the Asian Network, attacking Channel 4's response to the row. 'They have made a rather bland statement about condemning racism of any kind,' she said. 'But I am just wondering if on their last series, for example, the Tourette's sufferer had been called a "spaz" on a regular basis, whether they would have let that continue.' And former England batsman Geoffrey Boycott, who was a friend of Shilpa, also joined the debate, telling listeners that he had not been impressed by what he had seen. 'It is totally alien to most Asian girls, in particular Shilpa Shetty who's known in India for being a really nice girl; she's not full of herself', he said.

Shilpa Shetty won the Big Brother prize after polling 63 per cent of the vote. She later said Jade Goody did apologise and she had forgiven her. The Asian Network continued to follow her after the row died down, being on the red carpet for the London premiere of her new film 'Life in a Metro' three months later.

—◊◊—

In Birmingham another row was bubbling up – this time between the Asian Network and *The Archers* over noise. Both teams had their desks in the middle of the hangar-like building that was the Mailbox production office. The Bollywood and bhangra of the Asian Network's urban programmes were spreading from the speakers on the desks across to the bucolic peace of Borchestershire. The dispute was aired at the Birmingham Heads of Department meeting with Vanessa Whitburn, Editor of *The Archers*, squaring up to the representative of the Asian Network – one Mike Curtis. Emails were sent to the Head of Radio Factual and the Head of Radio Drama.

Bob Shennan and Michael Hill thought this was all rather amusing with Michael urging us to whack up the volume. Sitting in the middle of the Mailbox with various Archers production staff glaring over their partitions, it wasn't particularly funny, especially when *Countryfile* and *Points of View* joined forces with the soap complainants. I thought 'Please God, don't send a delegation led by John Craven'. I did actually have some sympathy and got on well with Vanessa, whose office was down the corridor and round the corner and thus out of earshot of the Asian Network speakers.

An Occupational Risk Advisor came to measure the noise levels. It was of course a particularly quiet day but he could see from the figures why *The Archers* were having problems. For the record, the background noise levels gave an average of 59 and 60 decibels which apparently is high for an office (normal should be 40-50 dB). Normal conversation (and our team were also accused of talking loudly to each other or on mobile phones) is 60-70 decibels but if they were talking against a background of music it would require an increase in volume.

We were urged to compromise by listening to output on headphones, which was not practical or sustainable. We did remind the Asian Network team to be good neighbours but the only practical solution to what I called this 'urban/rural conflict' was for one of the teams to move elsewhere in the Mailbox. That was not practical either so the stand-off continued until '*Silver Street* ' was axed and *The Archers* could escape down the corridor to the quiet pastures of the former Asian soap's desks. The Asian Network subsequently expanded across the old Archers production area and began to annoy someone above us from *Gardener's World* instead.

A year after 'TransformAsian', further changes to the schedule were implemented. Adil Ray's Drive programme was declared to be primarily a music programme and would not touch serious news. Instead the news team provided three new mini -'Wrap' programmes which were 15 minute bulletins on the hour. The Network's news provision, which was now commissioned from BBC News, was making an impact at the centre with several exclusives. These included the first interview with Mirza Tahir Hussain, the Leeds man who had been on death row in Pakistan for 18 years and who was subsequently paroled after a campaign by relatives, and a report on sex-selective abortions being behind a drop in the number of female babies born to Indian mothers in the UK.

One of the biggest stories of the year was the return to Pakistan in October by Benazir Bhutto. The Network's Manchester reporter Rahila Bano was at Karachi airport when Bhutto flew in, and was able to report live into Nihal's phone-in programme. Three months later, Benazir Bhutto was assassinated in Rawalpindi while campaigning ahead of elections in Pakistan.

Although the Network was committed to an equal split between speech and music, it was clear that music was getting a higher profile. Dharmesh Rajput and his small interactive team were told to focus their website energies on what Bob Shennan and Michael Hill thought would bring more people to the Asian Network brand and that was definitely music. Michael said the Network was going to be single-minded about becoming a fully fledged music station with a website, TV presence, mobile content and podcasts to back it up.

Interactivity went a step too far when a listener texted a picture to the Breakfast show of an erect penis coupled with some obscene comments. We told other programmes to watch out for the same mobile number to ensure the texter did not get on air and passed the evidence to the man I called 'Hennigan of the Yard' – Tony Hennigan, a former policeman with BBC Investigations who patiently handled numerous Asian Network cases over the years. Those moved to text pictures of their genitals would get the surprise of their life when confronted with a bluff Yorkshireman ringing them up to ask why they felt the urge to behave so pathetically.

One of the documentaries commissioned by the Asian Network in 2007 delved into a world of sequins and silicon breasts to meet British Asian drag queens. Called '*Life's A Drag*', it was a fascinating and provocative look at the Asian drag queens where they talked frankly about their experiences and aspirations in what was perceived by many in the Asian communities as a freakish sub-culture. The phrase 'chick with a dick' after nearly two and half minutes got cleared for broadcast along with an indelicate reference to castration, but three 'shits' were bleeped out.

The weekend schedule went big on Bollywood with four hour programmes on both Saturday and Sunday mornings. '*Love*

Bollywood', hosted by Raj and Pablo, would be broadcast from Yalding House, the home of Radio 1 in London, in the hope of getting more big name interviewees as they passed through the capital. A somewhat surprised George Mann, the journalist who was the Network's London assistant editor looking after the phone-in, was asked to oversee these programmes as well. He promptly organised a Bollywood 'awayday' round the corner in the Horse and Groom pub on Great Portland Street, hosted by one of those earnest BBC 'facilitators' brandishing a jar of a particular spreadable yeast extract as an example of divided opinions.

We were gradually being brought into line with other network radio stations, including the requirement to ensure that 10 per cent of our output (excluding news and the phone-in) went out to the independent production companies. The simplest way to achieve this was to offer up our eleven hours of devotional music, plus a bit of the Saturday night specialist music shows and some documentaries. The devotional strand was won by Fresh Air Production, an established Swindon-based company led by Neil Cowling. Despite his experience, the world of Hindu, Sikh and Islamic music was certainly new to him. At least he would be working with the three long serving devoted devotional presenters who were, nevertheless, not particularly keen on this new commercial arrangement.

As part of widening the scope of the music, the Saturday night *'Mic Check'* programme was awarded to another well known independent company called 'Somethin' Else' which would also be broadcasting the show from Yalding House. Meanwhile the music team also got out and about more to music festivals such as Glastonbury and Bestival. It took a lead role in partnerships for events like the London Mela, Regent Street Festival and Newham under the Stars (in east London). It staged a concert in conjunction with the BBC2 *'Desi DNA'* programme at the Scala Cinema near Kings Cross in London featuring Outlandish, Jay Sean, Swami, Sona

Family, Bishi and Tigerstyle. This event made two 30 minute television programmes and a created a bucketload of material for the Asian Network across February 2008.

The star for me was Bishi, dressed entirely in gold and beguiling all with her song 'Nightbus'. It was a powerful showcase for Asian music and deserved wider coverage than a couple of late night slots on BBC2.

Bobby Friction liked Bishi too, blogging: 'Bishi (one of my Future Frictions) was the surprise success as a lot of the crowd seemed to only be interested in Bhangra or Outlandish – but after her stunning and glittery performance, I was approached by many young Desi females who all said she was different but great. She's like a cross between a UK folk singer & a Bengali poet in high heels! Tigerstyle showed why they are constantly at the top of the game Bhangra wise with a powerful performance by loads of great musicians and a 'no keyboards or electronics' rule that saw their Punjabi folk stripped back to its essentials. Last (cue the screaming!) were Outlandish who did a performance defo aimed for the viewers at home. It was all subtle raised eyebrows and finger pointing – they must have literally hundreds of hours of experience at this sort of stuff, and the crowd loved it'.

The Indian International Film Awards bounced around the world from India to Thailand to Amsterdam to Toronto to China. But in 2007 it came to Yorkshire which made it easier for the Asian Network to cover and also to keep an eye on the staff that were sent to report on it. The stars' first glimpse of Yorkshire was Doncaster's Robin Hood airport and there were events at the Royal Armouries in Leeds and a celebrity cricket match at Headingly before the big bash at Sheffield's Hallam Arena.

—⁂—

'Asian Nation' was an ambitious project across the summer of 2007 and which also pulled in independent partners. It was a multi-media offering that aimed to mark the 60th anniversary of the Partition of India and would highlight the stories and opinions of British Asians. Many BBC radio and television outlets went back to the sub-continent to look at life there and how the countries had evolved since the bloody events of 1947. The Asian Network decided to stay in the UK and ask its audience about their understanding of history and the issues that affected them in Britain.

With the slogan 'My life, my roots, my music', Asian Nation aimed to use audio, video, images and stories collected by young and old across the UK. The hope was that it would boost the reach and reputation of the Network by attracting cross-promotion throughout the BBC. Independent production companies helped with the collection of content and with the interactive 'mini-website' while the reporters, producers and presenters all contributed to short reports and 25 minute documentaries.

An ICM survey of 18-34 year olds done for the Asian Network at the time revealed that 87 per cent of white Britons would marry someone outside of their race. However only 53 per cent of Asians said they would marry someone from outside of their communities. On the back of that survey, Gagan Grewal's Hindi-Urdu show ran a debate about the lengths that people would go to hide the fact that they were not a virgin. A later documentary looked at hymen replacement among young Asian women.

'Asian Nation' produced some excellent stories and a fine documentary pulled together by Harjinder Mann. But it never really took off as its own project. The staff never got behind it enough and the audience did not respond in large numbers to give it a strong on-line legacy. With hindsight, the Asian Network should have just covered the 60th anniversary of Partition with a good phone-in, documentary and appropriate news coverage rather than complicate things with the Asian Nation project. It was an initial venture in the 'visualisation' of radio and neither the staff nor the audience were quite ready for it yet.

Even so, the documentary won a Bronze at the Sony Radio Awards the following May, and The Guardian's radio review of 2007, written by Paul Robinson, the managing director of Kidsco, said: 'The final word goes to the BBC's digital 'Asian Network' which demonstrated in superb style how radio can transport you anywhere with its evocative commemoration of the 60th anniversary of partition of India'.

CHAPTER 21

accusAsian

'*Film Café*', the Saturday morning forerunner of '*Love Bollywood*', broadcast its Bollywood awards in February 2007. The winner of the Best Actress category was lined up to do an interview with Raj and Pablo over the phone but it fell through and she could not do it. The programme's producer therefore made the runner-up as winner as she *was* available to talk to live on-air. In the Best Supporting Actress category, the voting figures were 'misread' and the true winner lost out.

The communications regulator Ofcom was quite busy with BBC competitions. '*Blue Peter*', the children's TV programme, 'found' a competition winner amongst a group of visitors to the studio after viewers phoning in were unable to get through to the live studio. The BBC was fined £50,000. '*Blue Peter*' also ignored the winner in an online poll to name the programme's cat, preferring Socks to Cookie. Radio 2 and BBC London were also heavily fined for running phone-in competitions on pre-recorded programmes, and a 6 Music programme was criticised for making up the name of a winner in a competition for concert tickets.

The Asian Network's misdemeanours in the '*Film Cafe*' programme were overshadowed by the bigger television and radio culprits and it did escape a fine. However Ofcom said that there had been a willingness to exploit audience trust in the *Film Cafe* programme and knowingly mislead it. It said there had been a "lack of regard" for Ofcom's broadcasting code. The producer responsible was disciplined and moved to another programme.

Frankly, it was a relief when the BBC banned competitions. While the big stations were offering foreign trips for some winners, the Asian Network enticed listeners with a pathetic CD or a book which may or may not have been signed by someone interesting. And even then, some programme staff were failing to get the prizes out to people. Gagan Grewal was worried that the failure to get prizes out to winners could cost him listeners on his Hindi Urdu show.

After Ofcom passed judgement, Jenny Abramsky asked all stations to send details to HQ of any programme going back to July 2005 where the management had any concerns about listeners being deceived. Meanwhile the publicity over the fines imposed on the BBC prompted an Asian Network listener to write to the BBC's Complaints Unit saying that he may have won a rigged competition a few months earlier, again on the *Film Café* programme.

He had phoned in with the correct answer to the question 'What was the name of the producer of '*Shakalaka Boom Boom*?' (the film, not the racehorse...). He then recalled being phoned by the producer 45 minutes before the end of the programme to ask where he lived, which was in Cumbria. He said he joked to a friend that they had obviously decided that he had won before the competition had even ended. He thought it could be something to do with his English name. Either way, he was very pleased to win and get his prize.

The Complaints Unit passed me the email for action and I duly replied to the complainant that we were taking his concerns very seriously. I could also tell him that the BBC had suspended all phone-related competitions and I was sure he was impressed to learn that all 16,500 programme and content staff throughout the

BBC were facing a new mandatory training course to remind them not to deceive the audience and to uphold all the BBC's values and editorial standards. We heard no more from the competition winner but the allegation was referred to the top of Radio and Music under the new policy.

This particular luke-warm potato surrounding *Shakalaka Boom Boom* actually found its way to the desk of the Controller of Radio 4 no less, Mark Damazer, who was called upon to pass judgement. In a flurry of emails, I established for him that the reason that the *Film Café* producer rang to ask the winner where he lived was not a postcode prejudice but to ensure that he was not overseas and listening through the internet. The programme apparently had introduced its own policy of not posting prizes abroad (to ensure only UK licence fee payers won) and it appeared that such calls to contestants were routine. There was no further investigation as the producer concerned was already suspended for another lapse (failing to edit the f-word out of a pre-recorded interview before it was broadcast) and was out the door not long afterwards.

After a crisis at the BBC, staff would expect a flurry of initiatives. These usually took the form of mandatory courses which everyone involved in production would have to attend and have their attendance formally logged on a central database. Sure enough, the competitions fiasco spawned 'Safeguarding Trust'. Trainers were despatched around the country to host sessions with staff to enable them to draw the line between what it called legitimate media artifice and unacceptable audience deception. It also created 'ITACU' which staff enunciated in the style of Vic Reeves' 'Iranu' on '*Shooting Stars*'. It stood for Interactive Technical Advice and Contracts Unit and provided advice on running competitions, votes and any other use of premium rate phone calls.

The presenters of *Film Café*, Raj Dhanda and Pablo Sat-Bhambra, changed their BBC 'conflict of interest' declaration forms more than most with their outside involvements in live shows or consultancies around the Bollywood business. They were not BBC staff or fulltime with the Asian Network so were free to help Selfridges with a Bollywood month, set up 'Bollywood on Ice' at Somerset House in London, and run their own Bollywood club nights in London.

So it was no surprise when a film company contacted them about getting involved in a publicity deal for a Bollywood film which would be produced in Hollywood. The plan was to meet the company's representatives for lunch in central London but before that, a woman involved in the project arranged a phone conference with Raj and Pablo. She spent some time unpicking what they did and what they could offer. When they got round to talking about their Asian Network radio programme, they said it was the number one show where 'if we say the movie is going to flop, they (the listeners) don't go and watch it'.

The woman, calling herself Alison, said she hoped they would n't say that her film would be a flop and asked about getting advertising on the show, raising the 'conflict of interest'. Pablo replied that anything to do with the radio show would be in the hands of their producers.

The woman said that the film was actually quite weak and asked about Raj and Pablo reviewing it across their newspaper columns and on the radio. They said they would probably review it even if they had not had this conversation. 'Alison' asked if their review would be included in the deal with the film company, but Pablo again said that anything on the radio would be down to the show producers. When she asked if they could emphasize the positive aspects of the film, Pablo replied: 'We would have to watch the film'.

The proposed lunch meeting never happened. Instead a recording of the phone conversation was sent to the BBC with a claim that this taped conversation showed Raj and Pablo were prepared to give a film a good review on their BBC radio programme because they were being paid by the film company to handle all of its publicity. We had the whole recording transcribed and a group of us went through the 15 pages line by line with the pair of them.

It was now clear that this phone call had been an attempt at 'entrapment' to get them to incriminate themselves but, to their credit, it failed. It was also felt that it had been encouraged by a connection inside the Asian Network. Consequently BBC Security checked through the numbers phoned from extensions in Asian Network production offices and from BBC-owned mobile phones that were issued to staff. This confirmed a couple of suspicions but it was inconclusive as to who made the calls or whether they were connected to this particular saga.

It was clear that, however the conversation developed or was 'led', Raj and Pablo always said that their producers would have the last word as far as the radio show was concerned. They had not said they would automatically give the film a good review. All the allegations against Raj and Pablo were investigated by the BBC and found to be groundless.

The *Eastern Eye* newspaper based in west London regularly ran negative stories and gossip about some Asian Network presenters and managers across its middle page spread under the by-line of Asjad Nazir, the paper's entertainment journalist who had written so passionately about Sonia a few years earlier. In June 2010, Nazir – describing himself as 'one of the leading Asian showbiz writers in the world' – wrote a long email to Director of Radio Tim Davie and DG Mark Thompson outlining a number of allegations against some Asian Network people. The *Daily Mail* had a sniff at the claims but did not follow-up or publish anything. It took a letter from the BBC's legal team after one actionable outburst to finally shut him up.

There were a few Asian Network staff who felt some presenters got what they deserved in the gossip columns of *Eastern Eye*. The Asian Network was no different from any other radio station in that some of its presenters threw their toys out of the pram at some time or another. Any editor or producer across network radio would regale you with stories of presenter petulance without too much prompting. On a couple of occasions, we took a presenter off-air for a week or so after they overstepped the mark in their behaviour towards their production team. Staff felt Controllers indulged presenters too much as they were the front line in getting the listeners and thus securing the reputation of the Controller and indeed the whole radio station. The complaints of programme teams were usually answered with: 'I'll have a word', or more likely: 'I'll have another word'.

Once the upward elevation and the fame arrived, presenters would get themselves an agent to ask for more money and more time off. That summer while deputising for Vijay, I was asked by one agent for a 'short notice' day off for a presenter and also a week off to allow time for some other media work. I turned down the 'short notice' day off but agreed to the week-long request as it would give the programme team a break.

Getting a short-notice deputy to cover a programme could be difficult at the Asian Network as the replacement often lived hundreds of miles away. If the stand-in was needed in Birmingham, you could bet your bottom rupee that the only available cover was in London. Breakfast editor Jonathan Aspinwall highlighted his angst at trying to get short notice cover for Sonia one morning after she fell ill. He tried four people – 'one could n't do it, one always said no, another just said no without explanation and another would n't because she had been rejected in the past for presentation duties so why should she do it now?' In the end the golden voiced Sonal Patel expanded her usual newsreading role to present the whole programme. This run-around reached Bob Shennan who said it made us 'look like Mickey Mouse'. It was time for a completely new system of booking presenter cover.

Among the regular stand-ins who were called in, and enthusiastically agreed to help when they could, were Satnam Rana, Amanda Hussain and Yasmeen Khan. Aasmah Mir popped back from Five Live to cover the phone-in occasionally, and Rajini Vaidyanathan from the BBC's political unit helped with the weekend Bollywood shows.

Another newcomer in 2007 was Noreen Khan who was initially brought in to front the Saturday chart show from the London Asian commercial station Club Asia. Noreen, with a reputation for big hair and striking couture, was soon hosting the weekend breakfast show and later took on the weekday Drive programme, making her one of the Asian Network's best known top name presenters.

Away from the programmes and presenters, the first signs that the money bonanza was coming to an end were emerging. The schedule changes in May pushed music at the expense of costly speech. There would be no new fulltime appointments – any vacancies would be filled by contracts or internal attachments. And the Assistant Editors could not buy in casuals to cover holiday or sickness. If someone was away for up to three weeks, they had to make do with the staffing that was left and just muck in themselves. A plan to share the costs of the 'station sound' operation (on-air trails and the like) across both Five Live and the Asian Network was implemented and saved the costs of one post.

The Asian Network was being asked to identify £150,000 in its budget to cover the growing costs of presenters, the overspend on the casual budget and to keep a respectable contingency fund to hand. The cost of hiring casuals in the 12 months up to April 2007 was at well over £100,000. In the next financial year up to March 2008, the Network was spending the same amount on *Silver Street* as it was on News – the drama and journalism costing £1.3 million each. More than 30 per cent of the station budget (£2.3 million) would go on programme staff costs including casuals and relocation expenses. People agonised again over the cost and inconveniences of running a three-site station. Sangeeta Kotak, now the Network's own finance assistant, identified £25,000 of savings in the station's mobile phone bills alone (being the Asian Network, there were a lot of overseas calls) and she was unpicking other areas.

In the wider BBC, DG Mark Thompson announced in October 2007 that up to 1,700 BBC jobs were to be lost as a result of drastic plans to save two billion pounds. Thompson said the savings were needed to fill the 'black hole' left by a below-inflation settlement in the licence fee. The BBC had only just come through an earlier redundancy process triggered in 2005 which affected some 3800 staff. Most of the job losses this time would be in London. It was also announced that the BBC would be selling off Television Centre in west London.

At the Asian Network, the spending was already being reversed and the weekly audience figures were refusing to climb above

500,000. In the last three months of 2007, it dropped to 441,000. The extra investment at a time of big cuts elsewhere was not delivering the target of 750,000 listeners a week. And another major upheaval was heading our way.

CHAPTER 22

conversAsian

The BBC Trust approved the plan for five London-based departments to move to Salford in May 2007. It was confirmed that one of these five would indeed be BBC Radio Five Live. This triggered much speculation about which senior managers would actually want to head up the M6 permanently. Even though the actual move was some four years away, the senior team at the Asian Network wondered if the announcement would herald a mass bail out at the top of Five Live.

Moz Dee, the managing editor, was the first to go, announcing in November 2007 that he was off to Talksport, Five Live's main rival in sports coverage. Less than a month later, it was announced that the Controller himself, Bob Shennan, was leaving to head up Channel 4's new digital radio package. Bob was out the door almost immediately, going on 'gardening leave' (or 'golfing leave' in his case) until finally starting at Channel 4 four months later. Michael Hill, who I felt would not be keen to move north so soon after bolting together his new home in Kent, followed Bob to Channel 4 a few weeks later.

Andy Parfitt, the Controller of Radio 1 and Radio 1Xtra, was asked to look after Five Live and the Asian Network until a new Controller was appointed. He came to meet the management team of the Asian Network in the Mailbox before Christmas when a couple of us asked him about staying under his control going forward. Like Radio 1, we had a young audience and made much of our music. And the new Controller of Five Live would no doubt be focussing on the move to Salford and therefore not have his or her eye on the Asian Network ball.

When Adrian Van Klaveren was revealed as the new Controller of Five Live, the Asian Network's petitioning to go with Radio 1 gained more impetus. Van Klaveren, a former Head of Local Programmes at Birmingham and thus known to quite a few Network staff, was going to have enough on his plate getting to grips with a station the size and breadth of Five Live. He was also supposedly committed to personally moving to Salford, where the Asian Network had no production centre and no plans for one. Jenny Abramsky was persuaded by the logic of permanently moving the Asian Network under Radio 1 and so it came to pass that Andy Parfitt assumed control.

Having got used to the headquarters team at Five Live and built a working relationship with them, the Asian Network had to start again with the Radio 1 bunch at Yalding House, just up the road from Broadcasting House. Andy had a different way of working to Bob – he was more precise and concerned with detail. He chaired a fortnightly 'Board Meeting' with the senior four at the Asian Network, who also used to go to his Radio 1 management sessions every week. He liked people to be on time – and if they were given two minutes for their area updates, he used to actually time it.

For a while I joined the Radio 1 meetings with Vijay, Husain and Mark, sometimes pushing through the crush of paparazzi and fans outside Yalding House when stars like Maria Carey dropped in for an interview. The meeting usually ended with the summoning of George Ergatoudis, Radio 1's head of music, who brought in the latest controversial song releases to get the thumbs up (or down) from the hierarchy. I often wondered how I came to find myself sitting in a Radio 1 meeting room at 11am listening to Akon's 'I'm so paid' at high volume and being asked if I thought it should make the Radio 1 playlist. Andy must have wondered too and I was 'stood down' when the meeting was reconfigured and slimmed down a few months after he took over the Asian Network.

I did learn from Radio 1 that I was probably 'restless' verging on being a 'scenester'. There was a 'music industry cone model' which divided listeners into three segments and which Andy introduced to the Asian Network to define who might be listening when and why. The thin narrow end of the cone was the 'scenester' segment and represented the artists, broadcasters and people involved in recording, publishing, advertising, broadcasting and writing about the music scene. The middle segment housed the 'restless' which covered the active music fan who sought out new music and read music magazines. Finally you had the 'contented' who were the mass market who wanted an 'easy' listen of songs they recognised and loved – for the Asian Network, the Bollywood and bhangra brigades.

One-to-one meetings with about 50 of the staff produced an avalanche of feedback for Andy Parfitt about the direction that the station had taken since 'TransformAsian'. Many took the opportunity of the arrival of a new Controller to vent their frustrations at the output and the weekly audience figures. For all the investment and new staff, many felt the Asian Network did not know itself or its audience. It was Radio 1 one minute and then Five Live the next. It had an identity crisis and was 'all at sea'. It was targeting the young, trying to be hip and 'too cool for school'. Its output was too trivial and frivolous and it was losing its traditional audience. It needed to play more Bollywood and attract more of the 'contented'.

Despite Bob Shennan's plan to get the whole station pulling together in one direction and sounding all joined up, the reality was that each show was sounding very different to the next one. Breakfast was too young and trying to be hip like Radio 1, the Nihal phone-in debate (commissioned from News) sounded like Five

Live, and Nikki Bedi's excellent afternoon arts show was just too Radio 4. *Love Bollywood* (also commissioned from News now as it was coming from London like Nihal) was sounding too serious. Many staff were convinced that some of the traditional audience had been pushed away by the new younger sound and the output was not coherent across the day. The current strategy still seemed lost on many of the team.

People said there was no systematic review of the output, and that staff were all over the place chopping and changing around programmes. It wasn't always clear who was producing which show at the start of each day. There were claims that the Assistant Editors continued to encourage the 'silo' mentality, only caring about their own areas and not the rest of the radio station. Some senior staff decided not to move house from London to the Midlands where their job was based, meaning they were not visible and thus available to their teams as much as they should have been. On top of it all, the Asian Network was a technical nightmare with a complicated and unreliable transmission system between Birmingham, Leicester and London – and a playout system that continued to fall over.

Andy Parfitt realised he had a huge challenge in the face of this staff outpouring. He had to increase the audience, improve the station's audience approval factor, rescue staff morale and get it focussed, break-even on the tightening budgets and meet those SoPPS (Statement of Programme Policies – or Promises, never quite sure). It was my responsibility to fine tune the SoPPs every quarter to ensure they were realistic and looked as though they were being achieved without prompting questions from Radio and Music headquarters. They included aiming for 40 per cent of the music played to be by British Asian talent, maintaining a 50/50 split between speech and music, and running an average of between three and five hours of language programmes each day.

At Radio 1, Andy had nearly all his staff coming through the same front door of Yalding House each morning (some were in Manchester). He realized that many of the problems at the Asian Network arose from the fact that the station had numerous front doors around the country. Staff just did n't know each other and felt that other Asian Network output from other cities just did not concern them.

At a hotel near Leicester, Andy hosted an awayday 'brain-storm' with the Asian Network Leadership Group. The night before, he invited Vijay, Husain, Mark, Dharmesh and me to a meal to get to know more about each other and put the world to rights before the Assistant Editors bowled up the next morning. After Andy retired, the rest of us each stood a round of brandies (defiantly not on expenses) and sorted everything in an hour, firing half the staff in the process. On the television in the hotel bar, Blues fan Mark tried to ignore constant replays of Chelsea's defeat on penalties against Manchester United in the Champions League Final earlier in the evening.

The leadership awayday the following morning had the flipcharts, post-its, PowerPoints and mood boards. It had break-out groups, capture points and waterhole moments. It had audience research, media consumption overviews and Audience Segmentation (that cone again). The aim of the day was to draft a refreshed vision and strategy for the Asian Network and agree a plan going forward.

With hindsight, Thursday 22nd May 2008 was one of the most significant dates in the history of the Asian Network. What came out of that day was the new strategy strapline from the Assistant Editors – 'A Friend of the Family'. The Asian Network should have the Asian family with young children at the centre of its new policy, spiralling out to friends of the same age, teenage cousins, older parents and Auntie-ji. It needed a balanced, familiar and popular Asian music policy across the day that 25-30 year olds in the Asian communities love, carefully introducing new British Asian music. There was nothing wrong with some older tracks and the occasional mainstream track but there should be no hard underground music at breakfast.

The independent research among listeners and former listeners threw up four distinct groups. In an echo of 2002's mythical IT consultant figure, they were represented by four fictitious people who were named Shareeti, Shazad, Jas and Mala. Shareeti was the 21 year old who still lived at home and listened to the Asian Network, particularly Adil Ray, Bobby Friction and Raj and Pablo. She was the daytime target. Shazad was 31, lived with his wife and baby son and who listened to the radio but not so much to the Asian Network these days. Could we attract people like him back to the daytime core hours? 18 year old Jas was passionate about music and liked melas and specialist Asian music events – he was in the 15-24 youth target zone for specialist music shows at the weekends or late nights. Finally Mala was 37, lived with her husband and three children, loved soaps and old Bollywood music, and she would like the language and old music programmes.

So the plan was to 'warm up' (radio shorthand for making it more accessible) the daytime output so that it could be on in any family home or car without the music prompting someone to switch it off. The Asian Network should 'cement Shareeti and pull in Shazad' – more radio shorthand from the marketing people. The average Asian household was five members so the Asian Network should be the sixth. It should 'shine' and be 'big, national and glamorous'. It should be bold, welcoming, celebrate big events and talk to top stars. It needed a new weekday Breakfast show and the rest of the core output should be more accessible – in other words sound less like Radio 1 and Five Live. The new strategy was bundled up into a little booklet and given to all staff. It was the latest required reading for any job interview.

'Which radio station has changed the most in recent years? My vote would not go to any of the obvious contenders but to a service with only 452,000 regular listeners – though one that is as brave as it is small. The BBC Asian Network, which began a generation ago in the Midlands to offer Hindi and Urdu programmes to immigrant households, has changed from regional to national, from analogue to digital, from middle-aged to young and from sitar to guitar'. So wrote Paul Donovan, radio critic for *The Sunday Times* in July 2007.

It was a neat summary of the Asian Network journey so far and I used the quote in the paperwork for the entry in the Sony Radio Award's Digital Station of Year category. We were nominated again but did n't win again. By the time the judges were reading through and listening to our entry, the station was facing more changes to its output under its new Controller.

The first schedule shake-up was at the weekend. From mid-May after the football season ended, the Saturday afternoon *'Kickin' Off'* show was kicked out and replaced by a requests show with Zee TV presenter Murtz. Tommy Sandhu was brought in to host the weekend breakfast show and *Love Bollywood* was cut back to a more manageable three hours on a Saturday and Sunday. The changes to the weekdays would take another eight months to implement. Meanwhile, Jas Rao from the London Asian station Club Asia had taken over weekday Breakfast after Sonia Deol departed for new challenges (she'd be back again).

The outreach events were costly but important in taking the Asian Network out to its potential audience. The annual London Mela got bigger and bigger and the branding got more classy and flashy. Many of the 70,000 or so crowd poured away from Gunnersbury Park with Asian Network lanyards and whistles round their necks, some probably still thinking they had been at a Sunrise Radio event. Across the city, artists like Jay Sean and H Dami headlined 'Newham Under the Stars' where 15,000 people watched top stars on stage introduced by Asian Network presenters. The Baishakhi Mela in the heart of the east London Bangladeshi community was another important show for the Network but its London radio audience figures were still disappointing.

One of Andy Parfitt's first decisions was to change the Asian Network's management structure to bring it into line with what he had at Radio 1. Despite the BBC-wide cuts, he established a completely new post of Head of Programmes which had not been budgeted for. This figure would be the line manager for the clashing bunch of Assistant Editors who needed to be ejected from their individual silos and work together for the good of the whole station. Mark, as Head of Music, applied for it but it always seemed that Husain Husaini, the Head of News, was the anointed one. I took the opportunity of the shuffle to get my job title changed from Network Co-ordinator to the more understandable (internally at least) Network Manager to bring me into line with the similar but bigger jobs at Radio 4 and Five Live.

In his *Sunday Times* column highlighting the changes at the Asian Network, Paul Donovan specifically referred to the documentary strand '*Asian Network Reports*'. He had just listened to what he called a 'biting attack' on Asian racism, starting off with a white teenager in Glasgow who was abducted, set on fire and murdered by five 'Pakistani guys' as they were described on the programme. Other topics tackled in the strand included honour killings, shisha bars affected by the smoking ban, Asian-run pornography, binge drinking among young Asian women, and the Hindu plan to reclaim the swastika symbol.

'*Britain's Missing Girls*' was a documentary by Bradford-based reporter Sanjiv Buttoo into pregnant British Asian women who were turning to doctors in India for abortions if the foetus was female. It won a Gold at the Sony Radio Awards for 2008 output. Tim Gardam's 2004 report calling for the Asian Network's journalism to be more ambitious had surely been achieved by its documentaries alone.

The phone-in made national headlines ahead of the elections for London Mayor when the Tory candidate Boris Johnson told the host Nihal Arthanayake: 'My children are a quarter Indian – put that in your pipe and smoke it. You can't out-ethnic me!'

CHAPTER 23

denominAsian

A few months after Andy Parfitt took over, a group of past and present employees of the Asian Network lodged a formal complaint that it was operating an anti-Muslim policy. They claimed a 'mafia of executives' discriminated against Muslims by sidelining or dismissing Muslim presenters and reporters in favour of Hindus and Sikhs. They sent their complaints to the top – the Director General Mark Thompson.

Some of the Muslim part-time staff regularly complained that their religious festivals were not covered properly or that news bulletins carried too many negative stories about Islam. The complainants said that, out of seven daytime presenters early in 2008, only one was Muslim. Half of the eight or so reporters used to be Muslim – now there were only two.

The Labour peer Lord Ahmed supported the complaints and also wrote to the DG, saying he said he had originally raised the issue ten years earlier. He said there appeared to be a small 'mafia' that was promoting its version of a culture which was contrary to the diversity within the Asian community. Attempts to persuade the management to play Pakistani or Bengali music were allegedly ignored in favour of Bollywood and bhangra tunes which were more popular among the Hindu and Sikh communities.

The BBC said it took the allegations seriously and launched an internal investigation. It asked Stephen Whittle, a former Controller of Editorial Policy at the BBC until two years earlier, to listen to the evidence and report back. In my 14 years at the Asian Network, I never recognised such a policy as described by the complainants. There were personality clashes and management decisions that certain individuals might attribute to religious differences but to claim there was a 'mafia' at work was simply untrue. I did point out to Stephen Whittle in my contribution to the mafia inquisition that, before 'TransformAsian', the station had been run by a Hindu (Vijay), a Muslim (Ishfaq) and me – a sort of lapsed Anglican who, despite my father's calling, only really felt gripped by the music and the architecture. If you listen to Tomas Luis de Victoria's Tenebrae Responsories echo round a building like Lincoln Cathedral or Tewkesbury Abbey, you get the idea.

Anyway, back to reality. Stephen Whittle rejected the complaints but came up with proposals to avoid such grievances gaining credence in the future. He proposed a written policy for dealing with the various faiths consistently, with clear communication to staff on how religious festivals and editorial changes were handled by the Network. The roles and responsibilities of specialist music presenters and the process of music selection should be clarified and communicated to staff.

One of Whittle's most challenging proposals was to do with the status of the part-time presenters, a couple of whom had been at the centre of the complaints. BBC national radio stations had their presenters on freelance contracts with annual review dates but, at the Asian Network, nearly all the part-time presenters were actually on continuing staff contracts. This had been the result of an HR policy of the day many years earlier and it led to long running issues including how much holiday they were entitled to when they were only contracted for a few hours a week and also the inability to refresh the presenter line-up easily. Whittle proposed bringing the Asian Network into line with the rest of network radio and putting all presenters, including the language part-timers, onto freelance contracts. This was not achieved for another four years when the total staff number was cut by half.

Finally Whittle said the awareness of grievance procedures should be improved and a dedicated HR manager should be on site in Birmingham to ensure procedures were followed and offer support and guidance on how to communicate any concerns through the normal management chain. This was easier said than done as all the HR team for the Asian Network were based in London, but one lucky soul was sent up once a week for a while.

Religion always played a major part in the lives of the Asian Network's core audience, and this importance was reflected across all programming. No other radio station would devote so much to the devotional. Radio 4 may have 'Thought for the Day' and 'Prayer for the Day' and a Sunday service but those paled into insignificance against 11 hours a week of programming on the Asian Network. No other fulltime BBC or commercial radio station was committed to playing an hour of devotional music each weekday and three hours on both Saturdays and Sundays.

No other radio station had to consider the sensitivities of three major religions – and of their followers among staff and audience – like the Asian Network had to do every day. A throwaway comment on-air, a perceived slur in news coverage or a joke in a staff meeting could reverberate for days afterwards. There were also so many different elements within each religion which presented further opportunities to offend someone.

A few months before our devotional music programmes were dropped in 2012, I dealt with a complaint that our respected Sikh presenter was not referring to a particular Guru by the correct full title. The complainant said this showed a 'callous attitude' towards the community that followed this particular Guru, with phrases like 'ill discipline', 'blatant insult' and 'caste discrimination' sprinkled throughout the email. With the help and expertise of Sikh colleagues on the team, I drew up a tortuous but brief response, only too aware that a badly chosen word or phrase could set him off again. It ended: 'Our Devotional Sounds programmes are broadcast across the UK and ofcourse are available globally through the internet. We do therefore have to take a somewhat 'mainstream' approach generally while respecting the different opinions to be found in each faith'.

Religion figured in the Asian Network's Radio Service Licence under the section reflecting the UK's nations, regions and communities. It was duty bound to 'respond to the diversity of the UK Asian population in terms of geography, interests, ethnicity and religion. Its coverage of religion should aim to put British Asians in touch with each other and their spiritual roots'.

We were often asked if we could break down our audience by their religious belief but the BBC did not have the figures. You could take a guess from the ethnic breakdown. The average weekly audience figure across April, May and June of 2008 was 473,000. Indians made up 28.2 per cent of that figure, Pakistani's 36.6 percent and Bangladeshis 4.6 per cent. We aimed to give equal treatment to the Hindu, Sikh and Islamic religions but there were also Jains, Buddhists and Asian Christians in our audience.

The main religious festivals were always included in the forward planning discussions and the management was diligent in being equally fair to the three main religions relevant to the core audience. If any balance was occasionally lost, it was down to cock-up rather than conspiracy. Navratri, Diwali, Ramadhan, both Eids, Vaisakhi and the Births of the First and Tenth Sikh Gurus were all given particular emphasis. You had to remember and respect that across Ramadhan, colleagues were fasting. When I was News Editor, I was aware of the potential welfare issues of sending a Muslim reporter on an assignment who had been without food and water since the early hours. All would invariably want time off to celebrate their respective festivals like Eid, Vaisakhi and Diwali. And everyone wanted Christmas off.

The Asian Network marked the beginning of the daily fast during Ramadhan. This often meant starting the day's broadcasting very early with more devotional music rather than crashing out of Five Live at 3am and bouncing back into it again a few minutes later. Marking the breaking of the fast each day was more problematic, depending on the time it ended. It did not sound quite right changing the tone of a hip hop and grime show like Mic Check on a Saturday evening to tell a third (?) of your audience that they could eat again. The Network posted the daily fast times on its website, based on the timings of the London Central Mosque in Regent's Park. But there was always a rider – like a commercial radio advert's 'terms and conditions apply' – that if you were fasting in the Midlands or the North, you should check your local mosque for times which could vary considerably between London, Birmingham and Glasgow. We were never really sure how many Muslims used the Asian Network to mark the beginning and the end of fasting across Ramadhan. We were also in competition with various month-long local Ramadhan radio stations.

Religion made the news regularly and also provided strong material for the phone-in. Topics included children fasting, conversion to another religion, parental influence on a child's religion, the significance of death and belief in reincarnation, faith schools, terminal illness, provocative dress styles, sharia law in the UK, inter-faith relationships, being gay and religious, wearing religious symbols at work or in school, and blasphemy. Was it right to eat in front of anyone who was fasting? Adil Ray – a Muslim himself – did a wonderful spoof phone call to a local McDonalds to see if they would provide some take away 'fast' food for people who were fasting.

MIKE CURTIS

One of the Asian Network's big projects in 2008 was 'Faith Week'. This explored how faith affected peoples' lives, what it meant to them, how it made them feel and what issues it presented for them. The week was bookended by two documentaries called 'Symbol-ed Out' and 'Beats and Beliefs'.

Back in 2005, the Asian Network had reported on the case of Shabina Begum who won her appeal against her school in Luton who had refused to allow her to wear a jilbab (a long loose gown). Three years later, she was at university and still a staunch defender of religious symbols. The documentary also reported on a recent case of a Welsh student who had been excluded from her school for wearing a Kara (a Sikh religious bangle). In the second documentary, Bobby Friction looked at Asian musicians making music that was deeply religious but still massively popular and cool. Many of the interviews that Bobby did with musicians over the years drifted into a discussion about their faith. It was the same with many Bollywood stars.

Ofcourse the coverage of religion was not all poems, prayers and po-faced promulgations. A Vaisakhi coverage brainstorm among staff would be dominated by celebration, family, fireworks, fun, lights, dance and top Sikh singing stars. At Diwali, the Melton Road in Leicester would be alive with lights, noise, fashion and food. Asian Network presenters would dip into each others' religions by fasting for a day or visiting a mosque, temple or gurdwara. In the early days of the website, people were encouraged to send in festival greetings which they duly did from all over the world.

—m—

In June 2008, the High Priestess of Radio, Jenny Abramsky, announced she was leaving the BBC after 39 years. Jenny had been highly supportive of the Asian Network and channelled a lot of funds into it since the turn of the century. I never had a great deal

183

to do with her directly and was never sure if she knew who I was as we passed in Broadcasting House corridors. I would go for the half smile pending a possible 'Hello Jenny' only for her to completely blank me. Greg Dyke, in his book *'Inside Story'*, called her 'infuriating'. He said: 'On some days she is charming and reasonable; on others her paranoia that radio is a second class citizen to television with the BBC makes her difficult to deal with'.

My initial experience of her was at my first Local Radio News Editors' conference in the grand Council Chamber of Broadcasting House. She was Editor of Radio 4's *'Today'* programme at the time and was invited to address the conference. She complained about the lack of 'actuality' (sound effects) coming out of local radio stations during the 1984 miners' strike. Where were the sounds of riots and dustbin lids crashing? Around me, news editors who had been on the front line of coverage in Yorkshire, Nottinghamshire and the North East were incandescent. It had all been there and they had run it on their own stations but producers on programmes like 'Today' did n't trust local radio, preferring to send their own reporters instead. In those days, many of the local radio editors (including me) had started in newspapers and pointed out that the editor of 'Today' had never been a real reporter tramping the streets and had never worked outside of London.

Radio and Music headquarters was strange place. Many found it daunting. You wandered in and a host of rather solemn-looking people uplifted their faces to see who had entered the Holy of Holies. The headquarters in the old BH was bafflingly quiet like an old library. Considering these people were overseeing all these radio stations, it seemed odd that noone had switched on a radio. Perhaps they were just spoilt for choice and gave up. The new headquarters for what was then Audio and Music in the new BH was smaller but still had an air of foreboding about it – perhaps because every time I went near it, the Asian Network was under threat.

The new headquarters was on the same open plan corridor as Radio 4 Extra, presided over by the effervescent Mary Kalemkerian. She had been in the BBC as long as me and was great company reminiscing over a drink about time past and times passing. Outside of BH one day, Mary introduced me to someone called Bobby Jaye, whose name immediately rang a peal of bells. Bobby Jaye was a former Head of Light Entertainment of BBC Radio who had been involved in so many landmark programmes and worked with so many legends. He oversaw the transfer to radio of many classic television shows like '*Dad's Army*' and '*Yes, Minister*' and nurtured innovative comedies such as '*Radio Active*', the brilliantly funny satire about a local radio station.

Of course Jenny Abramsky's departure sparked rampant speculation about her successor. Andy Parfitt, our Controller of six months or so, was a front runner. Would we end up with our third Controller within a few months?

Closer to home, the successor to Husain Husaini as Head of News was named as Kevin Silverton, the number two at Radio 1's Newsbeat programme. Kevin lived in Woking in Berkshire and, like Husain, would not move north to be near his Leicester newsroom and settled for gruelling commuting and hotels. Ultimately, that decision paid off for him as the Network got out of Leicester and the newsdesk moved to the new Broadcasting House. Two of the news team got married to each other – Harjinder Mann and Sukhi Hayer. Elizabeth Glinka, who went on to become the political correspondent for the BBC in the West Midlands, got some of her initial journalistic experience with the Asian Network newsteam.

Assistant Editor Jonathan Aspinwall got a senior editor job back at Five Live and was not directly replaced to save money. Another Assistant Editor, the long serving Ishfaq Ahmed, left the BBC in 2007. Stephanie Hyner, who had come from Five Live to help run the newsroom before TransformAsian, also bowed out, pursuing a new career in photography and charity work. Dan McEvoy secured a station sound producer role with Five Live and was Salford-bound. Audrey Dias, a broadcast journalism graduate, arrived to cover Dorcas Fatade's maternity leave and pick up the mind-numbing administrative processes relating to compliance and scheduling. Audrey eventually escaped to pursue her passion for journalism, working for Radio WM, Radio 4's *The World Tonight* and the Birmingham television newsroom. Lucy Blair from Radio Leicester came on board to work for me, covering Sangeeta's maternity leave.

After the expansion of TransformAsian under Bob Shennan, the new age of austerity started to kick in under Andy Parfitt. As the Asian Network went into the new financial year starting April 2008, it was clear that savings would now have to be made and the areas that had benefitted from the extra money would now be cut back again.

The annual service budget for the Asian Network in 2008 was £8.7 million. However the new buzz words were 'Continuous Improvements' – in other words more cuts across the Corporation. The Asian Network was no longer exempt. £200,000 was taken out of the drama budget for *Silver Street* which signalled the waning enthusiasm for the soap within the BBC. The end of the separate sports unit was heralded with the decision to reduce the team from three to two and not replace the Assistant Editor Caj Sohal who returned to BBC Sport in London. Documentaries would continue but there would be fewer of them and they would be funded by the centre.

There were also more costs coming back onto the Asian Network's Audio and Music budget. Andy had to find the money for his new Head of Programmes post, and the *Love Bollywood* programme and its six production staff were coming back into the Division from News. The weekday breakfast show was to be relaunched, and Andy still wanted to do the big outreach event, the London Mela.

The cost of booking casuals to cover leave and sickness was identified as one of the profligate areas, along with overtime claims by staff. All of these costs had to be reduced by half, with the cost of travel and transport – always an issue with the Network split between Leicester, Birmingham and London – coming down by a quarter. There was talk already of building a new staffing plan from the bottom up with a radical look at structures and how many people were allocated to each programme. For example, if Radio 1's Breakfast Show with Chris Moyles could operate with two producers, one assistant producer and 40 per cent of the time of a senior executive producer, then so could the Asian Network. By the end of March 2009, the Asian Network budget was down to £7.9 million which was still far too expensive in view of the audience figures that it was returning.

'TransformAsian' had left the Asian Network overstaffed, expensive and still unable to attract a regular half a million listeners. And there was a new Director of Radio and Music to convince.

CHAPTER 24

visualisAsian

Tim Davie was appointed to succeed Jenny Abramsky, who finally bowed out at the end of September 2008. Davie was a surprise choice for many as he had no experience of radio production. For the last three years, he had been in the BBC as the Director of Marketing, Communications and Audiences division. Before that, he had been Vice President of Marketing and Franchise at Pepsico Europe where he was credited with getting an Air France Concorde painted in Pepsi Cola colours. Now he was required to market and sell BBC radio in an increasingly crowded market place.

We were disappointed for Andy but secretly pleased that he was not going anywhere. We were getting used to him and his ways of working, along with his helpful team at Radio 1 headquarters like Tony Wood, Tarrant Steele and Nicola Di Tullio. Davie described himself as a 'passionate advocate of radio'. The DG Mark Thompson said 'Davie's drive, knowledge and sheer love of the medium will ensure BBC radio remains creatively strong and vibrant in the years to come'. Andy still went up in the world – to the top of Kilimanjaro with Chris Moyles for *Children in Need*.

Tim Davie got off to an awkward start when, within a month of his tenure, all hell broke loose around Jonathan Ross and Russell Brand on Radio 2. They made a series of prank calls to the actor Andrew Sachs, of '*Fawlty Towers*' fame, on Brand's pre-recorded Saturday night programme. In the voicemails they left, Ross swore and Brand said he had slept with Sachs' granddaughter. There were only a handful of complaints but once the newspapers got hold of it, more than 30,000 agreed they were disgusted too and Ofcom launched its own investigation.

The DG Mark Thompson cut short a European holiday and flew home to take charge of this latest crisis. As usual with a BBC calamity, the Prime Minister of the day was asked to comment and Gordon Brown duly condemned the behaviour of Ross and Brand as 'inappropriate and unacceptable'. Both presenters were suspended and eventually the Controller of Radio 2, Lesley Douglas, resigned. The Head of Compliance at Radio 2 also left the BBC, and after that, the word 'compliance' loomed larger for all of us. As the fall-out raged, we could all be sure that, at the end of the hand-wringing, it would mean yet more mandatory courses and new processes.

Meanwhile across at Channel 4, the plans for launching new digital radio stations were not going according to plan. The cost of the enterprise had spiralled and the directors were nervous. Around the time of the Ross/Brand saga at the BBC, Channel 4 shelved its digital radio project. Six months after joining Channel 4, its Director of Radio Bob Shennan had nothing to direct. With the top job at Radio 2 suddenly available, it was ' Bob's your uncle' from February 2009. The sound reputation of Michael Hill, who had followed Bob to Channel 4, also found him a place back at the BBC working on a News project before launching and leading UK Radioplayer Ltd.

Proteus was one of the software programmes that the BBC introduced periodically to speed things up and bamboozle staff. You probably only used 10 per cent of its potential but that seemed to be more than enough to cope with. Nevertheless it came into its own after Ross/Brand in that every radio station schedule and programme had to be entered into it and, if it was a pre-recorded show, it had to be signed off by at least two senior producers. Every swear word had to be logged and its context explained. If a theme or character nudged the boundaries of taste and decency, the producer had to write a long detailed explanation to justify its inclusion.

At the Asian Network, this particularly applied to *Pathaan's Musical Rickshaw* across the early hours of Sunday morning, *Silver Street* and the documentaries, but at the beginning, any pre-recorded piece over 15 minutes long was subjected to compliance. The 'live' programmes were another matter. Every so often, a guest would swear on the Nihal phone-in or on one of the specialist music programmes. This had to be reported to the centre which maintained a list of 'Managed Risk' programmes. The presenter was supposed to apologise to listeners immediately even for relatively innocuous words like 'arse' or 'bollocks'. The production team would also have to tell the interactive team and senior editors to decide if the offending programme should be removed from the website's 'listen again' option. The procedure was only to remove in very special cases such as slander. You did not want to lose a three hour programme for the sake of one 'Shit' so you put a naughty language warning note next to the 'click to listen again' button.

The weekly audience figure for the Asian Network had steadily dropped across 2008, ending on a miserable 379,000 across October, November and December. So the second part of Andy Parfitt's relaunch of the Asian Network schedule was looking crucial to a recovery. It got pushed back to early January 2009 because, the staff were told, the station had to get it absolutely right. The priority was to get the Breakfast presentation sorted. In September 2008, the contracts for Jas Rao on weekday Breakfast and Tommy Sandhu at weekends were extended through to January. Neither were in the frame for weekday Breakfast beyond January but the Network wanted to keep them both on board for other shows.

With Sonia Deol gone, Adil Ray was the lead presenter on the Network. Having started on late nights, he was now fronting the Drive programme with a lot of music and plenty of his edgy humour. So he was the front-runner to take over the flagship Breakfast show but his relationship with his production team was somewhat fractious at times. In September – some four months before the relaunch – it was agreed that Andy Parfitt and his Radio 1 Head of Programmes Ben Cooper would talk to Adil about the Breakfast opportunity but stress he would have to mend his ways with his team. Husain Husaini wrote after one management meeting; 'Action Point – Andy to meet Adil with brick and Ben Cooper'.

Bobby Friction, Murtz and Raj and Pablo were also considered for the Breakfast slot but it was given to Adil Ray. The Breakfast show was relaunched on 5th January 2009, immediately after the Christmas and New Year break. Three months later the rest of the changes were introduced including cutting the four hour Drive programme, which was a long haul for any presenter, back to three hours. *The Wrap* news programmes, which had been shortlisted in the news category in the Sony radio awards, were renamed '*Asian Network Reports*' to bring them into line with the documentary strand. The lunchtime programme moved to 1pm and a second 30 minute round-up was introduced at 6pm.

Nihal's phone-in was moved to lunchtime to see if it could pick up a bigger audience and Nikki Bedi's arts and entertainment show followed Breakfast. Still noone was sure where to put Silver Street which was now cut back to five minutes per episode, creating further problems with scheduling the 25 minute omnibus on Sundays. The weekend '*Love Bollywood*' shows were brought back into Audio and Music and moved into the Radio 1 studios at Yalding House.

The language programmes in both Birmingham and Leicester continued largely unchanged although attempts were made to integrate them more, especially with the news operation. These mid-evening and Sunday nights shows in Mirpuri, Bengali, Gujarati, Hindi-Urdu and Punjabi never really got the credit they deserved, overshadowed as they were by the mainstream core hour shows and bigger name presenters. People like Vasu Pattni, Dev Parmar, Zarina Khan, Changis Raja, Shawkat Hashmi, Mahbub Hussain, Jayna Shah, Sanjay Sharma, Affie Jeerh, Neelu Kalsi, Dipps Bhamrah, Surinder Sandhu, Mukhtar Ahmed, Anwarul Hoque, Gurpreet Grewal Santini, Jyotsna Chavda, Vinod Ghadiali, Mahesh Nathwani and Sukhi Bart worked for years on these programmes and deserve a curtain call in the Asian Network story.

Tony Gilbert, an engineer whose time was divided between Radio WM and the Asian Network, was earmarked as the unofficial Technical Co-ordinator for the Asian Network, thanks to a deal I had done with James Patterson, not the thriller writer but the helpful Technology Support Manager for English Regions. James and I also worked out a plan for a long serving Asian Network broadcast assistant, Makhan Panesar, to support Tony and the wider technical team as Makhan's old engineering role was rapidly being overtaken by editorial priorities. We desperately needed our own technical people to address the multiple issues around transmission, circuits, play-out systems and studios.

Tony had his work cut out. In Birmingham, more space was appearing as network programmes were pulled back to London. The move of the overnight Radio 2 show meant that the network studios equipped with the VCS playout system were available to the Asian Network. We were keen to use this VCS system as it would bring us into line with all the other networks. But the studios had to be hooked up the transmission network and people had to be trained how to use them.

In the end the Mailbox programmes were split between the studio downstairs using the increasingly unreliable Radioman software and the network studios upstairs with an old version of VCS. The servers would threaten to fill up and fall over and put us off air, especially when all the pre-recorded programmes for Christmas were poured into them. The production teams and presenters had to be able to use both. Technical life really did n't get any easier for them or the engineers.

The Asian Network was now broadcasting from Leicester, from Television Centre and Yalding House in London, and from two completely different studio set-ups in Birmingham. Programmes originating from London had to go up the circuits to Leicester then across to Birmingham before being heard. A special line between Leicester and Birmingham was then removed to save money so the circuit went through Nottingham.

A sympathetic Rupert Brun, the Head of Technology for Audio and Music, said it was a 'miracle' that the Asian Network got on air at all.

The Asian Network was still relying on the AM transmitters in the Midlands for the bulk of its audience, and those transmitters were sounding rough, particularly after dark in winter. A French station could be heard cutting across one of the AM frequencies, and reception maps of the Birmingham and Leicester transmitters showed a dramatic loss of acceptable coverage once the sun went down. Special processors called optimods to help boost the volume and stabilise the levels were installed on the transmitters but the improvements were minimal.

The 'visualisation' of radio was continuing apace. We all had to think about 'glanceability' while listening to the radio on our smartphones or computer screens. Dharmesh Rajput, the Asian Network's interactive editor, had to pull together a digital strategy for the Network for the next two years. With radio being consumed on more devices with screens, it was important to offer the right visuals to compliment the output. There would be on-demand videos of big name interviews and live music sessions, live text on what song was being played and links to Asian Network content on You Tube, Facebook and the fast-expanding Twitter. It all had to meet the RQIV mantra – reach, quality, impact and value. Production teams no longer just prepared and produced radio programmes, but had to sort the programme web pages out as well. Podcasts, newsletters, blogs were deployed – anything to get the Asian Network noticed and get its audience figures up.

Two stories broke one morning which Adil Ray linked in his usual quickfire style. A concert starring Gurdas Maan, one of the top Punjabi singers in the world, was cancelled in Canada after a group of Sikh fans refused to leave their ceremonial daggers (called the Kirpan) at the door. In the UK, it was announced that the first Sikh soldiers would be joining the guard at Buckingham Palace.

Adil poked fun, in a Indian/Canadian accent, at the situation in Canada, basically saying that as this group were not allowed to get into the concert, they probably thought 'sod it, we will go and join Buckingham Palace instead'. And there was another remark about whether the Sikh soldiers would take their Kirpans with them for guard duties. It was all too much for a listener from Peterborough who rang the programme team to complain, saying he usually enjoyed Adil's humour but he had no right to insult people's religions. He was assured that no offence was meant and apologies were offered for any distress caused.

That is where many a complaint would have ended but this individual went on, saying Adil needed to be taught a lesson and that 'people were ready to do him in', possibly at one of the upcoming Melas. The programme editor Khaliq Meer relayed this conversation to the senior team. We all knew that any perceived slur against a religious symbol had to be taken seriously and had the potential to escalate. So far we had received one phone call and one accusatory text.

The programme was revoked – in other words removed from the 'listen again' option. Experience had taught us that bits of the audio were often edited out of context and emailed around to generate further complaints and rouse pressure groups into action. The BBC's security teams in London and Birmingham were alerted, with the Mailbox team monitoring CCTV when Adil arrived at the studios early each morning. Audio and Music HQ was alerted and Mark Strippel, who had the responsibility for the Melas, revisited the risk assessments and security cover.

A group called the Sikh Media Monitoring Group weighed in, asking to hear the audio. As it had been in the public domain, it was sent a copy and duly complained and asked for meetings. More assurances were given that there was no intent to offend but it was not convinced. Adil was given a security escort for the Cardiff Mela, and the Metropolitan Police were tipped off about it all for the London Mela. In the end, nothing more happened and the issue went away but one throwaway line and one complaint had resulted in a blizzard of emails, meetings and expense.

Sunny Hundal, a well-known Asian journalist and commentator in the UK media, noted that The Independent had run the story and wrote that he had received emails asking why he had not covered it. 'You know why: because it's rubbish. Adil Ray is neither biased against Sikhs and neither would he be stupid enough to even go near denigrating or making fun of any religion. The problem is that there are Sikh, Hindu, and Muslim groups constantly watching the BBC Asian Network for any slip-up so they can accuse the station of bias against their community. After all, making a stink helps them get some recognition and support'. He concluded: 'The BBC really needs to start ignoring these people…but I suspect the controllers are too scared to do that'.

It was welcome support, saying something that we could not articulate in public. Every written complaint to the BBC had to be acknowledged within ten working days even if it was just a holding reply while further inquiries were undertaken. The BBC was clear that the listeners paid their licence fees and had a right to complain. There was a big unit in White City dealing with complaints to the Corporation, and the Asian Network was a regular and much valued customer.

CHAPTER 25

speculAsian

The Asian Network was sounding good. It had a strong new presenter line-up on weekdays with Adil Ray on Breakfast, Nikki Bedi on mid mornings, Nihal on the phone-in and Tommy Sandhu moving to Drive. It was getting big names for interview and its stories were being picked up by other BBC outlets. Its branding was given a makeover with the word 'Asian' being made more prominent. It was planning the launch of the world's first ever Asian Music Download Chart show in partnership with independent compilers. Its 'pimped up' ex-ambulance, which had been turned into a mobile studio, was helping to showcase British Asian music and the Network's music shows at Melas and in High Streets. The on-line offering and its interactivity was looking and sounding contemporary and relevant.

The phone-in was feisty and thought-provoking, asking the diverse UK Asian communities what they really thought about stories like Prince Harry and the *Strictly Come Dancing* dancer Anton du Beke using the word 'Paki' in private conversations. What did they think about the BNP leader appearing on BBC's *Question Time*? What was their take on the hit film *Slumdog Millionaire* which had swept the Oscars early in 2009.

The career of Bollywood's biggest star, Amitabh Bachchan, was celebrated with a special week. This included an exclusive interview with him on 'Love Bollywood' and a documentary on Amitabh's relationship with UK Asians fronted by actor and comedian Sanjeev

Bhaskar. There was another documentary to celebrate the success of Jay Sean who became the first British Asian artist to top the American charts with his single 'Down'. Our contribution to the 75th anniversary of the BBC's Maida Vale studios centred on getting Apache Indian back in those studios for the first time in 20 years. Peter Andre turned up on our stage at the London Mela (he was invited) and the Adil Ray programme camped overnight in Epping Forest. I can't remember why but they called it 'Curry on Camping' and they did their own risk assessment.

Channel 4's series *'The Family'* was a big hit later in the year and the Asian Network kept up with the Grewal family from west London. The young couple at the centre of the series, Sunny and Shay, were later booked to present weekend programmes for the Asian Network, reminiscent of the move to use Herjender 'Gos' Gosal as a radio presenter after he was ejected from *Big Brother 3* household six years earlier. Anton du Beke's *'Strictly'* dance partner Laila Rouass, who accepted Anton's apology for his misguided banter with her, took up an invitation to host a special Christmas Day programme on the Asian Network.

Zoe Williams in *The Guardian* called the Asian Network a massive success story but admitted she had rudely shrugged it off because she never listened to it. She had a particular aversion to phone-ins but had caught a recent Asian Network one which, unfortunately for Nihal, had Sonia Deol standing in as presenter that day. The BNP successes in the European parliament was the topic and a BNP voter came on air to tell Sonia that she ought to be voluntarily repatriated to a country she'd never even been to. A teacher from Leicester who had come from Uganda followed and 'calmly and methodically wiped the floor' with the BNP voter. 'That's what's missing from other phone-ins: it's not sensible people, it's the triumph of good over evil. Normally what you get is the slightly less daft being shouted at by the daft'.

—⚡—

But the Asian Network's audience figures were still hugely disappointing. Across summer of 2009, the weekly figure reached an all time low at 357,000 and the BBC Trust pointed out that the audience had dropped by 20 per cent in one year. Its cost-per-listener-per-hour (CPLPH) was consequently getting embarrassing and noticeable, at 6.9 pence towering above all the other networks apart from Radio 3. The Asian Network finished the year on 360,000 a week, way off the half million mark and even further from the initial target of 750,000.

The vultures were circling and there were suggestions in the media that the Asian Network could be closed. Tim Davie rejected the speculation, saying there was no truth in it. He added: 'The Asian Network is incredibly important in providing news, debate, music and entertainment to British Asians and is growing its audience following a major schedule change'. No-one stopped us re-commissioning Devotional Sounds out to the independent sector for another two years.

In November, Andy Parfitt announced that 'Silver Street' would be axed the following March. The drama budget would be cut and channelled into a once a month 30 minute plays. Andy said the production team, writers and cast should be proud of what they had achieved but it had been decided that there was a better way to deliver drama with the money available. The head of radio drama Alison Hindell said the new format would be ambitious in scope and would create a richer range of drama programming for listeners to enjoy. No-one still really knew where to put it in the schedule.

The radio station did benefit over the years from the skills of some of the soap staff whose duties sorting scripts and scenes ensured they had to be extremely methodical and pay serious attention to detail. Che Chumber, Nazreen Ahmed, Ravinder Mann and Majabeen Salim were among the Silver Streeters who came to work on programmes or administration at the Asian Network.

In another cost saving move, Nerm and Pathaan had their Saturday night and Sunday morning show contracts only extended up to 15th January 2010. Both programmes finally came off air in March, meaning the Network once again opted into Five Live on all seven nights a week. If sleep was evading you in the early hours of Sunday morning or you were recovering from some clubbing, *Pathaan's Musical Rickshaw* was a good place to go but there were not enough insomniacs tuning in and unfortunately it was an obvious place to start the cuts.

Unbeknown to us at the time, BBC Distribution which oversees all the transmission networks had been asked to look at the practical possibilities for the Asian Network being only broadcast in five areas of England on both medium wave and DAB. The areas were London, West Midlands, Leicestershire, Yorkshire and the north-west covering Manchester and Lancashire. In a confidential draft document dated 22nd December 2009, the available AM transmitters and DAB availability were laid out along with the current costs.

In London, there was good DAB coverage but no available AM transmitter carrying BBC local radio. There was the 720 AM frequency which was allocated to Radio 4 and which had long been eyed covetously by the Asian Network. If the Asian Network could have the chance to go out on this frequency, it would make it available to more than two million Londoners. The line was that we would only want it for six months or so to get us heard in London more and ofcourse to 'drive up digital'. If you like listening to us on this crap medium wave signal, you will enjoy us a lot more by tuning into DAB. It never happened – putting a digital network onto a 'new' AM frequency was hardly 'driving up digital' and noone would grasp that particular nettle for us.

In Manchester there was no AM frequency available since the 1458 frequency had been given to the commercial sector years earlier. Elsewhere across England, local radio stations with AM frequencies as well as their DAB and FM service were identified as possible hosts for Asian Network programmes. Nottingham, Stoke, Hereford and Worcester, Humberside, York, Lincolnshire, and Lancashire were all included in the report, as well Derby, Leeds and Sheffield which were already carrying Asian Network output on AM in the evenings.

Not all areas had good DAB coverage either. The roll out of DAB across the UK had been going on for ten years or so but at the end of 2009, places like parts of Derbyshire, north Lancashire and North Yorkshire were still awaiting their local launch. And where there was good DAB, in some places it was noted that the capacity on the multiplexes that sent the signal out was already tight without adding an extra service. The London DAB multiplex was assumed to be full already with no spare capacity.

That same month, Vijay had a meeting with an Audio and Music strategist who I thought looked about 15. It seemed to be the first indication that there was now a debate at the centre about the future of the Asian Network. Vijay detected a view that the poor audience figures demonstrated that the current Asian Network was not meeting audience needs nor satisfying the BBC mission to serve all sections of the UK audiences. In a note to Tim Davie and Andy Parfitt, she said such a view was simplistic. It did not take into account the Network's unique contribution to BBC journalism, the engagement of the Asian communities every day which was not found anywhere else on the BBC, the commitment to Asian music and drama, the outreach events like the Melas, the language and religious programming, the powerhouse of recruiting Asian talent and the 'healthy contribution to BBC output originating outside of London'.

Vijay also highlighted the Asian Network's contribution to the BBC's strategy for Diversity. Was there a view that the discreet services such as the Asian Network and even Radio 1Xtra were actually impediments to achieving meaningful diversity within the BBC? Surely the Asian Network should be an important part of supporting and enhancing a broader BBC-wide diversity plan? In retrospect, it was the first salvo in the long campaign of banging the dhol to preserve a national Asian Network.

CHAPTER 26

damnAsian

It was a good scoop, apparently leaked by somebody in the DG's inner sanctum. On Friday 26 February 2010, *The Times* splashed the headline 'BBC signals an end to era of expansion'. Written by its media correspondent Patrick Foster, it announced that the BBC would close two radio stations, shut half its websites and cut spending on imported American TV programmes. £600 million of the £3.6 billion licence fee would be reinvested into higher quality programming. The third paragraph revealed that the two radio stations facing the axe were 6 Music and the Asian Network. There had been rumours and denials of closure of the Asian Network but for staff to see it spelt out so brutally and without warning was shocking and depressing. On the train into Birmingham New Street, I re-read it all several times.

Kevin Silverton, the Network's Head of News, said coyly he did not swear very much but felt 'that the situation seemed to merit a few expletives'. Kevin, who actually did n't seem to swear at all, was up to his neck in boxes preparing to move house in Woking when he got the news. He spent that Friday marshalling his removal men while checking with his Leicester newsroom that the Asian Network was handling news of its impending execution as calmly and responsibly as possible. After a phone hook round the senior team, Kevin held his news staff meeting over his mobile phone from his bathroom. Vijay was a week into a four week break in India so it was down to Husain, Mark and me to deal directly with the fall-out of the story on the shop floor.

The Times had clearly got hold of a copy of the whole strategic review which was now with the BBC Trust and was due to be published the following month. Mark Thompson was going to admit the BBC had got too big and had to shrink to give its commercial rivals more room to operate. 2010 was election year and the strategy had been drawn up by the BBC's director of policy and strategy, John Tate, who had been head of the Conservative's policy unit. Tate had written the party's 2005 manifesto with David Cameron and *The Times* stated that the review would be seen as attempt to show that the BBC did not need outside intervention to get its house in order and downsize.

The Times, part of the Rupert Murdoch organisation and thus no friend of the BBC, supported its front page splash with a leading article and a double page spread. The leader was entitled 'Big, Bloated and Cunning'. It did not mention the Asian Network by name, only stating that Thompson needed to 'do more than axe a few radio stations that no one has ever listened to' if he wanted his reforms to be taken seriously. It was a sloppy generalisation for a Times leading article when 357,000 people were actually listening but it suited the tone of what they wanted to say about the BBC. The Editor of The Times in February 2010 was James Harding. Three years later, Harding was appointed Director of News and Current Affairs of BBC News in succession to Helen Boaden. What goes around comes around – or something like that.

On pages six and seven, the paragraph about the Asian Network said that the review would state that the Asian population was too complex to be served by a single network. So that explained why the BBC's Chief Operating Officer Caroline Thomson had told the House of Lords Communications Committee a couple of weeks earlier that the Asian Network was trying to cater for many disparate groups simultaneously. 'We are wrestling with how best to serve this audience and whether one whole network is the right way to do it', she said, adding that a single station reflected a 'rather British view' that 'if you came from the subcontinent, you must somehow be the same'.

Tim Davie, the Director responsible for the two stations and their staff, sent an email to everyone at 6 Music and the Asian Network. 'Clearly it is disappointing and unsettling to read these stories in the newspapers' he said. 'Today I have spent time with the senior leaders of the key areas in A&M that are affected and tried to ensure that they can communicate the latest situation to you. Also I will ensure that once we have final and accurate plans, you will be fully informed. I will make myself fully available to discuss issues and listen to your comments'.

He went on to clarify the BBC's position. The plans would go to the BBC Trust in the coming days and it would stage a consultation period over the following three months during which the audiences would be consulted. Feedback would be considered and he conceded that some proposals may require further regulatory consideration such as a public value test (PVT). Most of the substantive proposals would not be implemented until the financial year 2011/2012 – in other words the cuts were at least a year away. Davie finished by reminding people why all their jobs were at risk. The strategy review would set out a template for 'a more focussed BBC that delivered better quality content' and it would guide the agenda after the digital switchover in 2012.

The BBC's formal public response on the day of *The Times* story was brief. 'Work on the BBC's Strategy Review is ongoing and we are not commenting on today's story'. Somebody was being paid a lot of money to come up with that line. 'Ooh, very good, very strong!' as the Director of Strategic Governance would say four years later in the BBC's comedy about itself, 'W1A'.

Over at Westminster, the Labour MP Tom Watson lodged an Early Day Motion (EDM) which attracted 33 signatures on the first day. 'That this House notes with deep concern recent newspaper speculation that the BBC is considering closing its 6 Music and Asian Network radio stations; believes that both radio stations offer outlets for independent and non-mainstream music; further notes that both 6 Music and Asian Network reach out to audiences not otherwise well served by the BBC; congratulates 6 Music and Asian Network for acting as a source of talent for the BBC and other media; recognises that the BBC has a duty to represent and give a platform to minority interests that need a mainstream platform to develop and grow; and calls on the Government to encourage the BBC to continue its support for 6 Music and Asian Network for many years to come'.

Among the comments posted below the EDM motion on Tom Watson's website was an attack on the Asian Network by one of its former producers, the long retired BAPS man Hisam Mukaddam. 'Dear Mr Watson, please let us not be confused by the popularity of 6 Music with the Asian Network. I am sorry and sad to say that the present model of Asian Network, in recent days, is serving Bhangha and Bollywood linked commercial groups. The service has moved away from its core BBC values of quality, universality and impartiality. They serve a tiny minority of the Asian licence payers in the main, daytime output in the guise of British Asian Music. You can fool some people some times…that is the situation'.

Mukaddam, who had been associated with the Asian Network for over 20 years, also told the Press Trust of India: 'It (the closure) was coming. The station had become a Bhangra-based Punjabi music station where the linguistic and information needs of the universal Asian community were severely overlooked". However he added that even though the younger audience had other sources to access Asian music, there was a need for dedicated Asian broadcasting, particularly because the Asian community put much trust in the BBC for news.

The General Secretary of the broadcasting union BECTU, Gerry Morrissey, said: 'It is obvious that the BBC is being bounced by its competitors and by the political climate ahead of the upcoming general election. It is not acceptable for the BBC to be offering up services and jobs as some kind of sacrifice ahead of the general election'.

Jeremy Dear, General Secretary of the National Union of Journalists, added: 'These plans smack of an attempt to appease commercial and political interests. Hard-working staff shouldn't be used as a political football and we will fight any compulsory redundancies'.

Commercial radio bosses seemed underwhelmed by the closure plans, branding them symbolic and believing that they would have only negligible impact on the market. 6 Music's playlists were very different to the big commercial stations and the Asian Network played a lot of new British Asian talent whereas their rivals concentrated on Bollywood and bhangra. Richard Wheatley, executive director of Jazz FM, welcomed the potential closures as a step in the right direction of the BBC reining itself in. 'It's generally good for commercial radio as it makes for a more even playing field, but it's not a silver bullet', he said.

The day after its scoop, *The Times* said that the BBC's plans to close the two radio stations were 'in chaos' as musicians vowed to stop the closure of 6 Music and the unions threatened to strike over job cuts. The campaign to save 6 Music got off to a quick start with many big names including David Bowie condemning the decision. For the Asian Network, the initial response was slow apart from some former staff and some commercial rivals supporting the closure plan. The BBC still refused to comment on the stories in The Times but the coverage did prompt the publication of the strategic review to be hurriedly brought forward to the following week.

The front page of the staff newspaper *Ariel* that week had a black background with bold headlines in red and white – one reading: '6 MUSIC : ASIAN NETWORK AXED'. *Ariel* was the staff newspaper but was nick-named Pravda over the years by staff who saw it only as a conduit for management to explain its decisions. In the old days, people picked up Ariel to see what jobs were available, glancing at the letters page to see which downtrodden soul in Television Centre was complaining that week about the price of a blueberry muffin in the BBC café going up by three pence. The jobs and the letters eventually went on line, followed by what was left of the paper in 2012. With no piles of *Ariels* greeting staff as they made their way in and out of work each Tuesday, the publication was largely forgotten on-line by most people.

While austerity caught up with *Ariel*, BBC News published a glossy A4 brochure every so often to trumpet what its newsrooms and correspondents were doing across the globe. No one seemed sure of the justification for this indulgence. Could n't these articles have gone on the BBC's Gateway web pages? Instead piles of unread News brochures built up in corners of newsrooms across the UK, picked up in idle moments by people outside of News who harrumphed about cost cutting and the vanity of senior news management.

The edition published after the Strategy Review had a couple of pages on the Asian Network written by Kevin Silverton. He highlighted the aspect which had been under-reported by all the other media, namely the preferred alternative for better serving the Asian communities. This was setting up five mini-Asian Network stations in areas with significant Asian populations. This, said Kevin, gave his team something to be positive about and it proved the BBC was still serious about serving 'this valuable bunch of licence fee payers'.

Kevin said many of his young team were even more determined to show everyone what a great job the Asian Network journalists did for the BBC and its audience. He was excited about the news stories being looked at for the following week – the significance of the Asian vote in the forthcoming General Election, why Asian children were waiting longer than white ones to be adopted, how gay Asians were the victims of racism within the gay community, and how Indian yoga devotees were trying to teach it to primary school kids in Glasgow. Kevin ended by hoping that this kind of journalism would continue to be a big part of the BBC's future. Certainly no other outlet was covering the Asian communities in such depth.

The BBC was obviously nervous about just closing the station and not replacing it. 6 Music would close and its best bits would be subsumed into Radio 1 and Radio 2. If the Asian Network closed, where would its best bits – its reflection of the UK Asian communities – actually go? The occasional Asian drama on Radio 4 or a weekly bhangra programme on Radio 2 were hardly a substitute. *The Times* said the BBC may explore the prospect of setting up a handful of part-time local radio stations in areas with high Asian populations but BBC Trust sources were quoted as opposing this move.

This was the idea that BBC Distribution had been asked to investigate a few months earlier. It now transpired that the Asian Network would indeed close as a national network serving the whole of the UK but would be replaced by five regional 'franchises' in London, Leicester, Birmingham, Leeds/Bradford and Manchester/Lancashire. In the Midlands, this would take Asian broadcasting back to the 1980s. It must have seemed a simple alternative to Thompson, Thomson, Davie and the strategists but it raised a plethora of questions about its practicality, costs, management, presenters, transmission, branding, exclusion of the Nations, and the impact on commercial rivals – in fact everything that generally put the wind up senior BBC executives and wound up hostile politicians. Most of us were beyond belief.

Three weeks before the closure shock, I had put the finishing touches to the annual Statement of Programme Policies for the coming financial year 2010/2012. This included the 'Controller's Vision' which was supposed to be a personal statement about the plans for the next 12 months. Andy Parfitt's ambition for the Asian Network was for it to become the broadcaster of choice for the UK's Asian community, recognised for its high quality provision and coverage of British Asian news, music and culture. By focussing on the achievements and culture of British Asian communities, Andy said he believed the Asian Network would grow to become a much valued and clearly distinctive service. He again stressed the 'friend of the family' strategy.

A new schedule was unfolding in which Sonia Deol would return once more, taking over the mid-morning slot from Nikki Bedi. In a rare move, I had actually suggested a presenter for the new British Asian Music chart show, namely Bobby Friction. This was picked up by Vijay, Husain and Mark and the show was duly launched with Bobby at the faders at the end of March. Tommy Sandhu was now on the Drive show and Noreen Khan took over weekend Breakfast. A new series of documentaries was lined up, looking at Asians in prisons, the spending power of Asians (called the Brown Pound), acid attacks on women, and the forthcoming General Election.

In the weeks before the closure announcement, there had already been a special day devoted to the leading Bollywood star Shah Rukh Khan amid all the publicity around his film 'My Name is Khan'. The actor had agreed to an 'in conversation' special with Raj and Pablo at the Radio Theatre in Broadcasting House where some 300 fans cheered their hero and pinched themselves about being so close to the man. Another day of music was devoted to

A.R.Rahman, who had provided the soundtrack for '*Slumdog Millionaire*'. And Adil Ray gave his community leader character Mr Khan his television debut in Paul Whitehouse and Charlie Higson's latest comedy '*Bellamy's People*'.

—ꝏ—

On the morning of Tuesday 2nd March, everyone gathered in meeting rooms or at their work stations to watch Mark Thompson deliver his Strategic Review as unexpectedly unveiled in The Times five days earlier. The initial shock at the Asian Network had subsided, not least with the suggestion of the regional franchises although there was little enthusiasm among the Birmingham and Leicester staff about possibly having to move to Yorkshire or Manchester. Andy Parfitt came up to Birmingham to talk to the Midlands troops.

Later in the day we sat through the Audio and Music perspective with Tim Davie but there was nothing new. Davie sent another note to Asian Network staff, saying we could imagine it had been impossible for him to get to Birmingham, Leicester or the London office that day but he knew it had been 'a very difficult and unsettling day'. He wanted to let us know that he was there to answer questions and was 'thinking of the team'. He also announced he was coming to Birmingham the following week, with the DG trailing in three days later.

Across the day in the Mailbox, the televisions showing the BBC News channel flashed the highlights of the Strategic Review – the strapline repeating '6 Music and Asian Network to close'. There was no mention of the five regional franchises which was buried in the Strategic Review statement with a line about better serving the Asian communities. It was a thoroughly dispiriting day for everyone, seeing the closure of your workplace flashed on screens above your desk.

The highlight of the day was BBC2's *Newsnight* with a classic

Jeremy Paxman performance grilling Mark Thompson. Jeremy questioned why, amidst all the cuts, BBC3 and BBC4 were untouched. After berating BBC3 as an expensive testing ground for the two main BBC channels, he asked the DG if he knew what was on BBC 4 that evening. Jeremy reminded him. 'It starts with the news; a repeat of a documentary; *Skippy – Australia's first Superstar*, a repeat no less; *Paws, Claws and Videotape* – a clips show about famous animals; a bought-in film; *Skippy, Australia's first superstar* again but with subtitles'. Channel 4 News had a dignified appearance by Bobby Friction on behalf of the Asian Network – just after 6Music presenter Adam Buxton challenged Mark 'Thommo' Thompson to a fight.

Nihal Arthanayake, the phone-in presenter, wrote an article for *The Guardian* the following day in which he said he was astonished that in 2010 he was having to defend the existence of the BBC Asian Network. In a country that largely respected and celebrated diversity, the idea that the BBC would want to dismantle the Asian Network would seem absurd as if it were to admit that it no longer considered the Asian community worth bothering about. He dismissed critics who said the BBC was misguided in setting up a station that could never appeal to so many cultures, languages and religions.

'Every day I host the Asian Network phone-in and for two hours we discuss subjects from the most traditional and religious, such as the bar on menstruating women from entering places of worship, to Asian takes on the most mainstream and popular topics – did, for example, *Eastenders* get its Muslim wedding right? Atheists, Buddhists, Christians, Hindus, Muslims, and Sikhs call in, young and old: far from being unable to cater to seemingly disparate communities, the Network draws them together'.

Nihal said there had been a history of tinkering with the Asian Network that had undermined its focus and led to a lack of morale. And now, just at the point where it had the strongest daytime line-up it had ever had and was looking forward to re-engaging with, and increasing, its audience by providing a unique service, the BBC seemed to want to move the goalposts yet again. He added that the five franchise idea ignored the reality that Britain's different Asian communities are not simply segregated geographically or regionally. 'Local is an attractive buzzword but the connections are national'.

Journalist Malik Meer, also writing in *The Guardian*, noted that support for Asian Network was negligible compared to the 6 Music reaction. The Network's core audience was still on medium wave in the Midlands and its listeners were not by nature active 'tweeters'. 'Is it all in Urdu?' one *Guardian* colleague asked him, 'underlining the point that few had heard its lively phone-ins, genuinely funny breakfast show (with Adil Ray) or its late night specialist shows or agenda-setting documentaries'. He said the decision raised questions about management support and trust, and the BBC's failure to serve and include British Asians on the rest of the 'mainstream' networks. And it should not be axed to save some cash in case the Tories won the election.

A few days after the confirmation of the closure plan, the Asian Network campaign got a significant boost from more than 100 prominent British Asians. Taking up a full page in *The Guardian,* the paper followed up an open letter sent to the chairman of the BBC Trust, Sir Michael Lyons, urging them not to close the station. Actors Meera Syal, Sanjeev Bhaskar and Laila Rouass, boxer Amir Khan, Bollywood star Shilpa Shetty, film director Gurinder Chadha, comedian Shazia Mirza, cricketer Vikram Solanki, BBC sport presenter Manish Bhasin, and singers Jay Sean and MIA all expressed their profound shock at the announcement. Other signatories included Sir Mota Singh QC, Britain's highest profile Sikh member of the judiciary, Lord Patel and Lord Dholakia. The Asian Network provided 'a key platform for the national Asian community and offered creative British Asian talent an outlet which is demonstrably under-represented in the more mainstream BBC. 'This would all be tragically lost if these proposals are agreed'.

The letter said that reducing broadcasts to just a few hours a day would be a retrogressive step, leaving only the commercial Asian stations. 'These stations will not and can not deliver a comprehensive service as the BBC Asian Network does. This is a vital part of what you (the BBC) offer in the name of public service broadcasting. We, as loyal licence fee payers, trust you will not let us down'. One week on, about 20,000 people had signed up to the 'Save the Asian Network' page on Facebook. 140,000 had joined the Facebook campaign to save 6 Music.

Sunrise Radio founder Avtar Lit took the opportunity to rubbish the Asian Network, describing its output as 'mediocre'. He said it had been given 'a bloody nose' by its commercial rivals and he did not think that the Asian community 'would give a toss' if it closed down. He highlighted the money that the BBC had spent and offered to run it for three million pounds a year. At the time Sunrise was getting about 480,000 listeners a week – 120,000 ahead of the Asian Network.

Sunny Hundal, the editor of the 'Asians in the Media' website, said the Network had a confused music policy, did not focus enough on news and current affairs and was not doing enough to develop new talent. 'But its biggest problem has been poor management', he wrote. 'That is now evident even more since the management has failed to make a case internally to keep the station'. However, even though he had been a constant critic of the station, he felt it was 'vital' that it survived as a platform for British Asian culture and as competition for the commercial Asian stations. It also was a source of Asian talent coming into the media and it brought stories to the rest of the media that mainstream news journalists would be unlikely to cover.

The way that the BBC ran the radio station was blamed by the Birmingham Post columnist Ammo Talwar, chief executive of Punch Records, who said that on the air the Network had a clear line-up of winners, all setting the pace for UK Asian music culture.

MIKE CURTIS

'In the back office, the BBC management has no clue what the station is for, and partitions its airtime from above like Mountbatten in 1947'. He said the BBC needed more Desi programmers and managers at top level.

The febrile atmosphere increased in Birmingham at the end of the week with the discovery of a disguised recording device in the Asian Network operations area next to the downstairs studio. On close inspection, it appeared to be a little black box held together with some brown tape. Inside was a mobile phone with a 'pay as you go' sim card, a battery pack of three AA batteries to power it, a small antenna and microphone held in place with insulating material.

The microphone was facing out of a hole in the box, which was not much bigger that the space required for an average size mobile and the three AA batteries.

The device was removed and someone from the BBC Investigations team arranged to have it picked up for analysis. Meanwhile a programme producer had complained to their union representative who contacted me for details, saying there was 'considerable vexation' about this device. I wondered if it had been an elaborate hoax at the end of a bruising week for everyone. Rumours flew that the management was bugging staff and presenters to find out what they really thought of the closure plans. Others suspected staff bugging each other.

After asking everyone for an anonymous confession to get an explanation, one came forward. The line was that an offspring was being bullied at college and the staff member had constructed a device to try and get some of the bullying recorded to take to the college principal. It had not been a good move to accidently leave it at work, especially that week.

CHAPTER 27

obfuscAsian

Tim Davie came to Birmingham a week after the Strategic Review was formally published. He began by apologising for the leak to *The Times* and went on to give his version of life on earth. The BBC Trust could close the Network completely so we had to have an alternative proposal – anything but a national proposition which was completely off the agenda. His idea was the five franchises and he urged everyone to engage in this proposal. He said the review was not about cutting costs but about how we best served the Asian communities.

The strategy revamps and the relaunches had not worked, and the nine million pounds for 350,000 listeners was not sustainable. He said the Trust was not convinced about the national service anymore but the key component going forward would be syndication across the five areas.

What about the Asian listeners outside the five areas? Scotland, Wales and places like Luton which had some of biggest Asian populations but would not be able to get the Asian Network on their radios any more? He could only agree that there would be an impact on those 15 per cent of listeners outside of the five franchises. My view, shared by most at the meeting, was that Tim Davie wanted to offload us. We were a blemish on his portfolio and something he did not really know how to market. As we were now going to ignore Northern Ireland, Scotland and Wales, he could shove us back into English Regions with four million quid instead of nine.

The questions kept coming but the replies (not answers) were largely unsatisfactory or condescending or both. We struggled as a station split between three cities so now you want to split us over five instead? We keep asking to use the AM frequency in central London but nobody will support us – he was very confident he could now sort this one. Do we do local shows for each area? Are you seriously suggesting five breakfast shows and five drive shows? And then syndicated programmes for all five areas in between and organised by Audio and Music rather than English Regions? Will there be five separate news operations then?

What about the evenings? The Asian service might only be 12 hours a day starting at 7am and ending at 7pm. The solution to this one was the final confirmation for me that someone had completed their mission on Earth and was being recalled to their home planet. From 7pm, we would run a message on a loop for 12 hours through the evening and night telling people: 'You're listening to the BBC Asian Network. We return at 6am'. Can you go further than 'beyond belief'?

Tim Davie kept returning to the end of the national offering, saying at one point 'The game is up in terms of a national station, you can indulge your fantasies as much as you like'. That went down really well. The five franchises were 'the only game in town' and he was behind it and would drive it forward. It would all go out to consultation. How do people respond to the consultation in Asian languages? Well that had n't occurred to anyone but he would look into it.

Someone in the Leicester newsroom, on a video conference link, said the proposal seemed ill-informed and vague. Who had come up with all this? Davie said he had consulted with Andy Parfitt and Husain Husaini, who looked uncomfortable. Someone asked if Helen Boaden, the Director of News and the overall boss of English Regions, had been involved. Kevin Silverton, the station's head of news, said he had heard that Boaden had commented that the plans were 'less than sketchy'. Davie promised more clarity in three months and scuttled off back to London.

Three days later, Mark Thompson came to apologise for the leak to *The Times* and promised an investigation was under way. He explained the rationale behind the decision, saying the Asian Network was a unique and valuable service and he had supported all the changes, but the conclusion now was that it had not worked. The aim now was to serve 85 per cent of British Asians with the five franchises. He echoed Davie, insisting this was not about cuts but about better serving the Asian audience. He too wanted to free up the AM frequency in London.

Every question revealed more about the proposal being 'less than sketchy'. Staff were confused by the different franchises. How would programming work? Are you defining output for an area by the predominant religion or South Asian background? The answer was invariably the same – it needed to be worked through. The DG repeated the mantra that the status quo was not acceptable. Something had to change and he believed the franchise plan was an exciting and compelling option that the Trust would accept. Crucially, he was not prepared to wait for the new presenters and the new 'friend of the family' strategy to settle in and then review things in a year.

So as the BBC tried to 'drive up digital' and persuade people to buy digital radios, it was closing two digital stations. Tim Davie argued that, as a national station, the Asian Network had been less successful at building a sense of community for its audience than the local services it grew from. Listening figures had dropped and its relevance was being tested by the diversity of British Asians. He believed the money and output of 6 Music and the Asian Network would be better targeted at the Corporation's existing, hugely successful national channels, offering extras which would entice listeners to digital services. He said a network of part-time local services would offer listeners 'a better, more tailored service'. However with the end of a national Asian DAB service, many feared that the voices of Asian Britain would disappear from the national airwaves. Mainstream newsrooms (national, regional and local) did not unearth the volume of stories from the Asian communities that the Asian Network could and did.

Elsewhere Tim Davie upset some people with his staunch advocacy of digital radio by saying he wished to make people without digital radios 'feel a little bit of pain', presumably by stressing what they were missing. An outraged listener from Leamington Spa wrote to The Times, saying of Davie's comments: 'This is insufferable arrogance on the part of the BBC towards its paying customers. Those who will feel Mr Davie's 'little bit of pain' will be the oldest and poorest listeners. Those who want and can afford pain can turn voluntarily to Miss Whiplash; they pay for other services from Mr Davie'.

At home I continually struggled to get a decent DAB signal, despite living in the middle of the country in an area well served by digital coverage. Digital radios would never work at the bedside, and I resorted to an internet radio in the kitchen. Elsewhere I had to settle for an unusual angle for the aerial and where I did finally find somewhere that seemed to work, the signal would intermittently start 'bubbling' for no apparent reason. The thick walls of our old house were to blame, I was told. FM was always reliable but I mostly had to listen to my own digital station on AM.

—m—

So how would the five franchises work and what issues needed to be unpicked to set them up? Initially three million pounds would come out of the current budget but had anyone actually costed five new regional services? The BBC Distribution document demonstrated there was a huge amount of work to done just to get the five franchises to air. Apart from ignoring Scotland, Wales and Northern Ireland, there were still significant gaps in coverage of main Asian areas. And many of the Network's listeners were in areas not associated with Asians but who found the programmes gave them a connection with their bigger communities – places like Lincolnshire and Northumberland.

Would the Asian Network logo and branding be retained or would there be five separate brand names like Asian Network London and Asian Network Manchester? Would there have to be five separate marketing campaigns? Would it keep one central website or have five offshoots? What would be the relationship with the local radio stations in the five areas? The Network would need their studios and other facilities like desks in the offices.

A sample schedule, showing the loopy evening and overnight loop message, indicated five regional Breakfast and Mid Morning shows, requiring 10 presenters. An afternoon phone-in and the Drive programme would be syndicated across the five franchises, along with evening language programmes ending at 7.30pm and all the weekend output. Regional news bulletins would be required across the weekdays, meaning more journalists to collect and read the news. Would there be five regional editors and five regional news and production teams? All these people would probably be on higher salaries than their local radio colleagues. The discrepancy between salaries in Audio and Music and English Regions had already led to mutterings at Radios WM and Leicester within earshot of Asian Network staff.

And how would all of this be managed? Who would have the editorial overview of the cultural and religious sensitivities and any inter-communal tensions? How would the different cultural, religious and language differences in each area be acknowledged?

Would the dominant Asian community in each area benefit at the expense of smaller groups who would then stop listening? Who would oversee the music policy and religious festivals coverage across the five franchises? How local should each franchise be? The questions were endless, and were all being raised by people who knew what they were talking about.

One of those people was Owen Bentley who had been asked to look at a similar plan for the BBC Charter Review back in 1991. This was part of a plan to expand Asian broadcasting but had failed because the BBC gave the 1458 medium wave frequency to commercial radio in both London and Manchester. This time round he recognised the argument that the franchise plan would bring Asian programming nearer to its audiences in the five areas, and the history of the Asian Network did indeed show that it was at its most successful when it dealt with local and regional concerns and tastes. But he described the franchise approach as conservative in outlook and said the reliance on medium wave for success was backward looking.

Owen outlined his views in a note to Mark Thompson and Tim Davie a week after the Review was announced. He included a copy of his report from twenty years earlier. He said the proposal involved 'big risks' and went on to highlight concerns around the management of the five areas and the syndicated service, the potential loss of on-air talent, the difficulties of recruiting new presenters and producers, the transmission issues including relying on medium wave in a digital age, direct competition with small local commercial Asian stations, the potential costs, and the dilution of the Asian Network brand.

The advantages of retaining the national service included continuing to serve even-handedly the Asian audience throughout the UK and facilitate a national conversation for communities and individuals. There would be clarity in the editorial focus and in management lines, it would be able to attract top presenter talent, remain a platform for British Asian music, a place to nurture writers, producers and documentary makers, a demonstration of faith in digital as the future, and the status and promotional opportunities through being a national network.

Meanwhile Mark Strippel was working on an analysis of the music policies of both the Asian Network and commercial Asian stations. This was somewhat difficult as most commercial stations did not operate a recognisable 'station playlist' structure with a revised weekly selection and rotation of identifiable core of music tracks. The DJ selected their own music and did not publish playlists or music policy. Consequently Mark and a couple of others had to listen all day and note down what was being played by stations such as London's Sunrise, Buzz Asia and Birmingham's Radio XL. Sample listening was done in the five franchise areas with Kismat Radio (London), Sabras (Leicester), Asian Sound Radio (Manchester), Sunrise and Masti Radio (both West Yorkshire). Some work was also done on small community based radio stations.

The research confirmed that the Asian Network had become much more distinct from its main rival, Sunrise in London, in the nine years since it went national. 95 per cent of Sunrise's daytime music was Bollywood compared to 50 per cent on the Asian Network. Sunrise did not have a commitment to the British Asian music scene but the Asian Network was committed to British Asian music accounting for 40 per cent of songs played. Sunrise had no specialist music programmes and no 'live' music commitment. These arguments applied to nearly all of the commercial stations and were not meant to denigrate them. It was all part of the campaign to prove to the executive and the BBC Trust that the Asian Network was very different and – a favourite BBC word – distinctive.

The actual words in the Asian Network portion of the Strategy Review stated that the increasing plurality and diversity of British

Asian audiences were stretching the coherence and relevance of the Asian Network. Reach was in decline and cost per listener was extremely high. The BBC therefore proposed to close the Asian Network as a national service, redeploying its investment and meeting the needs of Asian audiences more effectively. 'One option is to replace it with a network of five part-time local services with some syndicated national Asian programmes. These would be available on local DAB and local Medium Wave, serving areas with the largest British Asian communities. The consultation period would end on 25th May with the Trust publishing its provisional view and then its final recommendation by the autumn'.

The Review's discussion document used a handful of quotes to illustrate the ideological reasons for and against targeting an audience based on ethnicity. Someone in favour said it was one of the few clear ways that the UK provided a space and service for a community that had been here for generations and was an integral part of the British experience. Another said it was a small price to pay for diversity in the airwaves; another emphasised the national platform provided for music artists, news, debate and Asian culture. Someone in the middle said there may not be a 'need' for an Asian station in 20 years but there certainly was now; 'Unless of course they are willing to revamp the whole of the BBC output to be better reflective of their audiences'.

The negative views quoted in the Review were more striking and seemed chosen to deliberately support the closure plan. 'I'm not sure how Asian people making up 2.3 million in the population means they're entitled to a special service per se...is there a national black network? Should they be entitled to a radio station?'. *The Times* columnist Sathnam Sanghera was quoted from the day after the review was published and six days after the Times scoop: 'The idea of a BBC radio station dedicated to an 'Asian' community has always struck me as a bit odd...it has become a way for the BBC to ghettoise ethnic talent'. And to round it off, an unnamed commentator said bluntly: 'There really is no such thing as 'Asian' – a blighted term hated by everyone tacked under said label'.

With the closure plan out in the open, there was even more feverish anticipation around the next set of audience figures. We had to wait until 12th May to get the headlines for the first three months of 2010. The weekly reach was down again, back to 357,000 which is where it was the previous late summer and autumn. The 'friend of the family' strategy and the new schedule did not appear to be working and the closure plan seemed further justified. Thompson, Davie and the strategists must have felt even better about their proposal.

CHAPTER 28

consultAsian

The mood was indeed febrile and tense. The atmosphere was compelling with history in the making. Rumours flew left, right and centre. Journalists barked into mobile phones and realised they were in the wrong place at the wrong moment. Small crowds pushed and shoved near famous doors. Camera crews chased secret meetings and anyone who was anyone – or might indeed be someone – was collared for a quote or an interview. I decided it was the place to be that afternoon.

In London for the first of the Asian Network's public consultation meetings, I set off at a pace from the hell hole of the so-called Business Lounge in the BBC's Henry Wood House for Westminster. Six days earlier, the United Kingdom had gone to the polls in the 2010 General Election. It had proved inconclusive and now the two main parties were courting the Liberal Democrats to form a coalition. Whitehall, Parliament Square and College Green were alive with the world's media chasing every subtle twist and turn of the story. It was exciting and dramatic to be part of that scene if only for an hour or so on that sunny afternoon.

The drama of the Asian Network closure announcement had subsided and everyone at the radio station was just getting on with the job. Prime Minister Gordon Brown, on the election campaign trail for the Labour party in April, had been interviewed by the Asian Network and said he was 'interested in the BBC giving the widest possible range of services'. He added that the Strategy Review

225

decisions were for the BBC itself but believed the BBC had got a responsibility to serve all communities. For the management team, there were meetings with junior strategy people who were trying to unpick what made the Asian Network tick and how it might dissolve into five regional franchises. HR organised a session for staff entitled 'How to get that job!'

Twenty five people accepted the invitation to come to Yalding House on the evening of 11ᵗʰ May to discuss the Asian Network. The group – replicated at the other meetings around the country – were drawn from the Asian community and included representatives from business, education, religions, trade unions, councils, Melas, commercial media, voluntary organisations, the Asian music and record business and listeners. The aim of the meetings was to canvas opinion about the proposals for the future of the Asian Network. The sessions were chaired by the same independent facilitator, a former BBC English Regions editor Chris van Schaick, and lasted 90 minutes. Guests were assured that their view would be fed back 'as stated' to the BBC Trust. That particular promise was down to me, scribbling furiously in longhand with the occasional flurry of my old newspaper reporter shorthand.

Caroline Thomson, the BBC's Chief Operating Officer, came to the London session to see if anyone supported the closure plan. Vijay, Husain and I also sat at the back and observed, speaking only if asked for clarification of the Asian Network's current status, the proposals for the future or the 'five franchise' plan. Thomson was the most senior BBC executive to attend any of the five consultation sessions across the country but looked as though she would rather be anywhere else. The regional bosses in Leicester and Manchester came to their local meetings, along with the local radio station editors in London, Leicester and Birmingham. Leeds sent a senior broadcast journalist to the Bradford meeting.

The result of the five sessions was a 44 page bound booklet which I pulled together and which was sent to members of the BBC Trust and to the firing squad at Broadcasting House. People were overwhelmingly positive about the Asian Network, even those who hardly listened. They liked the journalism, the discussions about difficult subjects and the support for the Melas around the country. They felt the Network was important to Asian communities and that it had a bit of a global reputation with people listening on-line in South Asia and elsewhere. It was very important to the Asian music business.

People liked the national concept but wanted locality reflected too. There was a perceived lack of marketing especially in London and the north, and a lack of research in the potential audience, listening habits and demographics. They acknowledged it was a launch pad for Asian talent in broadcasting but they only seemed to mention Sonia Deol. They did not like DAB – everyone wanted the Asian Network on FM.

The evidence of the five meetings showed little or no support for the five local franchises idea. Some called it 'ghetto-isation' and said it implied that Asians 'did not deserve a national community'. They raised the issue of the rest of the UK being ignored and they were worried about the 'dominant community in each of the five areas being the sole beneficiary of the output'. They did not like the idea of only 12 hours a day and firmly stated that the BBC Asian Network just did not exist in London – it was all Sunrise.

Who knows if everyone in the BBC Trust read all the comments or indeed if it was bedtime reading for Mark Thompson and Tim Davie? The BBC liked focus groups and these sessions were real people from the Asian communities having their say, not just about the Asian Network but about the wider BBC.

Tim Davie made much of the fact that the two Asian representatives on the BBC Trust at the time did not support the

Asian Network. He said that his colleagues on the executive including the DG were surprised when the closure plan got the support of Mehmuda Mian and also Chitra Bharucha, who was Vice Chair of the Trust at the time and about to depart. He brought this up at every staff meeting which convinced us to target Mehmuda who was going to be around for a while longer and would thus be part of the final decision. She was duly invited to come and meet the team and get briefed on what we actually did rather than rely on the spinning of strategy papers and the admittedly disappointing audience statistics.

Meanwhile some of the staff were consulting among themselves through message boards and anonymous blogs. A handful were trying to get their colleagues to boycott the impending staff brainstorms. Why should they turn up to brainstorm 'this stupid idea' of the local proposal and thus give the management ideas on how to run it? Those exchanging views across the web nevertheless wanted the station to survive as a national service and wanted 18 to 20 hours a day rather than just 12. The prevailing mood was not to boycott the staff meetings but to get in there and fight because they knew and understood the audience better than anyone.

Another contributor to the on-line banter wrote (8.32 am: 1st May 2010) that some of the Assistant Editors could not take a decision, delegated all their work to their teams and left work early. It did not get any better with some of these individuals accused of 'going to meetings and pretending to be important, sucking up to higher management, taking credit for the hard work of other staff, letting presenters rule over producers just to keep them happy, fighting one another for content, and throwing out scraps of sandwiches from one of their pointless meetings because no one has the balls or vision to make a decision'.

Untouched sandwiches that were ordered from the BBC café and left over from management working lunches were indeed offered to the troops afterwards. This, along with fruit and crisps, was meant to be a goodwill gesture but was interpreted by some as 'crumbs from the rich man's table' (as the Gospel of St Luke would have it). Eventually these sandwich bonanzas were scrapped on the grounds of cost and indeed because of the bad taste they left in the mouths of everyone – philosophically and literally.

—ɯ—

The next phase of the 'friend of the family' strategy was implemented early in June when Tommy Sandhu took over the weekday breakfast show from Adil Ray, who left to further his career in comedy writing and acting. He later shone at a comedy session in front of the right BBC television people at Salford which in turn got him the commission for the first series of '*Citizen Khan*'. I got a call via Radio 2 from one of the senior members of his TV production team a few months later, asking me if I could put them in touch with a 'sensible Muslim'. Adil was pushing for a particular joke in '*Citizen Khan*' which they felt was a step too far. I gave them a connection who in turn was able to offer a second opinion and apparently the line came out.

Adil 's edgy humour had its place but that was not on a family friendly breakfast show. Many of the team felt he was put into that slot by Andy Parfitt to try and give the Network the 'Chris Moyles effect ' that had been so beneficial for Radio 1's audience figures. Adil did initially edge up the figures a bit but the family audience wanted something more populist and plenty of recognisable music at that time of the day. Andy acknowledged Adil's huge contribution to the Asian Network over the past eight years and wished him every success for the future.

In turn, Adil thanked his team and his listeners. 'It is with their love and support that I am able to go on and explore the exciting world of comedy and acting', he wrote in a note to all staff. ' I feel now the time is right to take on these challenges and hope to be working across a number of BBC platforms and beyond. I wish the station and everyone connected to it all the very best for the future'.

One of Andy Parfitt's favourite expressions likened a team to a bus and the people on board. He wanted the right people in the right seats on the bus, all moving forward in the right direction.

Tommy Sandhu was a safer bet for Breakfast and more family friendly. 'My dad used to come into my room in the morning, pull the duvet off and tell me I was late. It was, without doubt, the most horrible way to wake up! But my listeners can be assured of a much better start to the day – it's all about getting up with the radio, singing along to your favourite song and easing yourself into the world. I'm more excited about it than my mum is in an Indian suit shop!' quipped the voluble Mr Sandhu.

Being the Asian Network, Tommy Sandhu's move to Breakfast was not the simple smooth transition that would happen on any other radio station. The weekday breakfast show was broadcast from the Mailbox in Birmingham but Tommy lived out Essex way. He was therefore spending many nights away from home and his new bride and understandably wanted to do his show out of London. In fact it became a rider in his contract that the BBC would move his show from Birmingham to London. There was no studio available at Yalding House at that time of day so Andy Parfitt had a word with Radio 2's Bob Shennan, across the road at Western House.

There was an option with studio 4B in Western House, next to 6 Music's breakfast show. But the technical and operational impediments were considerable and it was down to me to approach the usually amenable Rupert Brun, the aforementioned Head of Technology for Audio and Music. Rupert was very familiar with the nightmares associated with the Asian Network transmission and technology and therefore none of the Network's requests usually surprised him. But he did have another little project on the go – getting everyone temporarily out of Broadcasting House to allow technical work to be done ahead of moving all the BBC's network radio stations into the brand new bit of that building.

Project Request F316 to PAG (Project Approval Group) was to move the Asian Network's weekday breakfast show to Western House and comprised 10 separate technical requirements. It sat alongside another request (F200 actually) relating to the broadcasting of the Saturday and Sunday '*Love Bollywood*' programmes from Yalding House. We were working round the *Love Bollywood* issue so decided not to make a further fuss about it. But the Western House project was pushing it.

Rupert Brun referred up to Caroline Elliot, Head of Development at Audio and Music and another regular recipient of Asian Network tales of woe. Rupert wrote: 'I would be interested to know how we entered into a (presenter) contract that has an unfunded and unresourced technical requirement'. He wanted to know where the Asian Network move was in the priority list and was it appropriate to be putting this much effort into moving such large amounts of Asian Network output to London now, ahead of the big migration into new Broadcasting House?

Andy, Vijay and Husain believed that Tommy Sandhu was the man to revitalise Breakfast and thus get the daily schedule off to a strong start. He had made his first impression at the Asian Network as a reporter on entertainment news and gossip with the Nikki Bedi show when it was broadcast in the afternoons a few years earlier. Tommy lived in the south-east where nearly half of the UK's Asian population lived and so, it was hoped, he could help nurture and grow the London audience. Hence the contract agreement and thus the technical requests – the Controller has spoken. After talking to Rupert, he agreed to assess the minimum amount of work required by his team to achieve this, but Caroline said that, because of the new BH work, there was a freeze on all new projects and the earliest start date would be the following January – six months away.

None of the options were good. How about treating it like an outside broadcast every day and playing the music in from Birmingham? Lease an independent studio which would still need hooking up to the transmission network? Use the BBC London studio at the Rich Mix building at the north end of Brick Lane in east London? Bush House? Television Centre? Tell Tommy the bad news and offer to release him from his contract early, or persuade him to hang on in Birmingham until the new year?

stagnAsian

'Undercover Lover' was typical of the attempts to lighten up the Asian Network's output and draw in the audience more. On the webpage for Sonia Deol's programme, there was this: 'Who is the love of your life? Are you happy or heartbroken? Share your anonymous Undercover Lover story here and we'll do our best to read it out and play a relevant song. Remember: We'll never mention names on air'. Furtive glances across the office, secret assignations near the water cooler and unrequited passion between couples wanting to bridge the religious and cultural divides had their opportunity to anonymously voice their angst after midday on Sonia's show. 'I'm frightened to talk to him but I know he listens to your show. Please read this out', appealed one young lady.

The business of actually running the radio station and broadcasting quality material was continuing as all the uncertainty swirled around it. The new drama series got under way with one play a month written by new and established Asian writers. Some of the best-known UK Asian actors got involved – people like Indira Joshi (Kumars at No 42), Nitin Ganatra (Eastenders) and Kulvinder Ghir (Goodness Gracious Me). For example, Kulvinder starred in 'We're not getting married' – a 30 minute drama about parents pushing couples together in the hope if not expectation that they will 'click' and get married. The whole drama series reflected situations that were very familiar to the Asian audience and were all superbly written, acted, directed and recorded in Birmingham.

The station's 'In Conversation' series was extended, inviting listeners into the BBC to see top Bollywood stars such as Shah Rukh Khan, Kajol, Aamir Khan and Dev Anand. All these interviews were filmed and compiled into a 'Best of Bollywood' film for the BBC's Red Button which attracted more than 600,000 hits.

Ten documentaries were commissioned across the year including a celebration of the life and work of Ravi Shankar at 90, the importance of preserving South Asian languages in the UK, the crisis in Pakistani cricket, and the memories of South Asian veterans who served in the British forces in the Second World War. A special week in June celebrated the success of British Asian enterprise in the UK and spoke to five new Asian entrepreneurs as judged by the Dragon's Den star James Caan. The new British Asian Download chart was up and running, and huge crowds were coming to the eleven Melas where the Asian Network was the main partner. Over 110,000 attended the Baishakhi Mela in east London's 'Bangla-town' – for many of them their only connection with BBC radio in 2010 and, for the station's own Bengali presenters like Shawkat Hashmi and Anwarul Hoque, a chance to muse on how many of that huge crowd were regular listeners of their shows.

The revamped weekday line-up settled in well with Waqas Saeed acting as the early hours warm-up act for Tommy Sandhu's Breakfast, Sonia Deol in her old mid-morning slot, Nihal and his phone-in early afternoon, Noreen Khan (from Weekend Breakfast) filling the late afternoon slot, and Gagan Grewal and Bobby Friction rounding off the evenings.

At the Sony Radio Awards in May, Nihal's phone-in won a Gold. The judges said: 'This programme consistently engages with its audience so powerfully that you have to stop everything and listen. Issues are addressed that you'll rarely, if ever, hear on mainstream radio, channelled through an exceptional presenter who is sensitive and challenging in equal part and, above all, informed. Quite brilliant'. It was a ringing endorsement for the programme team and the station, coming less than three months after the closure announcement.

The programme continued to tackle subjects that seldom got an airing among families or communities. People could come on the show anonymously and be harrowingly honest about situations that they were in or dilemmas that they faced. People who felt they had been cheated out of thousands of pounds by faith healers who advertised in the Asian press asked listeners across the country for advice because they could not tell their own family. Girls came on to ask if they should be completely honest about previous relationships with a new boy friend. It amplified reports like the one that claimed caste discrimination was rife in the UK with more than half of those from traditionally lower-status Asian backgrounds finding themselves victims of prejudice and abuse.

The documentary '*Passport to Murder*', presented by long time Asian Network journalist Poonan Taneja, won a Bronze at the same radio awards. Broadcast in December 2009, this looked at allegations that some British Asians were going back to India and plotting to murder spouses or relatives. The judges said the programme exposed, through strong case studies and some truly shocking stories, the unsolved cases of missing or dead British Asians, giving a voice to families of silent victims. 'The production team responded well to events which emerged during the conducting of the investigation, and it is testament to the power and relevance of the programme that it prompted a police investigation into the issue'.

The news team also commissioned the biggest ever poll of UK Asian voters ahead of the General Election. Despite a record number of South Asian candidates standing in the 2010 election, it found that this historic development appeared to be doing little to encourage the Asian communities to actually vote. The findings were in sharp contrast to the high Asian turn-out at the previous election five years earlier, suggesting that just over four in ten Asian voters intended to head for the ballot box. The news team also got an exclusive by being the first inside the UK's first Sikh temple school, and it had extensive coverage of the devastating floods in Pakistan and the subsequent impact on the affected communities both in Pakistan and the UK.

The interactive team was pushing the multi-platform digital brand to connect with the audience. Online, mobile phones, digital radio, digital television, Facebook, Flickr, You Tube and Twitter were all being used to 'big up' the Asian Network brand. Apart from the Bollywood Red Button hit, a film about the Melas and its star names got 570,000 hits and another about the UK Asian Music Awards topped 742,000.

In the middle of it all, a musician called Ranvir Singh Verma from the band Universal Taal walked backwards from London to Birmingham in protest at the plan to shut the network. His slogan was '4 Words Not Backwards – Save the Asian Network'. The total journey was nearly 130 miles and he did it alone with just his sat-nav and some cream for his blisters.

We had to wait until the evening of Wednesday 4ᵗʰ August to get the audience figures for April, May and June 2010. Across those three months, the weekly reach had gone up by 80,000 to 437,000 compared to the low of 357,000 in the first three months of the year.

I responded to the news that evening with a strange shaking fit at home which prompted my partner Jo to summon the paramedics. I had been feeling off-colour for a couple of weeks and by the end of the month was in hospital on industrial strength antibiotics to deal with a type of appendicitis and peritonitis. After five days to stabilize me, I was allowed home and returned to hospital two months later to have the whole thing whipped out and cleaned up. 2010 really was a terrific year.

In May, David Holdsworth, the Controller of English Regions and thus an interested party in the five franchise proposal, was tasked to investigate the practicalities regarding actually getting the programmes to the listeners. In a note to BBC Distribution, who had been asked to look at the five franchise idea the year before, David said he was chairing a small working party that was 'wrestling' with the proposal – a pertinent choice of word. Could they tell him which areas in the five regions were reliably covered by medium wave and DAB and where the transmission 'holes' were, and how many people were in them. He also asked if there was scope for the BBC to basically stick up more MW and DAB transmitters, and where would BBC local radio have to give up its medium wave to accommodate the Asian Network.

Back came the detailed maps and the problems, such as the BBC having already given away 1458 AM frequencies in London and Manchester. Another idea thrown up by someone was using the digital television platforms to 'regionalise' a feed of the Asian Network on Freeview but that could not be done. It would apparently need 'serious surgery to the coding and multiplexing to split the feed on digital television'. Therefore there could be only one 'flavour' of the Asian Network – not five. The technical talk went over the heads of most of us but the conclusion was pretty clear.

On 5th July, more than four months after the closure announcement, the BBC Trust announced its initial response to the Strategy Review. It rejected the plan to close 6 Music, saying the station was making an overall contribution to digital radio listening similar to other BBC digital only services. The Trust was not convinced that removing it and reallocating its budget to other aspects of digital radio would make a decisive difference to digital take-up. There were a few riders about music strategy and distinctiveness which allowed it to water down the reversal but ultimately it was saved.

The huge public response to the closure announcement must have influenced the members too. Apart from David Bowie and other musicians complaining about the plan, the Shadow Culture Minister before the election, Conservative Ed Vaizey, became an 'avid listener' of 6 Music after being lobbied by fans. He had never heard it before, initially describing the strategy review as intelligent and sensible. The high profile campaign also gave it pages of free publicity and the audience figure almost doubled, going from 600,000 a week to a million.

The Asian Network closure plan was approved by the BBC Trust which stated that the service was performing poorly and that its audience had fallen away. The percentage of Asian adults who were listening had dropped from 18 to 12 per cent and the younger audience was dropping faster. Its initial report stated: 'If the executive has concluded that the station's problems are such that they cannot be addressed effectively, then we expect them to come forward with a different proposition for meeting the needs of this audience in more effective ways'.

The Trust acknowledged that the Asian Network did deliver some real value to its audience. For instance, 48 per cent of its listeners did not listen to any other BBC radio station – and only Radio 1 reached the Asian community at all effectively. Awareness of all BBC radio stations had fallen over the past few years but the Network's had fallen from 41 per cent among Asian adults in 2005 to around 27 per cent at the moment. Meanwhile commercial Asian stations and community radio had been relatively successful.

As part of the consultation since March, the Trust received 1572 online responses, 1437 emails and 42 letters about the Asian

Network. A key theme that emerged was that the radio station nurtured the idea of being a British Asian rather than just a member of a local community. It also underlined the diversity within the British Asian communities. There was a risk that this British Asian idea would be lost if it was closed, but the Trust approved the closure anyway.

The BBC Trust's initial response was relayed by Andy Parfitt and Tim Davie as good news. Although the Asian Network would be closed as a national offering, it would survive in some form which was good for jobs and good for its audience. Discussions were already underway with people like David Holdsworth at English Regions to work up the franchises idea and ofcourse they wanted staff to be fully involved. Tim Davie addressed another staff meeting in Birmingham but only further convinced people that he wanted to send the Asian Network back into English Regions. His meetings with staff became notorious for phrases like 'Not for outside this room' as if he was letting slip some confidential nuggets from the top of the BBC.

Mark Thompson said the BBC would proceed to draw up detailed plans for the closure, which would also have to go to the Trust for final approval. The Trust would probably require a public value test before any changes were implemented, which could add another 6 months to the whole drawn-out process. The Asian Network was not going to be closed immediately and there would be opportunities for staff elsewhere in the organisation.

It was clear the Asian Network had few friends of influence in the BBC. People like Mark Thompson and Tim Davie appeared keen to get on with the closure, particularly in view of the about-turn with 6 Music. People at the top of Audio and Music offered sympathetic mumblings as though offering condolences on a death in the family. The increase in the Asian Network's weekly audience figure of 80,000 a week barely registered at the top. The Network's bid for some money from the Audio and Music Innovation Fund to underwrite ambitious one-off projects was rejected, along with bids to host people from other Networks under the division's 'Sound it Out' scheme.

The Sunday Times radio critic Paul Donovan used his column to demonstrate how other ways could be used to meet the needs of the Asian audience in the UK. He trawled through the schedules of Radio 4 looking for anything Asian to make his point. Book of the Week was *'We are a Muslim, Please'* by investigative journalist Zaiba Malik, and there was a documentary called *'Desi Pubs'* about Punjabi drinking dens in the Midlands – actually presented by the Asian Network's Bobby Friction. In the Saturday schedule, he found *'Never mind the Bhangra'* which considered the lack of Asian faces in British rock apart from Queen's Freddie Mercury who was born in Zanzibar to Indian parents.

Among the presenters, Donovan found Bidisha Bandyopadhyay who had just made her debut as a *Woman's Hour* presenter, and Ritula Shah who was now a regular anchor of *The World Tonight*. A documentary on laundrettes called *'Sud-U-Like'* was fronted by Yasmeen Khan, a regular stand-in presenter on the Asian Network. Noting that Radio 4 schedules were planned long in advance and therefore his findings were all coincidences, he said it proved that if the individual was good enough and the editorial was strong enough, it was an easy switch from marginal to mainstream. In a nutshell, he thought all the good news and speech on the Asian Network should go to Radio 4 and the music to Radio 1.

It was an interesting observation but Paul Donovan was only highlighting the handful who had succeeded in some way at Radio 4. What his skimming of the Radio 4 schedule overlooked was the significant number of young Asian presenters, producers and support staff for whom the Asian Network had been their entry point into the BBC. With more than 80 per cent of its team from the British ethnic communities, the Asian Network was important in attracting and nurturing these people, many of whom would then go on to work on the mainstream network and local radio stations, interactive teams and regional and national television. Some very good people would only apply to the Asian Network as it was within their comfort zone and they probably would not have to move away from their community if they got the job.

At the 2010 Radio Festival, which is the annual gathering of all UK radio industry figures, the name of the Asian Network was not mentioned. A handful of Asian Network assistant editors plus Vijay and Mark went to the event in Salford and felt it had already been expunged from the BBC network radio portfolio. They were not asked how things were or what was happening. People seem to avoid looking them in the eye. A speaker at one session was our Controller Andy Parfitt. When he was introduced, it was as Controller of Radio 1 and 1Xtra – there was no mention that he was also Controller of the doomed Asian Network.

The same month Gillian Reynolds, radio critic at *The Daily Telegraph*, previewed one of the new dramas on the Asian Network with the line: 'The axe will fall on this network next year but the actual output gets better every day'.

Elizabeth Mahoney of *The Guardian*, who had been very supportive of the Asian Network over the years, returned to its future in a column in September. 'These must be frustrating times to work at the Asian Network. Never supported as noisily as 6 Music, when the closure of both stations was mooted, the Asian Network remains doomed despite increased audiences and some terrific output. Last night's *'Mind your Language'* (documentary) presented by Konnie Huq, was a case in point; a well researched report on the survival of mother tongue languages among British Asians…

'…What distinguished the report from, say, a Radio 4 programme was how it spoke directly to its specific audience. We heard that community colleges, where much language teaching takes place, offer more than linguistic coaching. As one researcher explained, they provide a forum for discussing wider issues such as what it means to be British and Asian: 'That was a safe space for them to turn that over and explore it'. This is what the Asian Network offers too and what a pity to lose it'.

manipulAsian

The Asian Network staff did not know it but, by the autumn of 2010, even the five franchise plan appeared to have been dropped. The new big idea was not to have any Asian Network 'franchise radio stations' at all. Instead Asian content would be prepared in a 'hub' and then be guaranteed airtime on other BBC services and pulled together on-line. Around 50 of the 85 fulltime jobs would be lost.

While the radio industry executives were enjoying their annual festival in Salford in October, the Chancellor of the Exchequer George Osborne announced the new licence fee settlement that had been hurriedly drawn up and agreed with Mark Thompson. It was fixed at £145.50 for six years and included the BBC taking financial responsibility for the World Service, BBC Monitoring and the Welsh language television channel S4C. Thompson admitted it was tough but said it gave the BBC six years of financial certainty and real protection for the Corporation's editorial and operational independence. There was a rider clause in the agreement which Osborne relayed to the House of Commons: 'The BBC also agreed to reduce its on-line spend and make no further encroachments into local media markets, to protect local newspapers and independent local radio and TV'.

As if the staffing costs, limited hours and transmission difficulties were not enough to make the five franchise plans unworkable, this agreement not to encroach on existing local media surely sealed its fate. Direct local competition against local Asian commercial stations was one of the first and obvious flaws in the original plan. Even three franchises – London, Midlands and North – would be more credible (and cheaper) as the BBC could argue the services were regional and thus not competing with local commercial operations.

In the summer I had drawn up a list of negative points about the five franchise plan but had only shared it with Vijay. I did not want to contribute any arguments to actually bringing down the only serious alternative to the national offering (or so I thought at the time). These included the loop message across evenings and overnight, telling listeners we would be back at 7am. Some people said that Five Live Sports Extra did it but that was a false comparison – nearly everything on that network were commentaries for specific events like football or cricket matches. And those events were trailed heavily as and when on Five Live. To have 12 hours of a looped message was just insulting to the Asian communities, went against the line that the changes were all about delivering a better service to them and would simply send listeners elsewhere, probably for good.

This ludicrous looped message exercised my mind more than perhaps it should. Was this really a serious proposition? I started to speculate as to who should record it and how many languages it should be broadcast in? Should one of our presenters like Tommy or Noreen read it straight? Sanjeev Bhaskar in 'They are all Indian!' mode or 'Skipinder', the drunk Punjabi kangaroo from *Goodness Gracious Me*? Gulshan Grover, the Bad Man of Bollywood, delivering it with menaces? Should it be Adil's comedy character Citizen Khan? How about Steve Coogan's Alan Partridge? 'They're not here! They've ruddy well gone home to watch the lovely Nina Wadia on the *Eastenders*…ahh' (not Ah-ha). And so on. I knew I should get out more.

One document said the new franchises would see the end of the on-air 'mocking tones' – presumably a reference to Adil's style but he had departed and, anyway, poking fun at friends, family and institutions was part of everyday life and had a place in a radio entertainer's repertoire. The new services should also refrain from playing 'niche' music but it did not clarify what that meant. Did 'niche' mean specialist and new, which of course underlined the Asian Network's distinctiveness from its commercial rivals?

The importance of getting a medium wave transmitter in London was repeatedly emphasised but nothing appeared to have been progressed. Had the impact of taking AM frequencies away from BBC local radio been analysed? Why was Radio Derby's 1116 AM frequency being allocated to the West Midlands franchise rather than Leicester and the East Midlands? What about the playout system for the five franchises? We would want to do it on network radio's VCS system but local radio was still using Radioman – and the plan to roll out VCS to the regions had been delayed by costs. And there were the issues around the management of the whole enterprise. They had got no further than suggesting an Asian Content Editor who would report to the Controller of English Regions.

There had been a lot of talk about radio cars to enable reporters to broadcast directly from the heart of the communities. Some costs for the new generation of satellite link radio cars had been flagged but there were no indications that anyone had gone into the real costs of five vehicles, ongoing maintenance, receiver kit, garaging, branding, training and the project management of ordering them and getting them, possibly up to 12 months to sort.

—ɷ—

By October, the leading players had pulled together enough feedback to realise that the five franchise option was, in Andy's words, 'not going to fly'. People like Steve Mitchell, deputy director of news, wondered aloud if the BBC would commit to the cost and whether commercial competitors, particularly in London, would tolerate it. But he felt the franchise plan was more logical than the 'content hub' idea. Mitchell said the franchise idea better addressed the Trust's anxieties about serving the Asian audience, had the virtue of going back to the origins of the Asian Network and would be easier to monitor for performance against agreed criteria. He felt that it 'pragmatically appears to have more chance of success'.

Steve Mitchell's concerns about the 'Mainstreaming Asian Content' option, as the latest sparkling idea was named, were shared by many and were indeed included in the paperwork. Without a television or radio platform to guarantee broadcasting what was produced, it would be difficult to judge its success and what the target audience actually thought about it. It would require a strong commitment from English Regions and Network News to use material from this Asian content hub.

The guarantee that Asian content would actually be broadcast prompted feverish debate among the group that was tasked with formulating proposals. Andy Parfitt talked to Bob Shennan at Radio 2 and devised a development – or a 'build' as they called it – on the content hub idea. How about guaranteed Asian 'opt-outs' on the five local radio stations serving the five franchise areas? This would be cheaper than setting up five separate Asian Network operations. He described it as 'perhaps a contemporary hi-tech version of the original Asian Network model – back to the future but turbo-charged'.

The plan was for Asian listeners in the five areas to get high quality journalism and cultural programmes on limited but guaranteed hours, probably just in the evenings and on medium wave only. David Holdsworth agreed with 'the thrust of a souped-up Option 2'. (After 'turbo-charged', this was beginning to sound like *Top Gear*). He wondered if the plan could be expanded to ensure Asian Network journalism could work on Radio 4 and Five Live? Could there be a commitment from Radio 2 about a Bollywood programme? The plan still depended on getting medium wave frequencies in London and Manchester – and so it never flew either.

So 'Mainstreaming Asian Content' became the lead option for the discussion paper that would go to the DG's executive board at the end of the year. First, this latest plan for replacing the national Asian Network went to the board meetings for both Audio and Music and also Journalism. Both meetings agreed the three options for discussion, with A&M asking for some early commitments from other BBC services to actually broadcast Asian content, and the Journalism group suggesting there should be a lead option.

The 'authors' of the discussion paper that was to be discussed by the BBC Executive meeting on 8th November 2013 were Vahini Sangarapillai, a new strategy analyst in A&M, and Husain Husaini, the Head of Programmes at the Asian Network. The paper's 'sponsors' were Tim Davie, Mark Byford (Deputy Director General) and Caroline Thomson (Chief Operating Officer).

It was surprising to see that the recommendation in this paper to Mark Thompson and the most senior people in the BBC was to get rid of any stand-alone radio service. The lead option was to ring-fence funding for Asian content which would then have guaranteed hours on other BBC services such as BBC News, BBC Online, BBC Network Radio, BBC Red Button and BBC Local Radio. There was also the potential to syndicate it on Asian community radio stations. This preferred option would save £3.6 million from the second year and mean the loss of 50 posts.

The protagonists of this plan stated it would improve the value delivered to Asian audiences across BBC services through an online BBC Asian service that pulled together the best of the BBC's journalism and content that was relevant to British Asians. It would be a fresh TV newsgathering resource to provide output for the BBC Six O' Clock News, the News Channel and BBC World News. There was a commitment to cover at least three Asian cultural events a year like Melas. There would be a weekly Asian music programme on BBC Radio 1Xtra, more news stories on Five Live, and documentaries and dramas on Radio 4, Radio 3 and 4Extra. The Asian programmes on 12 local radio stations would be enhanced, and partnerships with Asian community radio would be developed.

In the small print, there was a reference to an Asian morning opt-out in the Midlands on its current AM frequencies. There would be two Asian stories a week on Five Live and 18 feature slots on *Woman's Hour, You and Yours*, and *Front Row* on Radio 4. How about an annual season of 12 plays on Radio 4Extra, some of which could make it to Radio 4 and Radio 3? And £100,000 reinvested in local radio to support Asian language programmes to mitigate the negative impact of closing the national Asian Network. It claimed all of this met the BBC's favourite criteria – reach, quality, impact and value.

This was radio by numbers, ticking the Asian checkbox across the BBC. And the arguments that dogged the Asian Network throughout its lifetime would still be valid – if you are doing this for the Asian communities, what are you doing for the African Caribbean, Chinese, Polish and other growing ethnic groups? The document acknowledged the biggest challenge would be for the content produced to 'maintain visibility and impact' within the BBC without a dedicated service outlet. This risk could be mitigated by securing those guaranteed hours across a number of BBC services. You could imagine editorial planning meetings and daily news conferences resounding with cries of: 'Have we got the Asian angle?'

The remains of the plan that had been offered to the staff at the Asian Network was included in the document under 'Other

Options Considered'. This was what the staff had been told by Tim Davie to get behind because it was the 'only game in town'. The five franchises had actually come down to two – London and Midlands/North. This would save £1.3 million from the second year of implementation and result in the loss of around 35 posts. This was described as two distinct morning schedules focussing on UK Asian news with a concentrated effort to deepen the BBC's connection with Asian communities. The target audience would shift from the under 35s to 25-50 year olds.

Having stated that, the authors and sponsors of this discussion paper said this option (called 'Radio Plus') was not being recommended. The main reason was the impact on the 25 Asian local commercial and community stations as this would go against the agreement with the Government about the BBC not encroaching on local media any more. The risk would have been mitigated by being part-time (6am to 7pm) and the focus on journalism where commercial rivals did not compete. Anyway all of that was irrelevant as Radio Plus was apparently not being recommended.

The third option was not being recommended either. This was simply the closure of the Asian Network and no ring-fenced funding for Asian content. This would challenge BBC outlets across all platforms (TV, radio, online) to improve appeal amongst Asian audiences. It would be an opportunity to transform the way in which the needs of diverse audiences were considered across all BBC services. There was a further vague nod to covering Melas, investment in Asian journalism within BBC News and keeping the Asian programmes on 12 local radio stations. These ideas were not recommended because BBC services may be 'unable to reprioritise within their budgets to improve value delivered to Asian audiences'. There were also risks to the reputation of the BBC as a broadcaster that aims to service all audiences, and there were clear risks in terms of losing diverse staff and talent – points which any observer would conclude that the whole saga was already risking anyway.

A week before the Executive board meeting, Vijay secured a meeting with Mark Thompson. It was an opportunity for her to remind the DG what he, and Tim Davie, had said to staff back in March. Although she had been on holiday in India, people like me had made notes and logged the quotes and assurances, and the team had certainly not forgotten what was said to them. Staff had obviously been shocked by the closure plan but took comfort from both the DG and Davie stating that there was a plan to maintain a radio output even if it was only 12, 16 or 18 hours a day. The five franchise proposal was also the plan that the Asian Network

Vijay Sharma with BBC Director-General Mark Thompson at the new BBC offices in Leicester.

management team had taken to the opinion-former meetings in the five areas – and now it was not even being recommended to the DG's board.

Vijay said that her staff had believed him and Tim Davie about the radio options and 'put our faith in those assurances from our senior leaders'. Because they were told they did have a serious radio option which had the support of both the DG and the Director of Audio and Music, staff did not mount a protest campaign like 6 Music. She also pointed out that Tim Davie, Andy Parfitt and herself had made public statements about the radio plan.

In an email sent to the DG two days after the meeting, she recapped her points and suggested that he might wish to press the 'pause' button for further reflection on what had changed since March. Specifically the audience figure had gone up by 105,000 to 362,000 a week with a subsequent decrease in the cost per listener. She also asked about the opportunities presented by the BBC taking over the funding of the World Service and S4C. Regarding the World Service, she pointed out that the BBC could end up better serving the Asian diaspora in India, Pakistan and across the globe than the British Asian licence fee payers. And did not the responsibilities for S4C raise the question of parity of service provision principles for minority interest services?

Vijay was reassured by the DG's promise to talk to her again before any decision was taken but in the meantime could she highlight a couple of related issues? The radio franchise proposal had been informed by audience research and the opinion former meetings, but no such audience insights had informed the 'Mainstreaming Asian Content' option. Surely, she said, the Asian audiences deserve the same level of due diligence?

The second point was diversity. If the BBC was really going to walk away from a radio option, it should take into consideration the disproportionate impact on Asian audiences, the British Asian music industry which was championed by the Asian Network and also the effect on the predominantly Asian staff and presenters at the station.

At the very least, the BBC should consider a rigorous Race Equality Impact Assessment. This was a way of systematically and thoroughly assessing, and consulting on, the effects that a proposed policy was likely to have on people depending on their racial group. The main purpose of a race equality impact assessment was to pre-empt the possibility that a proposed policy could affect some racial groups unfavourably. The Trust had hinted at a public value test about the changes to the Asian Network to work out the value to the public and assess the impact it could have on the wider market. A PVT could delay things by six months but it would surely throw up the anger of local commercial Asian radio stations. The BBC liked to talk about diversity but that was not the same as undertaking a properly constituted Race Equality Impact Assessment.

The evening before Vijay sent her summary to Mark Thompson, she got a call from Tim Davie who assured her that he would be championing the radio option. Once more I was called in to help fashion another email record of a Vijay conversation with the upper echelons. These conversations and the follow-up summaries played a significant role in gradually turning the tide against closure.

This time Tim Davie was reminded again of the improved audience figures and the knock-on effect on the cost per listener figure, the fast growing Asian population in the UK that the BBC should be serving and which showed an appetite for radio listening, and the impact on the British Asian music industry. She asked why the strategists had not warned him very early on about opening BBC regional franchises directly against small commercial stations. Why did they wait until now to use it as argument for supporting the non-radio plan? As with Mark Thompson, Davie was reminded that no audience insights had been collected on this 'Mainstreaming Asian Content' option.

Mark Thompson had heard enough. He pulled the Asian Network discussion paper off the agenda of his Board meeting on 8th November. It was the first indication that the Asian Network may yet follow 6 Music and survive as a national radio station. Or it could confirm that everything was so bloody complicated and difficult that the best solution would be to take the Asian Network to the guillotine immediately.

CHAPTER 31

frustrAsian

The BBC's plans for serving its Asian audience were now looking to me like the proverbial 'omnishambles', a word that finally made it to the Oxford English Dictionary after springing from the BBC's political satire '*The Thick of It*'. The central argument for closing the Asian Network (its diminishing audience) had been overthrown by a 30 per cent rise in the past 12 months. The alternatives initially put up had been exposed as ill-conceived and unworkable, and the new idea of the 'content hub' had crept into the discussions without the staff being aware.

Three days after Vijay had met Mark Thompson, and the day after her emails to both him and Tim Davie, Andy Parfitt rang to confirm that the Asian Network discussion paper was indeed off the executive agenda for the following week. They had to revisit the proposals and come up with something else. Tim Davie now 'did n't know what to think', according to Andy. In the Mailbox in Birmingham, David Holdsworth, the Controller of English Regions, told me that the plans were in disarray.

Hosting a staff meeting by video link from Yalding House, Andy Parfitt sounded quite gloomy. It was the day after the Executive board had not discussed the Asian Network but he thought closure was likely even though there were still options to be explored. Elsewhere the BBC was facing strikes ahead of Christmas over the changes in the pension scheme. Record low temperatures were recorded in the UK as the country endured a big freeze.

On the day of the staff meeting, Tommy Sandhu was talking to Asian actor Jimmy Mistry about being voted off '*Strictly Come Dancing*' at the weekend. On her programme, Sonia was discussing interfering mothers-in-law and how to deal with them. The news team were following the story of a Pakistani cricketer who was seeking asylum in the UK after claiming he had received death threats for not agreeing to fix cricket matches. Nihal's phone-in contemplated the *Eastenders* storyline which highlighted the issue of gay Asians entering marriages of convenience. Reporter Sanjiv Buttoo visited a Bradford curry house that had featured on a Gordon Ramsey TV show.

Looking further ahead, the Asian Network was still making big plans for the following year. It had £100,000 to spend on big events – either a one-off Mega Mela probably in Birmingham or four smaller shows in significant Asian cities. How about a month-long season of wedding-themed programmes, launched on Valentine's Day? The next Cricket World Cup was looming in February and the film '*West is West*', a follow-up to the 1999 classic '*East is East*' starring Om Puri again, was due for release the same month. A comedy week featuring the best Asian comedians was discussed, along with a 'Curry Cook Off' to celebrate home cooking in Asian kitchens. An Asian Network 'Hall of Fame' was seriously discussed, with the stars of '*Goodness Gracious Me*' being the first nominees to mark the 15th anniversary of their first radio show. The idea was quietly 'put on hold' after I pointed out that they could be the only nominees – ever – if the radio station was closed down.

—w—

The BBC Trust held one of its regular meetings in Birmingham in mid-November. The chairman, Sir Michael Lyons, hosted a meeting of staff from throughout the building facing questions about cuts, pensions and the future of departments in the Mailbox. I was away having my troublesome appendix whipped out but did n't miss anything. Sir Michael, who lived in the West Midlands, could offer no assurances about the future of the Asian Network and remained non-committal. Trust member Alison Hastings, standing alongside him, paid tribute to the hard work being undertaken by staff in the face of huge uncertainty.

One of the senior producers, Stin Mattu, asked a general Asian Network question but followed it up with a written invitation to Sir Michael to come and visit the Asian Network. Stin got an email back from him a few days later, saying he would be happy to meet with some of the Asian Network staff. He wrote: 'In terms of timing, I'll get back to you in the New Year when there will be greater clarity over the Executive's proposal for the future of the Asian Network and the Trust will therefore be in a better position to engage meaningfully with staff and other stakeholders'.

It sounded as though Sir Michael certainly knew about the confusion among senior managers over the plans and he too was awaiting 'clarity'. Anyway he had already announced two months earlier that he was off, declining a further year in office. It was probably worth getting to him as hopefully the Trust would have something in front of it before he departed in May 2011. 'The BBC Trust will make the final decision' became a management mantra across the whole period of instability for the Asian Network.

A month after her meeting with the DG, Vijay followed it up with yet another summary of what they had discussed. Apart from repeating her points, Vijay rounded off the email with an appeal to the DG to seriously consider the Radio Plus option or challenge the Asian Network to slim down its offering and costs as part of a pan-BBC requirement to tackle the financial challenges ahead. She was not seeking special treatment for the Network but wanted him to take the final decision with due regard to fairness and equal treatment. She again asked him to take account of the likely disproportionate impact on the actual and potential UK Asian audiences, the British Asian Music industry and of course the predominantly Asian staff and presenters at the radio station.

Vijay appealed to the DG for fair and equitable treatment with other minorities that were targeted by the BBC. I suggested querying if the Asian Network was viewed through the same criteria as the Scottish Gaelic service Alba, Radio Cymru and the Welsh language television channel S4C. The BBC was due to take financial responsibility for S4C in Wales which had been funded by the Department of Culture, Music and Sport to the tune of something like £90 million a year. The weekly number of viewers of S4C in 2009 was 549,000. The Asian Network cost well under £10 million a year and was heading towards half a million listeners.

I also compiled some information around the audience that Vijay could use to support the case for keeping things national. Ethnic minority communities were projected to grow rapidly from 8.6 per cent of the population in 2001 to 16.3 per cent in 2016. The Indian community was forecast to be the largest ethnic group in England and Wales the following year (2011) – 2.8 per cent with the Pakistani communities at 2 per cent. The whole south Asian population was expected to reach 3.5 million in 2011 and 57 per cent of them were under 35. BBC research on the Asian Network's 'audience story' concluded in November (2010) that 'BBC Radio does have an Asian issue'. So why is the man in charge of radio wanting to remove the one dedicated 'in-road' into Asian communities and alienate the 462,000 who were now listening each week?

Another piece of work that I fed into the fight was a simplistic comparison around weekly audience figures for other stations. The Asian Network's latest official weekly figure was 462,000 but the unpublished total for October (the first of the final three months of

2010) was 540,000. Monthly figures came with big health warnings about reliability but this was at least indicating a continuing upward trend. Nevertheless, 462,000 a week was more than the combined weekly reach at that time of the BBC local stations for Birmingham, Leicester, Oxford and Coventry & Warwickshire. I did not include Radio Oxford out of affection for my first radio station but because it was the home station for the DG – he lived round the corner in North Oxford.

In fact the Asian Network's top line figure for the last quarter of 2010 was up again, averaging out across October, November and December at 477,000. It was a figure we used to compare in detail with other radio station audiences from that period. The Asian Network on 477,000 was targeting a UK Asian population of around 2.4 million while Radio Wales, on 486,000, was targeting the 2.9 million Welsh population. BBC London was getting just over half a million of the 7.7 million Londoners. While Asian Network was on 477,000 a week, the combined audience of Radio Leeds and Radio Leicester was 454,000 and that of Radio Manchester and Radio WM was 435,000. The DG's local station in Oxford was getting 62,000 but the point was that he was not planning to shut any of these radio stations.

It was an unsophisticated argument that did not tackle the money issues but it did make the point about a significant group of listeners who were paying the licence fee.

Looking through the document that was ultimately pulled from the agenda of the Executive Board a month earlier, Vijay asked Mark Thompson where was the evidence that UK Asian audiences would actively search for the content listed in the recommended option? She also argued that, in 2010, other BBC services should already be reflecting Asian music, drama and news as a matter of course. For example, the existence of Radio Cymru did not stop the BBC from portraying Welsh people and stories in the mainstream.

The arguments were piling up, getting somewhat repetitious but also more compelling. If the reason for not recommending the franchise option was the perceived market impact on commercial rivals, why had it taken eight months before it was flagged as a reason for not supporting the franchise plan? Despite the Chancellor's requirement in October, surely senior management at the BBC recognised the potential arguments about competition when the franchise plan was first drawn up?

Vijay emphasised the difference between the outputs of the Asian Network and its commercial rivals, not least in journalism and British Asian music. She warned that the high cost per hour per listener figure could not be tackled with a part-time radio station. It needed a strong on-air presence to make an impact. Otherwise the BBC was running the danger of setting up something to fail.

The BBC taking on the funding of the World Service from the Foreign Office provided more ammunition. Could the BBC find itself in the position of UK licence payers funding World Service output to the South Asian diaspora overseas – while those same UK licence payers from the Asian communities here would not have a serious BBC radio service reflecting their growing populations? And a recent report by the 'think-tank' Migration Watch had highlighted the huge number of primary school children in places like London, Birmingham, Leicester, Bradford, Oldham and Luton where English was not the mother tongue. The Asian Network was broadcasting in the Asian languages that were the prime one every day.

She concluded that things had changed since March and the arguments for closure were 'no longer stacking up'.

Tim Davie was copied into Vijay's email to the DG and replied a few hours later with a couple of observations. He said they needed to recognise that the financial climate had changed dramatically since the first announcements in March – a reference to the licence fee settlement in October. He said it was clear that the staff knew that if they could not 'sell' the franchise proposal to the Trust, then closure was a real threat. 'The truth is that we have tried to get traction for it but it has proved hard. The truth is that we must look at other options. I am sure that you are talking to Andy (Parfitt) about a credible proposal that we can sell'.

Tim Davie, Husain and Vijay had a phone hook-up on 8th December to look at new options. Among the ideas from the centre was a new franchise proposal which excluded the North – so only London and the Midlands would be served. Even then, it was suggested again that these franchises take the World Service South Asian programmes from 12 noon to 7pm. As Mark Strippel noted, this was like putting Radio 1Xtra bulletins on Radio 4. Just because the word Asian was in both brands, someone at the top thought it was all the same. Another phone hook the following week included Andy Parfitt and Helen Boaden, the Director of News, and the 12 hours a day option (7am-7pm) was back on the table. Vijay said that the lack of support for the national radio station from Helen Boaden was particularly damaging.

The BBC Trust published its strategy review conclusions on 14th December. It endorsed the management's plan to close the Asian Network as a national service. Tim Davie told Asian Network staff that there was no change to what they already knew and that 'A&M leadership are working on a proposal to take to the Executive committee in January 2011'. Mark Thompson addressed all BBC staff on the 20th December about 'Putting Quality First' before chairing a meeting on the Asian Network with Caroline Thomson, Tim Davie, Andy Parfitt, Husain and Vijay. Everything was delayed due to the announcement of the death from cancer of the BBC's highly respected Diplomatic Correspondent Brian Hanrahan, famous for counting out and checking back in the same number of Harrier jets from HMS Hermes during a Falklands War mission in 1982.

The Asian Network meeting did not go well with the DG walking out after 20 minutes, clearly not impressed with the latest concoction and the lack of clarity. Only two of the ten PowerPoint slides in the Audio and Music presentation actually got shown before Mark Thompson, said to be in a 'ferocious' mood, stated that he could not take this to the Trust or indeed the Executive board. Andy Parfitt hardly spoke. Vijay Sharma contributed no more than pointing out that the latest proposal excluded the north of England and did nothing for London. Caroline Thomson could only murmur 'Don't worry, Tim' after the DG left the room.

Tim Davie later said there was 'tension at the centre' because the group who had met the DG were not united. He accepted before the meeting that Vijay would not fall into line as she was repeatedly highlighting the shortcomings of the alternatives and bringing them to the attention of the man at the top. Husain said the strategists were still the enemy, especially A&M's Will Jackson who was said to be openly negative about the Network. There was talk of keeping a national service but it could not be on the national DAB network – it would have to use local DAB multiplexes. Was this just a cunning plan to pretend it really was n't national any more?

Vijay told Mark Strippel and me that she thought the DG was now 'on-side'. She said he had considerable editorial 'nous' and a political head on him. She was sure that he was being persuaded by the improving audience figures and all the supporting information to at least give the Asian Network another chance as a national enterprise, despite what others might be whispering in his ear. Maybe there was a chance of a couple more years with strict targets on audience figures and costs?

Bill Rogers, the former BBC News executive who had got involved with integrating the Asian Network newsroom into the

BBC News operation six years earlier, had some encouraging words on his respected blog on the day the BBC Trust published its review. 'I know it's anxious and stressful to work for all sorts of organisations under threat of change. However, I ask you to spare a thought for the excellent people who bring you the BBC's Asian Network, condemned to closure, apparently, in a leak of a BBC strategy paper to The Times in February this year. Today, they were offered the gracious view of the BBC Trust in their Strategy Review Paper. 'We will also consider carefully any formal proposal to close the Asian Network'. 13 words, no ifs, no buts, or rationale'.

The campaign to save the Asian Network got a subtle unexpected boost at the end of the year. Mark Thompson was appointed chair of the Cultural Diversity Network, an alliance of leading broadcasters and independent production companies. Its aim was to improve the representation of ethnic minorities on television, both on-screen and behind the camera. Surely the new chairman could not start his two year tenure by shutting his Asian radio service and putting loads of ethnic BBC staff out of work?

The Network got a national 'plug' on Christmas Eve when Raj and Pablo appeared on the National Lottery programme. Its future at the end of 2010 was still unclear but suddenly looked a little brighter. I contemplated that the decision to simply close down the national Asian Network now looked 'courageous', as Sir Humphrey Appleby of *Yes Prime Minister* might have described it. Or as Sgt Wilson repeatedly cautioned Captain Mainwaring about his plans in *Dad's Army*, 'Do you think that's wise, Sir?'.

CHAPTER 32

clarificAsian

The Asian Network was going to close and other departments in the Birmingham Mailbox were already measuring up to move into its production area. Tim Davie's deputy, Graham Ellis, and the Head of Factual in Birmingham, Andrew Thorman, had been seen walking round the area, pointing and muttering. This was clearly another sign that the Network was doomed. *The Archers* were going to reclaim their old territory and live quietly in peace there without the dull throb of bhangra sweeping across the fields like a rave in a distant barn or the thump of Euro-pop across a Mediterranean bay that had promised peace and tranquillity.

The Ellis/Thorman expedition was genuinely seen as a bad sign by some Asian Network staff. By the time this rumour got to me, Andrew was away for a couple of days but so I had to wait to collar him for an explanation. The truth was, needless to say, very simple but also a secret. Camilla, the Duchess of Cornwall, was due to visit the BBC in Birmingham (well, The Archers specifically) and the pair had been working out the best route round the Mailbox for the Royal visitor.

A month later, the Duchess duly arrived, sweeping past the Asian Network area on her way to Borsetshire. Vijay frantically waved staff over to introduce as many as possible in the shortest space of time. Charming and friendly, Camilla stopped to chat. Vijay waved her hand expansively around her assembled troops and declared; 'As you can see Your Royal Highness, the Asian Network is a very young team'. The Network Manager, who had stayed at his post, slunk lower behind his computer screen.

—m—

While the Asian Network staff awaited their fate, the New Year brought big cuts elsewhere in the BBC. In one week in January, 360 job losses in the on-line community were announced with more than 600 in the World Service. The same week, beginning 24 January, the BBC's Director of Human Resources Lucy Adams visited Birmingham but could offer no news on the Asian Network.

Ariel's deputy editor Sally Hillier decided to comment on the Asian Network's July to September 2009 all-time low audience audience figure of 357,000. Praising the weekly audience figures of Radio 3 and Radio 4, Hillier zeroed in on the Asian Network's 'less rosy' picture. 'Rajar results swing up and down from one quarter to the next but any further fall for the Asian Network would be bad news indeed', she wrote. Why would the deputy editor of the staff organ be moved to write that? Pravda indeed.

People asked what the mysterious Head of BBC Diversity actually did and why she had n't she been to see the Asian Network team? Perhaps she had removed it from her list – Audio and Music's target was to get 12 per cent of its staff from the ethnic communities whereas the Asian Network was already on 88 per cent.

Lucy Adams was later much maligned in the media in the fall-out over big management pay-offs but we had no issues with her. At least on her occasional visits to Birmingham, she actually came to speak to us and we found her approachable and unpretentious. However I felt the top level of HR managers in Audio and Music were noticeable by their absence at the Asian

Network in the three difficult years from the start of 2010 to the end of 2012.

Considering the uncertainty and stress that the BBC had dumped on its predominantly young staff, it was 'disappointing' that these senior people failed to come and talk to people affected and make themselves available. I tried to hijack one who turned up in the Mailbox but, barely pausing to stop as she strode past the Asian Network, she said she was only there to see the Radio 4 team that day. Maybe I naively expected them to be sort of social workers for the beleaguered staff. As it was, the responsibility of dealing with a tortuous saga of redundancies and wholesale re-recruitment was largely delegated to one part-time HR middle manager Laura Friedner and a couple of inexperienced young assistants – all pleasant and helpful, and facing 'restructuring' themselves.

One of the big problems we had around staffing after the closure announcement was that HR would not let us fill any vacancies with full-time appointments and later even short-term contracts. There was a ban on new substantive posts as they would mean more redundancy pay-outs as the staffing was slowly reduced. Money-wise it made sense but it left programme teams unsettled, and scrabbling around and sometimes competing for the services of a handful of available freelance journalists – people like Durba Banerjee and Farah Mehmood – who effectively propped up a lot of the programme production for months.

Ahead of the cuts announcements, Mark Thompson staged one of his all-staff meetings via the BBC's internal ring-main system. One of our London producers, Sheetal Parmar, got in a question about the Asian Network's future. Thompson replied: 'What's happening now is there's been a process of dialogue and consultation including the leaders of the Asian Network absolutely in the picture and some fresh audience research.

We've always said with the Asian Network the important thing is we don't want to lose eye contact or ear contact with this audience and we want to come up with the right solution for them".

Nearly a year on from *The Times* scoop on the closure plan, he added that they were doing some more audience research and that it was going to take time before a decision could be made. 'I take the point that it's been a long time coming and the sooner we can get clear answers on the Asian Network the better".

By February 2011, complaints to the BBC about the closure plan totalled 922. This comprised 617 after the first announcement last March followed by 305 since the Trust announced last July that it accepted the proposal. But 95 per cent of that second figure had come in across January after a renewed push on-air and on social media by presenters and staff. Listeners were urged on Facebook and Twitter to phone the BBC's complaints line to protest about its likely closure. *The Guardian* ran a story about supporters planning one last push to highlight the plight that the Asian Network now found itself in.

One insider was quoted thus: 'The mood at the station is even worse over the last six months than when the closure was first mooted. The brand has taken a kicking, not just in the media establishment but inside the Asian community. People are sending their CVs out and expecting to be made redundant. All this at a time when its listening figures are going up'. A reporter from the in-house paper *Ariel* had asked to do another feature on the Network but pulled out of the assignment. 'I'll get back to you next month once a few big Ariel deadlines have passed', she emailed me mysteriously. She never did.

It was true that morale was probably at its nadir at the start of 2011. For all the praise about audience figures, there was a real feeling that (those of us who did) were now drinking in the last chance saloon. Staff were vaguely aware of ongoing talks but were not being told that anything positive was emerging from them. Working on the Radio Academy Awards seemed to me like polishing the obituary for the station. In the supporting paperwork for the Digital Station of the Year entry, there was an opportunity to outline 'Special considerations or hurdles encountered in fulfilling remit.' I wrote: 'BBC announced in March 2010 that Asian Network would close as a national DAB station – probably at the end of 2011. Nearly a year on, the exact future of the Network remains unclear. All the achievements and day-to-day broadcasting in 2010 were conducted against this backdrop of uncertainty, including the threat to people's jobs'.

In the midst of all this, at the start of 2011, came the latest rehearsals for covering the death of a senior member of the Royal family. Each network radio station had to provide a presenter and production team to take part in an exercise which ran through how it would announce the demise of one of the top four, how it would change the tone and music of its output and how it would elegantly join the national programme being presented from London. All the Controllers would assemble in the Council Chamber in Broadcasting House on a Saturday morning to listen to their respective radio networks dealing with a couple of possible scenarios.

This required a lot of technical work to ensure that the Controllers could hear the rehearsals down the line without any of it actually going out on air for real and precipitating incarceration in the Tower of London. It always seemed to be a risky endeavour and, needless to say, the Asian Network was the most complicated one, being based in Birmingham and Leicester. Its Head of Programmes also wanted to listen across the line from his home in Wimbledon. Most of this was achieved by specially allocated ISDN lines but there was always a fear that someone somewhere who was doing a 'live programme' would open the wrong channel fader on their studio desk and broadcast the rehearsal. The exercises were launched by text messages to selected senior staff. At home I got a text about the wellbeing of the Queen and called another colleague as part of the exercise. My partner, on the phone to a friend, heard me and she assumed immediately that this was real life. I stopped it going viral.

—ᚙ—

As staff waited to hear their fate, the Asian Network found itself in the middle of a new storm of controversy after a discussion on the English Defence League on the Nihal programme. One of Nihal's guests was Guramit Singh, a Sikh who was an official spokesman for the EDL at the time. He criticised the ideology of Islam and another contributor, a Muslim who had phoned in to take part, cut across him, expressing surprise that the BBC had allowed him to make derogatory remarks about Islam.

It was one of those robust debates encompassing racism and religion that Nihal was so good at hosting but which had the potential to generate days of controversy within a second. Guramit Singh's comments and Nihal's handling of the debate attracted well over 1,150 complaints to the BBC. An organisation called the Peaceful Arts Association hand-delivered an 11 page legal notice to the Asian Network in Birmingham, accusing the Nihal programme of being broadcast with 'intentions to fuel and spread racial and religious hatred'. It demanded, without irony in view of the Network's situation, that the station be closed down, that everyone associated with the programme be sacked and that apologies for the programme be offered across TV, radio and newspapers.

It said it had instructed a firm of Birmingham solicitors to act on its behalf and to look at both civil and criminal action against the

EDL and the BBC. We passed all this to the BBC's legal department but, unsurprisingly, heard no more from the Peaceful Arts Association or its solicitors. The daily complaints dwindled after a week or so. Nihal had apologised during the same programme for the offensive remarks of the EDL spokesman and admitted that he should have cut him off earlier.

The unpublished audience figures for January added to the depression among the management – down to 299,000 a week. But in fact, the overall official figures for January, February and March were stunning and continued the upward trend. Asian Network now had half a million listeners a week – the second highest figure for six years and the highest for three years. It had gone up by 143,000 in the 12 months since its closure was announced. The Network had also overtaken its main commercial rival Sunrise Radio in London which was down to 469,000.

These encouraging figures were not actually released until May, nearly two months after the announcement that the Asian Network had won a reprieve from closure. At the beginning of March, Andy Parfitt hinted that he knew what Mark Thompson was now thinking and that it was 'fair'. There were suggestions that Tim Davie was planning to make an announcement the following week and would come and talk to the staff. Davie visited Birmingham to talk to all Audio and Music staff five days before the Asian Network announcement but said nothing on that visit about the Asian Network plans.

At 9.20pm on 13 March, one of the strategists Caitlin Hughes sent a note to Tim Davie, Caroline Thomson and head strategist John Tate, saying she understood the DG had come to a decision about the future of the Asian Network and outlining what she thought was a fair record of what was agreed. The Asian Network would continue as a national digital station but would be set a tough two year challenge.

CHAPTER 33

rejuvenAsian

The reprieve of the Asian Network as a national station was a significant victory for Vijay and the audience and another U-turn for Tim Davie. Almost a year to the day that its closure was announced, the Asian Network followed 6 Music down the survival route. From being told that it had to stop being a national offering on DAB, it was now declared that it would continue in exactly that format. After staff were told repeatedly that the five regional franchises idea was 'the only game in town', that proposal (which had been downsized into a three and then a two regions offering) was long gone, shot to pieces by logic and cost.

The announcement came in the same week as Comic Relief. Staff joked about red faces rather than red noses at the top of Audio and Music. The Fake Andy Parfitt, some wag within Radio 1 who pretended to be its Controller, tweeted: 'I'd forgotten that I'm in charge of the Asian Network. Apparently it's still going to be on'. This tweet was taken at face value by one Asian media website who reported it as a quote from the real Andy Parfitt.

Officially the BBC preferred to call it a possible reprieve, saying that it was exploring whether the Network should remain on the national DAB and that the work around this was being done as part of the Delivering Quality First process, which had been spawned from Putting Quality First. It said no decisions had been made and any proposal would be subject (as ever) to approval by the BBC Trust. *The Daily Telegraph* said the BBC had performed another about-turn on its planned cost-cutting drive, noting it was the second time in a year that the Corporation had backtracked on its original decision to shut down two digital stations.

On the day of the formal announcement to staff on Monday 14th March, global news was dominated by the earthquake and subsequent tsunami in Japan. Thousands were dead and missing, and there was a nuclear meltdown at Fukushima power plant. The news footage of the terrible devastation that morning rolled across the television screens around the main production areas in the Mailbox in Birmingham. The fear and uncertainty about the future of the Asian Network and the potential knock-on effect on jobs and families and mortgages paled into insignificance against the lives of the casualties of this latest terrifying 'Act of God'.

As the uncertainty swirled around us that spring, I saw the West End revival of Terence Rattigan's play '*Flarepath*' which was set in a hotel near an RAF Bomber Command airfield at the height of the Second World War. It reminded me of the uncle I never knew – my father's brother Colin who was training to be a teacher when he was called up. He joined the RAF volunteer reserve and was trained to fly Wellington bombers. His aircraft was shot down over the North Sea on a night raid in January 1942. The aircraft and the six crew on board have never been found. He was nearly 23.

When I was 23, I was enjoying life as a young newspaper reporter, driving a Mini Cooper S (motor insurance companies loved me). '*Rumours*', '*Aja*' and '*Marquee Moon*' were on my Dansette stereo. '*Saturday Night Fever*', '*Annie Hall*' and '*The Spy Who Loved Me*' were on at the cinema. I flew in a Hercules with the RAF parachute display team who were in Lincolnshire as part of the Queen's Silver Jubilee celebrations – noone was shooting at us. I

what does this mean?

did n't know it then but the following year I would join the BBC. More than 30 years later, I was edging towards the end of a fulfilling career with 'Auntie'. Whatever life lay ahead of my 23 year old uncle was ripped from him as his blazing bomber plunged out of the night sky into the murky depths of the North Sea. Perspective. We did n't know how lucky we were.

I have often reflected on who was the most inspirational character I ever actually met or interviewed in my BBC career and always concluded it was a pilot. Roland Beamont was one of the 1950s British test pilots who first flew military aircraft like the TSR2, Canberra and the Lightning. When I was at Radio Lincolnshire, the Lightning was retired from service and its last base at Binbrook, high on the Lincolnshire Wolds, was closed. I contacted the long retired Beamont at his Wiltshire home to see if he would be happy to be interviewed about the Lightning. He replied by return of post and I drove down to see him.

Roland Beamont was a fighter pilot in the Second World War, flying in combat at the same time as my Uncle Colin's Wellington bomber was lumbering off towards Germany. He once faced a courts martial for flying a WAAF to a party at another airfield on his lap in his single-seat Hurricane. The charge was dropped because they needed him in the air for the Battle of Britain. Towards the end of the war, he was shot down and taken prisoner. Later, he became one of Britain's top test pilots, facing danger and uncertainty every working day as he pushed the boundaries of supersonic flight. He was the most modest, self-effacing character I ever met.

Talking to people like him and researching the story of my uncle always reminds me why I have found aviation so fascinating and why it brings me 'back to earth' and offers perspective on my own 'chairborne' working life. In my local radio days, I pursued my interest in aeroplanes and was privileged to get some 'media facility' flights with the RAF, and thus got a very small insight into the world of people like Roland Beamont.

MC after an hour's flight in the back seat of a 'Red Arrows' Hawk, RAF Scampton May 1992. The tube coming out of my middle connects to the jet and works the Auntie-Ji ★ suit which stops you passing out in very tight turns when your blood would otherwise drain south from the brain and pool in your lower body. (★Editor's note: 'anti-g' surely?)

Not long after the Asian Network was welcomed into the bosom of Radio and Music, some of us found ourselves at a big brainstormy 'away day' at a place called Vinopolis near London Bridge. We were broken up into groups to discuss the meaning of life, whom we would like to swap jobs with at the Corporation, what the BBC was for, and contemplate the 'big picture stuff' through clouds of 'blue sky thinking'.

Each person in my group was asked to describe their most memorable experience in life so far. The four people before me all plumped for the birth of their children, either giving birth or witnessing it. I mumbled that I was indeed proudly present when my wife Val gave birth to our sons Tom and Mark in the early 1980s but, I'm sorry, the hospital delivery rooms did not compare to being trussed up in the ejection seat in the back of a Tornado F3 and launched into an afterburner vertical climb off the end of runway 25 at RAF Coningsby. 15,000 feet in under 30 seconds. Awesome, as the younger son would now say.

Anne Rawlings, Vijay's longtime PA, spent the morning of the 14th March wrestling with the BBC system of booking rooms. Even though you were in Birmingham, you had to ring Manchester to book a room in the Mailbox. The Asian Network needed video conferencing to link Birmingham with Leicester, Television Centre, Yalding House and Millbank (the BBC Parliamentary Unit where our political reporter Adam Pasternicki was based). We had ended up with room 15 in Birmingham which was small and pokey, especially for a big staff meeting. Anne had been dealing with someone called Kurly in the Children in Need team about doing a swap for room 083B which was bigger. Kurly said no – she had a big team too.

However on the morning, there was no sign of Kurly and her Pudsey pals. Room 083B was clear – so the Asian Network grabbed it and Anne fired off an email to Kurly complaining about her insisting she needed the big room but then not using it. Kurly had cancelled the booking but not told Anne. The exchange of emails between the two of them, with me copied in suddenly, provided some light entertainment before the Asian Network team assembled in 083B. Kurly now said she was 'fully on board in an absolute team spirit way with other key meeting room bookers around the Mailbox such as yourself'. So that was all good then – in a very real way.

At the staff meeting, Andy stressed that what he was going to say was 'not for public consumption'. It would not be helpful for it to go outside the BBC and there would be no public announcement. This was somewhat surprising. Did they really expect to contain it within the BBC after the year that the Network had experienced? In fact, within an hour of the end of the full team meeting, it was all on the *Media Guardian* website. Two of the specialist music presenters arrived late and missed Andy's appeal for confidentiality and happily tweeted throughout the presentation.

Andy also stressed that the decision was still up to the BBC Trust. We knew that, and had targeted the Trust for months with Vijay meeting the chairman Sir Michael Lyons and members Alison Hastings and Mehmuda Mian. We had ofcourse invited Mehmuda to visit the Asian Network and convinced her that the Asian Network was actually working well now.

Standing outside the Mailbox during a fire drill three days earlier, I had fallen into conversation with Louise Hall, the magnificently titled 'Head of Governance and Accountability for the BBC Trust in the Nations and Regions'. We discussed the new Trust chairman-designate Lord Patten whom she thought would be great for the BBC – a 'big beast' who had held big posts. I reflected on the very funny parliamentary sketch piece in one of the newspapers that morning on Patten's performance at the Commons Broadcasting Committee the day before. A man of the people he was not, preferring programmes about agriculture on BBC4 to *Eastenders* and Radio 1. What would he make of the Asian Network? He probably thought it was something to do with Hong Kong.

Andy said the reprieve plan was complicated and challenging. The conditions were tough – we had to 'up our game' yet again. He used the analogy of four faders on a radio studio desk. We had to balance costs, weekly reach, cost per hour per listener and, that word again, 'distinctiveness' in our output. We would juggle with those 'faders' to get our costs down. Tommy Sandhu, on the video link from London, asked 'What makes you confident it will work?'. Kamlesh Purohit, on the Leicester link, noted that the whole episode had been damaging and how could we restore our image?'. Andy's response was basically that the performance of the past 12 months had shown it would work and that the reputation was already being rebuilt.

Sonia asked the best question – ' Is Tim happy?'. Andy stressed the positives but the question hung in the air. If we had been presented with this plan a year ago, it would saved a lot of money and anguish. If something was not working, go and sort it out. You have a year to push up the audience and settle the schedule and the new strategy, and indeed start on some cuts. We could have achieved that and, apart from cuts, we did. Instead the BBC backed itself straight into a corner in March 2010. A 'courageous' decision.

The staff felt vindicated and jubilant but the cost of the reprieve was brutal. Its programme budget would be cut from £6.6 million to £3.5 million over the next two years. The cost per listener per hour would have to drop from 6.9 pence to 1.9 pence in line with other digital stations, such as BBC 7 (1.7 pence) and 6 Music (1.5 pence). This would mean increasing the audience even more, targeting another 100,000 a week and getting them to listen for longer. To reach 600,000 listeners a week would apparently require 5 per cent growth in London and 11 per cent in the Midlands. The BBC also planned to spend £2.5 million on output across the whole of the Corporation to improve value to the Asian population, including more on-line, red button activity and journalism.

The plans were bundled up with the wider Delivering Quality First proposals for radio. At least, as others in radio awaited the outcome of DQF, the Asian Network staff knew what was in store for them after their year of waiting. It was still going to take another year for the changes to be fully implemented with everything in place or in the case of staff, half of them out of the door by early 2013. A due Service Licence review, which unpicked the reasons for having an Asian Network, would also be undertaken in parallel with all this, along with what the strategists liked to call a 'significance analysis'.

We were despatched to workshops to understand DQF and explain it to the staff. However much spin was put on the process, it was still about cuts of up to 20 per cent. The licence fee was fixed until the end of 2016 and the income would now have to fund the World Service, S4C and other services. 130 News jobs in London were already under threat by the move to Salford, and there were plans to move programmes out of Birmingham to Bristol.

Elsewhere in the world, the Asian Network followed the cricket World Cup in South Asia. Some staff following the India v Pakistan semi-final on the production office television in Birmingham got over-excited and noisy – and upset *Points of View* again. India beat Sri Lanka in the final a few days later but that was staged on a Saturday when there were no neighbours to express a point of view. Brian True-May, the executive producer of ITV's '*Midsomer Murders*', was suspended after attributing the success of the detective series to a lack of multi-culturalism and non-white characters. True-May apologised later and said his comments had been taken out of context, but it was the kind of story that was made for the Asian Network phone-in programme. Radio 7 was rebranded after a year's consultation as Radio 4 Extra, and the Asian Network failed to get any nominations for the Radio Academy Awards.

—ϻ—

Andy Parfitt formed what he called 'the Kitchen Cabinet', named after those inner circles of US Presidents and British Prime ministers, to organise the changes in the Asian Network. This consisted of Vijay, Husain, Mark, Kevin from News, and me. It met regularly to draw up the framework for another 12 months of consultation and change before dumping the final proposal for a slimmer Asian Network on the Trust the following year. Looking way ahead, the Network was contemplating no drama, no documentaries, no language programmes for the East Midlands specifically, and no early morning devotional music. The staffing would be cut from 82 fulltime posts to 46.

The news team would lose nearly half its journalists. There was a bid in for some extra investment outside the cuts to maintain original journalism (exclusives from the Asian community) and specialist reporters covering sport, entertainment and politics. Without this extra money, the erudite Kevin Silverton said: 'We're stuffed'. The effort put into news for the Breakfast programme would have to be reduced to ensure coverage across the rest of the week and they would have to use more material from the rest of BBC News rather than gather it themselves. The case for extra investment in the news operation rested on promising that, whatever stories that the Asian Network got, they were made available to the whole of the BBC. It would effectively become an 'Asian news hub' which also happened to do bulletins on the Asian Network.

The importance of the language programmes to the new schedule was also emphasised. Even while the first discussions were opening on how languages would be treated in the new era, the weekday language shows were tweaked in July 2011. Gagan Grewal's Hindi-Urdu evening show was given an extra hour at the expense of the regional languages shows which were cut to one hour only. Most British Asian households were bi-lingual or multi-lingual. According to a 2009 survey 'Ethnogue: Languages of the World', six of the 10 most common foreign languages used by Britons as their first language were South Asian. With the use of Asian languages growing in the UK, the Asian Network had to capitalise on this development. In the end, the Hindi-Urdu show was retained across weekday evenings with the other language programmes going into Sunday afternoon and evening.

For years, the station was committed to 40 per cent of the music it played being from British Asian artists but this was now going to drop to 25 per cent. The playlist across the daytime core hours had to reflect what British Asians actually wanted to hear and the 40 per cent commitment was too restrictive. UK acts accounted for between 5 and 9 percent of the airplay on commercial stations like Sunrise and Sabras – instead they were banging out the ever popular Bollywood tunes. That was the way to push up the audience but ofcourse went against the BBC's requirement to be distinctive from its commercial rivals. Still, the Asian Network would remain committed to supporting new and emerging British Asian artists, play so many hours of specialist music, and record live sessions in studios and at the Melas.

The programme title '*Asian Provocateur*' titillating re-emerged again. First suggested back in the days of 'TransformAsian', it would be the provocative and stimulating Sunday morning multi-faith discussion show – a sort of '*Any Questions*'. Once again it never got off the ground with everyone reluctant to remove any populist Bollywood from the weekend schedules and fearful of competing with the television show '*The Big Question*'. Vijay said there was no appetite for such a show which would probably kill off the existing audience at that time. The idea of a Tamil language show was also discussed again, not least as part of the plan to get more listeners in London where the majority of UK Tamil speakers could be found.

The question of where the new-look Asian Network would actually be based continued to perplex the BBC. Nothing had progressed since Tim Gardam's report on the BBC's digital radio stations back in 2004 which suggested that Birmingham would be the best location. Seven years later, the Network was actually broadcasting from five centres in three cities. Apart from London and Leicester, programmes were coming from Television Centre, Yalding House and Western House in London. Tommy Sandhu had got his wish to host his weekday Breakfast show from London but, because the required technical work was not a priority for the hard-pressed people working on the new Broadcasting House, he only had control of his microphone. The music was being played out more than 100 miles away in Birmingham. It was not until early September that Tommy had full control of his studio in Western House.

The plan in the middle of 2011 was to concentrate the Asian Network on two locations – Birmingham and London. Now that the Asian Network had been saved, it could broadcast out of the new BH like its parent station Radio 1. Before the closure was announced, I had logged with our Radio 1 colleagues that, based on current staffing on our three London sites, we probably needed 20 desks in the new BH. But after the closure was announced, the Asian Network fell off the plans to move into the new building and the 8th floor was configured for just Radio 1 and 1Xtra. Now we had to start again and negotiate for desks, training and a place in the moving schedule.

Alongside the plan to reduce the Asian Network's bases was another desperate attempt to simplify its playout systems. The Leicester newsroom was using the Radioman system which was the standard kit for local radio. The same system was used downstairs in Birmingham but upstairs (in the network radio studios) the staff had to use VCS. This German-made system was now the default playout system of all BBC national radio but ofcourse the Asian Network was left with an old version in the Mailbox. In Western House and Yalding House in London, the team were using a version of VCS called Highlander, whereas the phone-in programme in Television Centre was using a News version of VCS. People responsible for BBC Radio's business continuity (emergency planning) who asked for details of our playout systems lost the will to live quite quickly after I tried to give them even a simple answer.

In Birmingham, the two different systems (Radioman and VCS) could transfer music and audio between them thanks to a unique set-up by someone who had since left the BBC. Consequently the remaining engineers did not fully understand it and warned constantly that it left the Asian Network's programmes very vulnerable. The admirable Tony Gilbert, our technical supremo in the Mailbox, fretted frequently over this lash-up and never wasted an opportunity to unburden himself on any senior engineering figure in Audio and Music.

There is no doubt that Tony's dedication and attention to detail saved the Asian Network in Birmingham from falling silent on many occasions. Radio 1 and Radio 2 had dedicated Operations Managers but we had to share Tony with the English Regions engineering team as part of the deal to have him at all.

To add a further edge to this technical nightmare, the BBC was in the process of upgrading all of its computers. This meant more meetings in London to discuss 'PC Refresh' and hear tales of woe from other departments as they moved from Windows XP to Windows 7. Ofcourse our old version of VCS in Birmingham was not compliant with Windows 7 which meant any computer used in connection with actual broadcasting could not be upgraded. Instead these machines had to have a different version of Windows XP in order to work properly. All we wanted was to get the Asian Network in Birmingham and London onto the latest version of VCS like all the other networks. Everyone was also looking forward to 'Pull Printing' – a new way of printing documents using fewer printers which in turn had to be swiped with your ID card and which wished you a nice day.

—⟁—

While all this was bubbling along, another big change was brewing. I was on a day off to oversee the replacement of our old wheezing gas boiler when my mobile rang. It was the Controller with news that he was leaving. I had picked up the gossip in London the day before but Andy Parfitt was now ringing managers in his rather large BBC empire to tell them personally. It was typical of him. I had been particularly touched when he sent me a personal note as I recovered from my appendix aberration the year before, wishing me a speedy recovery and expressing appreciation for my work behind the front line at the Asian Network ('the glue that holds it all together'). Sonia once asked me what I actually did after I stopped being the news editor. I said I could n't tell her as it was government work. She indulged me and never bothered to ask again.

Andy had taken over Radio 1 at exactly the same time that I had started at the Asian Network – March 1998. After 13 years in charge, he was moving on to look for new opportunities outside of the BBC. A few months later he joined Saatchi and Saatchi as Executive Director of Talent. He had missed out on the top job in BBC radio when Tim Davie was appointed as Director of Audio and Music and many felt there was some tension there. Whatever the reasons, he said he had been thinking about it for some time and it had been a tough decision.

Radio 1 had to wait a while to see who would be its new Controller, but the Asian Network got its new boss straightaway.

CHAPTER 34

realisAsian

T he formal announcement on 21st July 2011 that Andy Parfitt was leaving the BBC included the appointment of Bob Shennan as the new controller of the Asian Network. Bob, who had been running Radio 2 and 6 Music since his return to the BBC in 2009, had been asked by Tim Davie to add the Asian Network to his empire. So for the second time in six years, the Asian Network was moved under Bob and consequently parented by yet another national radio station.

In his farewell note to the Asian Network staff, Andy said Bob had enormous affection for the station and had been a wise counsel for him while he was looking after the Network. He said Bob had made it clear that he understood the current 'friend of the family' strategy and did not plan to change that direction. This was reassuring for the staff whose first reaction had been that Bob Shennan had presided over the period in which the station had targeted younger people and lost listeners, triggering the whole closure saga.

In fact, it was a good decision to put Bob Shennan back in charge of the Asian Network. The so-called 'Man in Black' (a reference to his predictable sartorial style rather than any resemblance to Johnny Cash) knew all about its eccentricities, and the strengths and weaknesses of most of its staff, especially the senior ones. He was also now the most experienced of the Controllers and would be listened to when fighting the Asian Network's corner. Andy Parfitt's deputy Ben Cooper was eventually appointed as Radio 1 boss and had enough to do adjusting to his new responsibilities without having to sort out the Asian Network as well.

Andy Parfitt was out of the door pretty quickly, hosting his last staff meeting over a video conference from Yalding House a week after the announcement. He was perceived as part of the senior executive group that had gone with the closure plan but, under his leadership, the new strategy had turned things around and he was a popular boss. When Bob Shennan took over again at the beginning of August, the listening figures for that quarter (July, August and September) hit yet another high of 507,000 a week.

In the second week of that August, England was hit by serious rioting triggered by a police shooting in London. Three young Asian men died in Birmingham after being hit by a car while trying to defend their property from looters. The father of one of them made a powerful appeal for peace which many felt helped to calm the mood in the city. One of the Asian Network team knew the family and acted as a conduit for the station's journalists to cover the story. A shop in the Mailbox near the BBC offices was looted and steps had to be taken to get BBC staff in and out of the building safely, including putting the early team into a hotel attached to the Mailbox.

Bob summoned the 'kitchen cabinet' to talk through a programme schedule with half the staff and half the budget. Everything had to be done with £3.5 million a year but a case was to be made for the additional money to fund original journalism and red button activity. Bob said the plea for this re-investment money had to be written into the schedule document in the spirit of how 'we will turbo-charge the Asian Network reach in the next 18 months'. New Controller, same old '*Top Gear*' language – but also no equivocation. Tim Davie wanted a very clear and singular set of detailed messages about the Asian Network ready to go public in a few weeks time.

Bob Shennan grumbled to me about Vijay's 'hot line to the DG'. Vijay was keeping up the pressure on Mark Thompson, securing another meeting with him on 15th August. This time Mark Thompson asked her to drop him a note capturing the key issues around the future of the Asian Network. She pointed out that the station was now facing cuts of 48 per cent with the resulting disproportionate adverse impact on the number of ethnic minority staff (82 reduced to 46). She also urged him to seriously explore the possibility of getting the Asian Network onto an AM transmitter in London, if only for 18 months to allow people to sample the Network and to drive up the conversion to digital listening.

Having accepted the cuts as the price for survival, the separate re-investment bid was assuming more importance. Vijay wrote that to get the extra money (ideally £1.5 million) would signal the DG's commitment to deliver Asian content for the rest of the BBC. It would enable the BBC to invest in original and distinctive journalism to deepen the relationship with the hard-to-reach Asian audience. It would also reduce the perceived impact of the Asian Network having its budget halved – the re-investment would bring the cuts down to a less brutal 30 per cent.

The money would also enable the Asian Network to continue to do 'red button' activity which had proved popular, and also stay involved in big outreach events like Melas. A timely example was offered with the Network making a fuss of one of the biggest British Asian stars, Jay Sean, who was recorded and filmed in conversation in the BBC Radio Theatre and performing at the London Mela over the first weekend in September. Some 80,000 people turned up at the Mela, which also featured Jazzy B, Mumzy Stranger, Ash King and Hunterz, and the boxer Amir Khan.

It was the Asian Network's 'Time to Shine' according to the audience researchers and the marketing people, who were planning a big campaign early in 2012. With its closure plan shelved and its forthcoming new schedule, the radio station should make a significant contribution to the value of the BBC among the Asian audience. It should meet the needs of the Asian audience which was not being served by the mainstream. It should provide a bridge between communities within the Asian population and be the place where the UK's Asian communities come together. Sitting through yet another PowerPoint presentation, the staff were urged to feel 'vibrant and sparky' and boost awareness of their radio station in the Asian population.

Radio 4's *Feedback* programme featured the Asian Network with its presenter Roger Bolton visiting the Breakfast programme one dull grey morning. In a write-up for his report, he enthused; 'Tommy Sandhu, the presenter, was on his feet dancing around to the latest glorious Bollywood mix. I felt very overdressed, not to say grey and middle-aged. Well that's stretching it a bit. I think I was middle-aged before Tommy was born. It was impossible not to grin and start shuffling around in what approximates in my case to dancing. I was watching what broadcasting life is like after death, or at least after a death sentence has been commuted'.

Across the autumn and into winter of 2011, plans for the new look Asian Network gradually emerged. But staff were frustrated by the lack of hard facts, with every snippet of information carrying the rider that the BBC Trust would have the final say. The schedule would be simpler and have fewer, longer programmes but no decisions could be taken on staffing cuts until the schedule was approved. However staff were told that it was clearly possible to make radio programmes with fewer of them and on lower pay grades – and indeed this policy was being implemented across BBC radio.

The outline plan was to have a new schedule sorted by the following April then spend the next 12 months up to April 2013 going through the redundancy process. To help people expand their experience and better prepare them for going for jobs anywhere in the BBC, Bob Shennan talked to his fellow Controllers and other department heads about setting up a special attachment scheme for Asian Network staff. They could apply to go and work elsewhere for a few weeks – a simple idea which undoubtedly helped quite a few of the team who seized the opportunity and never returned to the Asian Network. The idea was that these people would not be replaced when they went on attachment, thus giving those who remained an idea of life after 48 per cent cuts.

—ɯ—

It was also finally decided that the Asian Network would get out of Leicester with the newsroom moving to the new Broadcasting House to sit alongside the Radio 1 Newsbeat team. The best selling point for grasping the Leicester nettle and moving the news team to the new BH was obvious. The team would cease being isolated from BBC News in Leicester and would work alongside colleagues in one of the globe's finest newsgathering organisations with brand new kit and opportunities to develop their careers in the same building. However it would be a big upheaval for staff that survived, with grinding commuting and hotel nights away from their Midlands homes.

The flight from Leicester would also mark the end of the East Midlands regional language programmes – the last remaining links with the original Asian programmes on Radio Leicester. It would also leave the new Leicester building half-empty.

The changes would also mean that ten per cent of the Asian Network's output would go out to the WOCC – what the BBC called the 'Window of Creative Competition' where independent companies and BBC departments could compete to produce programmes. The ten per cent commitment to the independent sector remained as well. It was initially thought that one of the main weekday sequence programmes such as Sonia or Noreen would be offered to the independent sector. It would be good for the image of the Asian Network if it was partnered with a reputable indie but the money on offer for such a commission would not be good so the idea was dropped.

Another idea that was briefly floated for the new schedule was repeating the Nihal phone-in at the end of the day. It would give the station another daily hour of output and offer those who missed it a chance to catch up with the issues of the day as they dozed off. But it would have to be edited and signed off for compliance, and the topics discussed at 10am may well have been overtaken across the day before a repeat at 11pm. It was quickly and unanimously dropped as a daft idea.

There was renewed talk of all the plans being put out to a Public Value Test which would delay things by a further six months as the public were once again consulted. This could be automatic if a budget on a service was to be reduced by more than 10 per cent, although it was hoped that any PVT could be bundled up with a Service Licence review. And there had to be a new Service Licence for the new look Asian Network.

Bob Shennan and Husain Husaini took the proposed changes to Mark Thompson and the BBC Executive board early in December. Their submission to the Trust on the Service Licence review was accepted and adopted by the Executive board. The decision not to complicate things by pressing for the London AM transmitter was agreed but the option remained 'on the back burner' for a time when, hopefully, the Asian Network would prove that the new strategy had been successful. Realistically though, it looked as though the Asian Network would never appear on a medium wave frequency in London.

Bob reported back to the senior managers in the team that the Executive board had been very complimentary about the new strategy. He wrote: 'I think you should all be aware that a number of Board members paid tribute to the way you have collectively run this station under the most difficult of circumstances, Tim Davie, Mark Thompson and Caroline Thomson among them. Well done all'.

Nearly two years after Caroline Thomson had told the House of Lords Communications Committee that the BBC was trying to decide whether the Asian Network was the right way to serve the Asian population, her words were still being used by another pressure group. Soundstart, a group headed by the former presenter of children's TV show 'Magpie' Susan Stranks, called for the Asian Network to be replaced with an 'inclusive radio network to serve and support young children and their families across all our communities'. She quoted two surveys from 2001 and 2010 which placed a radio station for young children and their families at the top of public preference for a licence-funded network and both surveys placed the Asian Network at the bottom. 'It's time to give the public what they want', said Ms Stranks.

Caroline Thomson, still the BBC's Chief Operating Officer, pitched up in Birmingham in November to talk to all staff about the changes at the Mailbox. The Asian Network team, who had been through so much and now knew roughly how their future looked, contributed nothing to this meeting and just looked on with an air of world-weariness. However some of the Radio 4 and Vision people, heading for Bristol, Salford or redundancy, were in truculent mood. They were not impressed when Thomson insisted that one of the five BBC production centres had to close, and that Birmingham had been chosen on the grounds of productivity and property. She said the BBC also wanted to consolidate around places where its reputation was strong – and Bristol had the Natural History Unit. It looked like *Countryfile*, *Farming Today*, *Hairy Bikers*, *Trawlermen* and *The Sky at Night* were no match for gorillas and penguins.

The year ended with the Asian Network highlighting Bangladesh's 40th anniversary as an independent country. Forty years on from George Harrison 's 'Concert for Bangladesh', there was a far wider understanding of the music of Ravi Shankar and other South Asian musicians. But also forty years on, there were still new and shocking stories from people like the Asian Network's Mintu Rahman who, as a child, had lived through the upheaval and hardship of the war that eventually created Bangladesh.

CHAPTER 35

inspirAsian

Vijay Sharma had been considering her plan to leave the BBC for some time. However she delayed her retirement until the future of the Asian Network had been secured and because she wanted to be there for her battered team. The station now had a future, the audience figures were at a record high and the output was sounding 'great'.

Her email to staff, sent on the morning of 18ᵗʰ January, said: 'It has been my absolute privilege and honour to take on a five hour-a-week service with three freelancers on Radio Leicester, grow it up to 80 hours a week, establish a Midlands regional Asian Network, lead the roll-out of the regional service on the AM transmitters in the East Midlands, the North West, South and West Yorkshire, Peterborough and Three Counties. Then of course came the move to national status, going out on DAB ten years ago. The constantly changing audience remit, and the expectations required from us, were the only 'constants' throughout this whole period – that is what kept it fresh and challenging'.

Referring to the last two years of uncertainty, Vijay praised the team for still rising to the challenges, staying focussed and producing excellent output. 'Your commitment and self-belief has been inspirational. Well done to all of you for keeping faith in the value and the relevance of a national BBC Asian Network. As the Asian diaspora grows and flourishes in the UK, the Asian Network needs to continue to reflect, entertain and engage with this very important audience.

'I have had an enormous pleasure and joy in recruiting and working with hundreds of colleagues over the years. When I see or hear ex-Asian Network colleagues on BBC Radio and Television, it gives me enormous satisfaction. And I have seen many colleagues move on to important production and support jobs throughout the BBC and beyond. The Asian Network has played a pivotal role in proving a platform to the British Asian artists and creative and journalistic talent. I am enormously proud of this. I have valued the wise counsel of Mike Curtis, and the tireless approach of Mark Strippel in positioning the Asian Network at the heart of the British Asian Music scene. All the senior leaders around me have played a pivotal role in delivering high quality editorial in programmes, news and on–line. I have enjoyed your support and that has been very important to me'.

The announcement took most staff by surprise. Vijay was urged by some to reconsider, saying the Network needed her experience, wisdom and 'political nous' to continue to defend the Asian Network inside and outside of the BBC. But Vijay had been developing outside interests in the health service, cultural and charitable fields (all meticulously declared) for some time. And after fighting battles within the BBC and balancing the diverse elements within the audience, she did not want to be part of forthcoming upheaval that was the price of survival.

Tim Davie generously said Vijay had been 'a formidable champion for the Asian Network, her staff and British Asian audiences over the years. She leaves a strong legacy as a creative leader whose team are delivering strong results and have proved themselves to be an important part of Audio and Music and the BBC'. Bob Shennan said Vijay had been 'a leading light in the BBC Asian Network', adding that he was 'particularly grateful to her for her inspirational leadership during the last turbulent 18 months'.

The day of Vijay's announcement coincided with a strike by BECTU union members in Birmingham over the plans to move all the network radio and television programmes to Bristol and Salford. Not long afterwards, Andrew Thorman, who had been responsible for the Asian Network's documentaries while running Radio 4 in Birmingham and the 'Countryfile' television programme, announced he was leaving too. On February 1st, the BBC opened a two month 'window' for Asian Network staff to express any desire to take voluntary redundancy. At the end of February, Trish Dolman, the long suffering music librarian for the Asian Network and Radio Leicester, retired after years of chasing Asian Network producers and presenters to log their music for the Performing Rights Society.

People were disappearing from the Asian Network all the time, with the smart ones taking advantage of the special attachment scheme set up by Bob Shennan. Sonia Deol announced that she was off as well, finishing in early March to head for Canada and marriage. Dharmesh Rajput, the station's diligent interactive editor, was made redundant, a unfortunate victim of the severe cuts in the BBC's on-line operation. The Asian Network's overstretched online team was reduced to two with Manish Pradhan and Mintu Rahman holding the fort, helped for a while by a freelance social media expert Kaushal Tailor.

February saw the culmination of a six year grievance by senior producer Devan Maistry, who felt he was not treated fairly in the recruitment process around 'TransformAsian' in 2006 when he was not short-listed for the Assistant Editor interviews. After several so-called 'formal capability procedures', he was eventually dismissed on the grounds of poor performance, despite a number of appeals which were heard by senior managers outside of the Asian Network. Every appeal failed but, once out of the BBC, he took his case to an employment tribunal. He filed a claim for 'religious or belief discrimination', which allegedly took place against his philosophical view that 'public service broadcasting has the higher purpose of promoting cultural interchange and social cohesion'. He also claimed that he was dismissed because of his age, and that he had been treated unfairly.

Eleven BBC managers and one presenter who were involved over the years were called to make statements at the tribunal, including me who had a very peripheral role in the whole saga. Devan had never worked directly for me but we had a cordial relationship, occasionally but briefly discussing music, news and politics. In May 2007, I had been tasked to talk to him about taking redundancy to resolve the issue and frankly to help him make a stress-free start somewhere else, but he chose not to take up that option. Devan's two line managers over the years, Neila Butt and Jonathan Aspinwall, were at the centre of the case and had kept immaculate notes across numerous email trails.

The BBC won on all counts with the Tribunal dismissing all Devan Maistry's claims of discrimination and harassment on the grounds of age and belief, and of unfair dismissal. The judgement was 86 pages long but, in a summary of the finding that the dismissal was fair, the members of the Tribunal did say: "We are satisfied that Ms Butt acted as a reasonable employer would do, and that overall therefore the decision to dismiss fell within the range of reasonable responses". The Tribunal said that the credibility of Mr Maistry was "generally to be poor" and that his evidence was 'inconsistent'. The whole process cost the BBC a lot of time and money, and the paperwork associated with it was vast. I don't know why Devan put himself through it. He seemed only interested in serious, analytical journalism and unfortunately could not embrace the Bollywood gossip and the 'skate boarding duck' scene (the light, funny stories which any news outlet has to juggle with the more serious side of life).

Surprisingly in view of the fact that the employment tribunal involved the BBC, there was no publicity. The Daily Mail had run a story in May 2011 after Birmingham employment tribunal chair Pam Hughes decided that Devan Maistry had a worthy case and gave him the right to a full hearing. She was effectively saying that rules to prevent religious discrimination could also be used to protect a belief in the BBC's ethos of public service broadcasting. In the end, no newspaper or agency reporters turned up at any of the hearings in February 2012. This was a complete contrast to the media circus around Miriam O'Reilly's victory after the 'Countryfile' presenter took the BBC to an employment tribunal over ageism.

Another upset with the Sikh religion did get the Asian Network back in the news. During the phone-in programme, presenter Nihal touched on the relationship between Sikhism and the other predominant religions in India in the 15th century. A text from a listener was read out complaining that Nihal had suggested that Sikhism was made up from other religions like Islam and Hinduism. Nihal said that it was and suggested to the complainant that 'with all due respect, I know more about your religion that you do'.

Lord Singh, a regular on Radio 4's 'Thought for the Day', complained about the remarks as the clip went viral. The BBC said it would 'bear in mind' the complaints from Sikhs but did not apologise. After more complaints, Kevin Silverton, the Head of News and the man responsible for the programme, issued another statement: "We have reviewed the transmission from the Nihal phone-in on March 13 and agree that this short excerpt was less than satisfactory. The debate show deals with difficult subjects on a daily basis and very occasionally we don't get the tone exactly right. We have spoken to the team about this matter and continue to strive to be as balanced as possible and sensitive to people's religious beliefs, always wanting to avoid any offence."

—⁂—

The Birmingham Mailbox became a depressing place to work. The Asian Network production area was in the centre of the building, away from the windows and natural light. It had its own deserted core where the Breakfast team used to be before they moved to London. Gradually more and more desks became vacant as people moved out on attachment or just left the BBC. And all around the building, more gaps were appearing as the cuts hit home in Radio 4 and television, and the programmes moved out. Getting to my desk around 9am, I gazed forlornly across the wasteland and made my plans.

It was clear from some meetings I went to at Audio and Music headquarters that 'Delivering Quality First' was going to be used to streamline management lines and reduce the number of grades within the Division. Indeed the Asian Network was held up as a shining beacon in this process. With its staff being halved, it obviously presented the perfect opportunity to shuffle everything. The organization chart that was being bandied about still had the job title 'Network Manager' on it but I was sure that would change as we got further into the shake-up. It was time to go.

First thing on 1st March (half way through Voluntary Redundancy Preference Exercise as it was called) I sent a courtesy note to Bob Shennan to let him know I would be submitting a request for voluntary redundancy. I said I felt the opportunity now offered would be an elegant way to bow out after 34 years continuous service. With Vijay leaving, my departure would allow the BBC to say that the 'Heads' level at the Asian Network was being cut by 50 per cent. I also offered to discuss a departure date that would be helpful to the BBC in view of the forthcoming transition that faced the station. Bob replied a couple of hours later, appreciating the warning and the offer around the timing. He said he had not anticipated it, but he understood why I thought it was a good time to go and suggested we meet the following week.

I did consider aloud and with some wry amusement that I was older than all of them – Bob, Tim Davie and Mark Thompson. Tim Davie was born in the year I became a teenager. I was happy with what I had achieved – in fact I felt I had probably over-achieved. Bob said graciously that it would be perverse to turn down my request and we turned to the potential carnage ahead of mass redundancy and re-recruitment. He was alright, was young Bob.

Director General Mark Thompson (three years younger than me) was obviously so upset that I was off that he announced that he would also be leaving the BBC in the autumn. He had been in the job for eight years, taking over after Greg Dyke resigned. His departure was not unexpected as the chairman of the BBC Trust, Lord Patten, said in January that the BBC was engaged in 'sensible succession planning' to find a replacement. Having spent a fortune on an external headhunting company to find the next DG, Patten eventually appointed the man down the corridor – George Entwistle.

People began talking about a concept called 'The Production Team of the Future'. Inderpreet Sahota was asked to lead on this for the Asian Network and enthused about her work with people from the management company McKinsey. I glazed over at the charts and work flows and let them get on with it. It all seemed to be about getting more productivity out of those who were left still standing. There were undoubtedly people who needed pushing but it was obvious that programme producers were going to be really stretched sorting out their programme and its on-line and social media connections, and filling in more forms.

In May, I took my eldest son Tom, a photographer and big music fan, to see Mike Scott and the Waterboys at Derby Assembly Rooms. Amid the upheaval and the new jargon flying around the BBC, the concert felt like a re-connection to the human spirit. The Waterboys, playing in a half-full venue that Mike Scott described as looking like a school gym, were superb, playing music from the heart and their Celtic roots and, through their latest album, broadening people's cultural knowledge by introducing them to the work of the Irish poet W.B.Yeats. While I was writing this book, I read Mike Scott's autobiography which unpicked his creative and spiritual journey from Scotland through London, New York and Ireland. I had seen pretty much all of the western music acts that I wanted to see in concert but the Waterboys in Derby seemed to transcend them all. From Derby, Mike and the band went on to Bournemouth and then around the world. I went back to the Mailbox.

More confirmation that I had made the right decision to go came at a meeting where the very sensible Head of Music Mark Strippel, whom I liked and respected enormously, suddenly used the phrase 'horizontal curation'. I had no idea what he was talking about. He'd been on a course.

As the Asian Network went through its transition, it continued to explore ways of pushing up its audience by pulling in big names. The Bollywood icon Madhuri Dixit flew in to record an 'in conversation' session for the radio and on-line. Pakistani cricket legend Shahid Afridi agreed to a similar experience at the Edgbaston indoor cricket centre where he also did some exhibition batting in the nets. Shah Rukh Khan returned to the Asian Network to co-host a three hour show with Tommy Sandhu. 'Summer with the Stars' continued with a number of emerging UK Asian comedians featured in special shows recorded at the BBC Radio Theatre and hosted by author and '*Goodness Gracious Me*' star Meera Syal. A small team headed off to report on the International Indian Film Awards again – this time in Singapore. Oh, and there was some coverage of the Queen's Diamond Jubilee and the Olympics.

The documentary strand remained strong. Poonam Taneja reported on British Muslims on the frontline with the British Army in Afghanistan – it was the first time a BBC radio reporter had been given access to follow Muslim military men and women. Two documentaries bookended a week called 'Get Healthy' which looked at the state of Asian health in the UK. The aim was to pull together all the health issues and talk about the preventable ailments that affected the Asian communities such as heart disease and diabetes. One programme covered the sensitive topic of male infertility among Asian men and the acute shortage of suitable sperm donors, while another examined the growing phenomenon of polygamy in the British Muslim community.

A few days before the BBC Trust published its service review on the Asian Network, Bob Shennan sent out the email telling everyone that I was leaving the BBC. His note contained two surprises – one that my career included a spell at BBC Religion in Manchester (it had not but HR records said I had) and the other was that I was pushed into second billing by Husain Husaini. The Asian Network's Head of Programmes, who had himself been on a career development attachment at Radio 4 Commissioning, surprised us by announcing that he was also taking voluntary redundancy. Not long after he left, he joined up with former BBC executive Matthew Bannister to successfully bid for the independent contract to provide the new mid-evening show for all of BBC Local Radio.

CHAPTER 36

culminAsian

The BBC's new plans for the Asian Network and the findings of the Trust's Service Review were published in May 2012. The senior managers in Audio and Music had finally agreed a way forward with Mark Thompson, and the BBC Trust had approved the revised proposals.

The station would broadcast from 6am to midnight each day, get rid of drama and devotional music programmes, reduce its documentaries and play more music (60 per cent of the output). The budget would indeed be slashed from £6.6 million to £3.5 million by April the following year, and the number of staff would be cut from 83 to 49. This 49 would consist of 26 Audio and Music people and 23 in News and the phone-in. The new schedule would actually be introduced some 6 months before the April 2013 deadline as staff took redundancy, got other jobs elsewhere in the BBC or successfully applied for the remaining ones at the Asian Network.

The pesky Cost per Listener Hour was already heading downwards due to the increase in audience. It was now at 5.1 pence but the next target was 2.8 pence. This would bring the Asian Network into line with the BBC's other digital networks like Radio 1Xtra (3.7p), Radio 4 Extra (1.3p) and 6 music (1.2p).

It was estimated that 16,000 were listening to the devotional music programmes across the week. Audience research suggested most listeners felt there was a limited need for this type of programming, with most only listening at key times of the year when there was usually other faith-specific media available such as the Sikh Channel or the Ramadhan Radio short-term licence. The Asian Network nevertheless pledged to continue to cover the significant religious festivals across the year.

The end of devotional music programmes did mean the end of the contract with the independent production company Fresh Air whose boss Neil Cowling had handled this unique commission with tact and good humour. It was also the end of the line for the long serving staff presenters who had faithfully fronted the Islamic, Sikh and Hindu music sections – Zeb Qureshi, Ravinder Kundra and Ashwini Mahli.

The statement about the new-look Asian Network also talked about strengthening the coverage of British Asian stories across the UK, and improving collaboration with BBC Local Radio. It was also the end of Leicester as a base for the Asian Network, with the news operation moving to London by the end of the year and the East Midlands language programmes being scrapped. The BBC Trust also approved the plans to 'remove regular sports coverage from the schedule'.

There was continued support for live events and music coverage such as the Melas, which had been positively received in the qualitative research by the Trust. Around three in ten of those questioned had used the BBC's Red Button service to watch Asian Network live music and events. Indeed these figures often exceeded the growing weekly audience figure for the radio programmes. For example, a Red Button special in January called '*Asian Network Gold:Iconic Asian Music from four decades of BBC archive*' had been watched by 790,000 viewers.

The BBC Trust issued its announcement on the Service Licence at 9am on Wednesday 16th May. At the same time, Bob Shennan sent out an all staff email outlining the changes while someone in HR briefed the union representatives. At 1pm, Trust member Mehmuda Mian appeared on the Nihal show explaining the Trust's decisions and underlining how much she understood and liked the Asian Network now. Someone else made sure that all the contract presenters and language staff who could not get to the staff meetings the following day were aware of what was going on. That evening the latest audience figures were available to senior managers. In the first three months of 2012, the Asian Network had got another new weekly record of 540,000 listeners.

After the staff meetings, everyone got a 20 page guidance pack on what was happening, covering the new schedule, staffing levels and structures, locations, and information on redundancy pay and notice, redeployment and pension implications. The big impact, which had not been clocked by everyone, was that all staff were actually losing their jobs and would have to reapply for the new ones within the new structure. No one outside the Asian Network could apply. Some people had thought that their role was so specialist or was the only such role on the station that they would be safe and not have to worry.

The long, tortuous and difficult re-recruitment process got underway as the nation celebrated the Queen's Diamond Jubilee and anticipated the European Football Championships and the Olympics. The Asian Network Bollywood team got back from the IFFAs in Singapore. In a somewhat ironic sense of timing and indeed cost, piles of 'postcards' appeared around the Birmingham Mailbox urging staff to take part in the latest staff survey, asking them if they were happy in their work and loved their managers.

None of us who were leaving had any input into the re-recruitment process apart from Vijay who was on the panel for the Head of Programmes post. That went to the only one of the four Asian Network senior managers within Audio and Music who was not leaving – Head of Music Mark Strippel. The three Editor roles went to Inderpreet Sahota (in charge of Birmingham programmes), Khaliq Meer (London) and Neila Butt (Live Events and Music).

My Network Manager post was replaced by a new role with the title of Production Manager, who in turn would be responsible for two production assistants. Sangeeta Kotak, who had been working with me and therefore understood the strange backstage world which I inhabited, went for the Production Manager role and prepared for her interview with impressive determination. She deserved her promotion after convincing the interview panel including the new supremo Mark Strippel and Lorna Clarke, the Network Manager at Radio 2.

Vijay and Husain left in July, basking in another record audience figure showing an average of 547,000 listeners each week across April, May and June. Meanwhile the re-recruitment process cascaded through the station. Among those who successfully made it through in programmes and news were Sabina Alderwish, Shabnam Mahmood, Deena Chohan, Harmit Gill, Bal Sidhu, Dil Neiyyar, Anish Shaikh, Sheetal Parmar, Rayhan Rahman and Ahmed Hussain. Some staff were making the most of the attachment scheme, working at *Strictly Come Dancing*, *Dragon's Den*, *Late Kick Off*, Radio 1 press office, Comedy, 6 Music Live Events, *The One Show* and even the Cairo news bureau.

The new Asian Network area on the 8th floor of the new Broadcasting House began to take shape with the realisation that it was going to be somewhat cramped with lots of hot-desking. The Asian Network's migration into the new BH was to be sprinkled across November and early December.

In Birmingham, the Mailbox was looking seriously lifeless. Rumours abounded of departments coming from London to fill some of the empty spaces. Many thought the BBC would be out of the Mailbox within five years despite being on a lease until 2026. David Holdsworth, the Controller of English Regions, assured staff there were no plans to sub-let either part or all of the BBC area for the remainder of this period. He pointed out that all the local BBC news programmes for the West Midlands, *The Archers* and the Asian Network would remain in the building, along with UK travel news, English News and Sport Online, and the Headquarters for the BBC Big Screens and English Regions.

Sangeeta planted the Asian Network flag in the old *Hairy Bikers* production area after they rode off to Bristol, and prepared to shift what was left of the Asian Network into the daylight overlooking the Birmingham canals. Asian Network assets in Leicester were also brought across to Birmingham, leaving a new gaping hole in the middle of the BBC building which had been home to the Asian Network for only five years. *The Archers* still were n't interested in heading east.

The radio station formally said farewell to Vijay Sharma in October in a room at the top of the new Cube building along the waterfront from the Mailbox. Owen Bentley and Bob Shennan paid tribute and everyone reflected on her years of inspiring and encouraging talented people from the Asian communities and beyond to enter broadcasting and to forge long careers. She has been a role model for many, being one of the most senior people in the BBC from an ethnic minority background.

Manzoor Moghal, chairman of the Muslim forum UK and a regular contributor to debates on the Asian Network over the years, was asked for a written tribute. 'From the beginning, I was impressed with her dedication to Asian broadcasting and her determination to be fair in dealing with various cultural and religious diverse interests of the Asian communities, which was not always an easy task. She was always a good listener and continually set high standards of service for her team in the interests of all South Asian communities'.

Shama Sharif, who was the chair of the Asian Network Advisory Council between 1997 and 2002, added her praise. 'Vijay's great knowledge, understanding of Asian communities, together with her experience of making quality programmes, has significantly contributed to the development of the station over the years, and the changing taste of the listeners. Vijay has demonstrated the utmost dedication and commitment to the Asian Network and its audiences, and has made a valuable and long-lasting contribution to the station'.

The City Mayor of Leicester, Sir Peter Soulsby, highlighted how Vijay had taken the Asian Network from small beginnings in her home city to the rest of the UK. 'Vijay Sharma's role and influence in developing Asian broadcasting can not be overstated', he wrote. 'She deserves enormous credit for taking the concepts and ideas she developed in Leicester to a national audience. The recent success of the BBC Asian Network – and the service now provided to hundreds of thousands of people across the UK – is fine testament to her vision'.

In fact the written tributes had not originally been gathered to mark Vijay's farewell. Word came down from Audio and Music headquarters that Mark Thompson wanted to nominate two BBC people for the New Years honours list – Nicholas Parsons and Vijay Sharma. I was asked to gather some tributes to Vijay for the paperwork that the BBC would submit to the Cabinet Office in support of the nomination. One person who eventually failed to send in a tribute actually rang Vijay to ask what it was all about, thus nearly spilling the beans. The cover story, that it was in connection with her BBC departure, therefore became the real reason. So far, there's been no national honour for Vijay but Mr Parsons did get a promotion from his OBE to a CBE a year later.

—⟋⟍⟍—

A month ahead of its tenth anniversary as a national radio station, the Asian Network announced the line-up for its new schedule. Tommy Sandhu, Nihal, Noreen Khan and Bobby Friction remained at the heart of the schedule during the week. In the early evenings, Bobby Friction would launch a new music and entertainment show with Anushka Arora from Sunrise Radio. Two other new presenters were announced. Suzi Mann would host the new Saturday Asian Download Chart Show and Yasser, a 23-year-old newcomer from Manchester, took over the Bobby Friction late night slot.

Ray Khan was retained to look after the late night Hindi-Urdu show from 9pm, and Gagan Grewal was moved to a new weekend Breakfast show. Raj and Pablo also hung on to the weekend Bollywood shows and Murtz continued with the Saturday Request Show. Panjabi Hit Squad, followed by Kan-D-Man and DJ Limelight, anchored Saturday nights and a new strand of language programmes on Sunday evenings would follow a couple of months later.

The Controller Bob Shennan said: "Asian Network is growing in reach and popularity and it's essential that we continue to celebrate, champion and reflect the lives of all the UK's Asian Communities. Our 10th birthday feels like the right time to refresh and re-energise our schedule, keeping our listeners' favourites at the heart of the network whist bringing some dynamic, exciting new talent to the airwaves."

And the new Head of Programmes, Mark Strippel, added this to the mix: "This is the right moment to build on our recent RAJAR results and an impressive summer of distinctive content with a new streamlined schedule focusing on the very best of Asian Network. It's important that we continue to evolve and strengthen our engagement with audiences. We'd like thank all of our departing DJs for their significant contribution and we wish them the very best for the future."

Three days after the new schedule launched on 22nd October, the latest audience figures were released. In the three months from the end of June to mid-September, the weekly reach had hit a new record high of 584,000. The old management team was leaving on a high. The last three months of 2012 saw the figures plummet back to 453,000 but they had recovered to another new high by the middle of 2013, touching 587,000. By the end of 2013, it had broken through the 600,000 mark.

The day before the new Asian Network line-up was announced, the BBC's new Director-General started work. George Entwistle, who had been in charge of BBC television, was to have a baptism of fire as the scandal around the sex abuse allegations against Jimmy Savile broke around him. Almost the last notes I wrote before leaving the BBC were on a pan-BBC briefing given by George Entwistle and the Director of Human Resources Lucy Adams. Entwistle talked of a complex and serious crisis, and it was down to him to get the crisis management under control. There was an obligation to ensure stars behaved. Inquiries were announced, public apologies were given, assurances were made that the sensitivities around those who were abused would not be forgotten, and senior figures like Helen Boaden and Adrian Van Klaveren were reshuffled.

Towards the end of 2012, it was announced that Tim Davie was to leave the top job at Audio and Music to run BBC Worldwide, the commercial bit of the BBC. In the fall-out from the Savile crisis and the subsequent *Newsnight* issues, Davie even ended up as acting Director-General for a while after George Entwistle resigned after 54 days in the job. Helen Boaden was moved out of News and dropped into Davie's old post of Director of Audio and Music, thus robbing Bob Shennan of a crack at the top radio job.

*Bye Bye BBC! MC at his 'chuck-out do' with Owen Bentley (left),
Vijay Sharma and Mark Strippel (far right)*

On the 31st October 2012, I stopped working for the BBC. There
was a respectable turn-out for my 'chuck out' party in the familiar
surroundings of meeting room 083 in Birmingham, where I had
spent so many hours 'brainstorming' stories and schedules, waiting
for video conference links to flicker into life, interviewing hopefuls
and the hopeless, unpicking grievances and gossip, listening to
senior managers giving replies but not answers, forward planning,
back-tracking, phone-hooking, chairing , swearing, laughing, eyeing
suspicious BBC sandwiches and head-banging against a virtual wall.

In my farewell speech, I produced my first ever BBC pay slip
from Radio Oxford in 1978 (an annual salary of £3,826 and a
monthly take home after tax of £221.62p). I noted that my BBC
career had run parallel with Ceefax (the world's first teletext service)
which started four years before I joined and was switched off eight

days before I was. I quoted a line from Sunderland MP Chris Mullin when he stepped down as an MP – get out while people are asking you 'why' you are going rather than waiting for them to ask 'when' are you going. I thanked my Asian Network friends for the best compliment I had been given, regarding me as an 'honorary Asian' and for the experience of working with the Asian communities for 14 years. Clutching various bottles, gifts of DVDs of 'Mad Men' and the BBC's Olympics comedy 'Twenty Twelve', and Neil Young's just published autobiography, I slipped out of the Mailbox and out of the BBC.

appreciAsian

From the start, I decided not to chase up the people peppered throughout this book for their take on the tale. However I am indebted to Vijay Sharma and Owen Bentley, two pivotal figures in the Asian Network story, for helping me to clarify the early days of the Asian Network in Leicester before I arrived in 1998. From March of that year, I was in 'the thick of it' and it could truly be a personal account.

There has been no desire to falsify, mislead, or over-dramatize, and I have no scores to settle. If anything clashes with how others remember it, then maybe some recollections have been befuddled by the passage of time and it is probably only to be expected of a man of my age.

I have written it all from memory inspired by documents and press cuttings collected over the years which sat in files and boxes at home, challenging me to do something with them or burn the lot. I left it a year before grasping the nettle in October 2013. I did not keep notes detailing exactly what had happened each day, but I did keep all my diaries with their scribbled comments and entries of meetings and appointments which tripped the brain cells into new trains of thought and reminiscence.

Where I have quoted articles from newspapers and magazines, I have endeavoured to correctly credit the writer and publication. In the course of this project, I enjoyed seeking out published books about this media life and found 'Radio Head' by John Osborne (which has a chapter on the Asian Network), 'When One Door Closes' by Peter Sissons, 'A Woman of Today' by Sue MacGregor,

'The Kindness of Strangers' by Kate Adie (the local radio years struck many a chord), 'Thank you for the Days' by Mark Radcliffe, 'And now on Radio 4' by Simon Elmes and Greg Dyke's 'Inside Story'. I would recommend them to anyone with an interest in BBC radio.

I have made every effort to respect the spelling of the names of everyone. The BBC's human resources (or Personnel as we used to call it) always struggled with names at the Asian Network, invariably finding it a challenge to enter correct spellings onto its database or getting confused that some people were known by two different names. Many presenters did not use their real name on-air. Some colleagues had subtle differences in the way they spelt their name – maybe just one letter but both versions acceptable. Ofcourse the computer would try to help me, insisting that the spiritual leader Sri Chinmoy should actually be spelt Sri Chimney.

I am grateful for the support of my partner Jo, my sons Tom and Mark and the number of friends and former BBC colleagues who told me to get on with it. On winter afternoons, Jo would emerge in my writer's garret at the top of the house, bringing tea in mugs with inspirational inscriptions such as 'I'm a Mug for Radio Oxford'; 'Radio Norwich – Up with the Partridge'; and 'BBC Working in Partnership' (Digital, Management, Artwork, Distribution, Print, Communications zzzzzzzzz).

The radio on the cover is the one from my teenage bedroom referred to in Chapter 1, and photographed by Tom Curtis.

Thank you to Mintu Rahman for the Asian Network photos from his personal collection. Others are from my own archives.

You can find the Asian Network on the web at: www. bbc.co.uk/asiannetwork and also on Facebook and Twitter. The website will also tell you how to actually listen to it – on-line, on digital TV, on DAB, and ofcourse on those still-surviving venerable medium wave frequencies crackling through the atmospherics across its original Midlands heartland. You will also find Asian programmes on several BBC local radio stations. Details on all BBC radio can be found here: www.bbc.co.uk/radio/stations.

In the words of the great Irish comedian Dave Allen, 'Good night, thank you, and may your God go with you'.